THE RABBIS' BIBLE

Volume Two: Early Prophets

THE RABBIS' BIBLE

VOLUME TWO: EARLY PROPHETS

Joshua, Judges, Samuel, Kings, Chronicles

by Solomon Simon and Morrison David Bial

woodcuts by Irwin Rosenhouse

BEHRMAN HOUSE, Inc.

Publishers   New York

For David, Judith and Miriam
and for Dorothy Diona Bial

2 3 4 5 82 81 80 79 78

Library of Congress Catalog Card Number: 66–20409
Standard Book Number: 87441–023–1

MANUFACTURED IN THE UNITED STATES OF AMERICA

PREFACE

Turn it, turn it again and again, for everything is in it.
Contemplate it, grow gray and old over it, for there is
no greater good.

PIRKÉ AVOT 5:25

THE BIBLE is a world in itself, rich, deep, wide, fulfilling. In a time when men are overwhelmed and surfeited with facts and find them unsatisfying, even setting the teeth on edge, the return to acquiring values built out of encounters with the world of the Bible and its wisdom is even more important.

This edition of the Biblical books, which deals with judges, kings and the early prophets, is intended as a textbook and companion for the young and adult study group, as well as a book for reflective individuals who seek the quiet pools and turbulent rapids of our millennia of Jewish history and religion. An abridged version of the Bible is arranged as continuous text across the tops of the pages with a continuing keyed commentary at the bottoms. That commentary explores the vast literature of post-Biblical interpretation and includes the two Talmuds, the Midrashim, medieval and modern Jewish commentary, as well as legend and folklore. Together Biblical text and commentary reinforce each other and out of their separate strands weave three thousand years of Jewish wisdom and tradition.

The Bible never tells a story for its own sake nor delivers stirring poetry for poetic grandeur alone; each verse is meant to teach a lesson, point a moral, record an important event or folk memory in the history of the Jewish people. With that in mind we have included law, history, ritual and ceremony—everything that bears on God and the Covenant, on ethical precepts and moral conduct, for there lies the Bible's central core and wisdom: Live rightly or die.

NOTE

The text is a new translation which avoids archaism but does no violence to the Biblical context by awkward colloquialism. Nor does the abridgment compromise the narrative or moral shape of the Scriptures as a whole. Occasionally verses have been slightly rearranged to provide for a more coherent narrative or moral shape of the Scriptures as a whole. This is especially the case in this volume in the use of the Book of Chronicles to support and broaden the historical books of Samuel and Kings. Biblical and place names are spelled as in the Jewish Publication Society (1917) translation. Otherwise the modern Sephardic pronunciation is used for Hebrew transliteration.

A Teacher's Resource Book has been prepared to make the study of the Bible even more accessible and meaningful to a contemporary reader. It clarifies the more profound meanings and subtle philosophies, the complex meaning of words and places, embodied in what is often a symbolic and hyperbolic Scriptural text. What is offered, then, is not apologetics but interpretation rich in ancient lore and replete with modern scholarship, so that throughout the student, teacher and reader will find new insight and understanding of the relevance of the Bible.

CONTENTS

1. JOSHUA [1–6]

THE COMMAND TO CROSS
THE JORDAN

IT WAS AFTER the death of Moses, [1] the servant of the Lord, the Lord spoke to Joshua, the son of Nun, the attendant of Moses, saying:

"Moses, My servant is dead. And now, arise and cross the Jordan, you and all this people, into the land which

---

[1] AFTER THE DEATH OF MOSES: In the days of mourning following Moses' death, many ordinances confused the people and they pleaded with Joshua to recall to them the forgotten ordinances and to explain the difficult passages. When he could not, the people sought to kill him. So Joshua prayed to the Lord, "Let Thy holy spirit descend upon me to explain the passages and to repeat what has been forgotten so that I may make these things known to the people." But God refused. Then Joshua reminded the people: "Torah is not in heaven but on earth. The commandments which the Lord gave you

מֹשֶׁה עַבְדִּי מֵת. וְעַתָּה קוּם עֲבֹר אֶת הַיַּרְדֵּן הַזֶּה, אַתָּה וְכָל הָעָם הַזֶּה.

I promised to give [2] to the Children of Israel. Every place which the sole of your foot [3] shall tread I will give to you, as I said to Moses. No one shall be able to stand against you all the days of your life. As I was with Moses, so I will be with you. I will not fail you, nor forsake you. Be strong and brave, because you shall cause this people to inherit the land which I swore to their fathers to give to them. Only be strong and very courageous [4] to observe and do according to the whole Torah, that My servant Moses commanded you. Turn not from it to the right nor to the left, that you may succeed wherever you go.

are neither hidden from your eye nor beyond your reach (Deuteronomy 30:11–12). Use the strength of mind with which He has endowed you to discover the commandments for yourself."

[2] WHICH I GIVE: Why does God once more point out that He is now giving the Children of Israel the land which He had long ago promised to Abraham, Isaac and Jacob? Because the Lord did not specify to the Patriarchs which generation of their descendants would inherit the Promised Land. Those who left Egypt with Moses were unworthy but the new generation had proved deserving and had sealed its bond by readiness to obey God's injunction.

[3] THE SOLE OF YOUR FOOT: When the Israelites were about to enter Canaan, the Lord commanded them to destroy its inhabitants utterly. They were neither to show them mercy nor make treaties with them, so that the Israelites might not be infected by the Canaanite pagan abominations (Deuteronomy 7:2; 20:17–18). But Joshua, remembering Moses' treatment of Sihon and Og, instead proclaimed to all Canaan that any nation which chose to leave the land might do so unhindered, that any nation which wanted to make peace could conclude a peace treaty immediately, and that any nation which chose war ought to make ready for it.

[4] BE STRONG AND VERY COURAGEOUS: God repeats this admonition and stresses courage. Conquering the land will take courage but

חֲזַק וֶאֱמָץ, כִּי אַתָּה תַּנְחִיל אֶת הָעָם הַזֶּה אֶת הָאָרֶץ אֲשֶׁר נִשְׁבַּעְתִּי לַאֲבוֹתָם לָתֵת לָהֶם.

This book of the Torah shall not depart from your mouth, and you shall meditate on it day and night, [5] so that you may observe to do all that is written in it; for then you shall make your ways prosperous and you shall succeed."

JOSHUA SENDS SPIES

JOSHUA SENT two spies [6] secretly, and said to them: "Go and look to the land and the city of Jericho."

They went and came to the house of

---

conquering the problems of living according to God's law will require even more bravery. Living a life of dignity and honor requires more courage than going forth to battle. The Rabbis wisely noted that the greatest fortitude is required to live according to the Torah, to do good deeds, to pray and to perform one's social tasks; in short, to live a righteous life.

[5] MEDITATE ON IT DAY AND NIGHT: The Romans condemned Rabbi Simeon ben Yohai to death because he had censured their rule and so Ben Yohai and his son fled for their lives. They hid in a cave for twelve years, eating the dry fruit of a carob tree and drinking water from a nearby stream. They spent all their waking hours in prayer and study of the Torah. After twelve years the decree was annulled and they left their cave to return to their native city. On the way they passed farmers tilling their fields and exclaimed: "Those people still neglect the eternal life and busy themselves with transient things." Shocked, Ben Yohai burst out: "Let these fields that lure men away from the study of the Torah be burned!" Instantly, flame from heaven consumed the fields. But then a voice from heaven was heard: "Did you come out of your cave to destroy My world? You have sinned by detaching yourself from daily life. Back to your cave!" There Ben Yohai was kept for twelve months, the maximum time a transgressor may be kept in Gehenna.

[6] TWO SPIES: Moses had sent twelve spies to search out the land; Joshua sent only two. The difference in number was because Moses wished to test the spirit of the Israelites to see if they were ready to

לֹא יָמוּשׁ סֵפֶר הַתּוֹרָה הַזֶּה מִפִּיךָ, וְהָגִיתָ בּוֹ יוֹמָם וָלַיְלָה.

a woman whose name was Rahab [7] and lodged there. The woman hid the men. She brought them up to the roof and hid them with the stalks of flax which she spread out upon the roof.

The king of Jericho was told, "Some men came here tonight from the Children of Israel to spy out the land." The king of Jericho sent to Rahab, saying: "Bring out the men who came to you, because they came to spy out the whole land." And she answered and said: "True, the men did come to me, but I did not know where they came from. When it was about time to close the gate of the city, just before dark, the men went out; whither they went I do not know. Hurry, pursue them, you may overtake them." And the king's men pursued the spies to the Jordan. When the pursuers had gone out, the city gate was closed.

Before the spies went to sleep, she went up to them on the roof, and said: "I know that the Lord has given you the land. Your terror has fallen upon us, because we have heard how the Lord dried up the waters of the Sea of Reeds before you when you came out of Egypt. We also know what you did to Sihon and Og, the two kings of the Amorites, on the other side of the Jordan—you destroyed them. When we heard of it, our hearts did melt, and no courage was left in any man. For the Lord your God, He is God in heaven above and the earth below. Now, since I dealt kindly with you, swear to me by your Lord that you will also deal kindly with my father's household. Give me a true token that you will spare the lives of my father and mother, my brothers and sisters, with all that belong to them."

And the men said to her: "Our lives for yours, if you will not tell about our errand. When the Lord will give us this

---

enter the Promised Land, but Joshua was concerned only to find out the preparedness of the Canaanites. Joshua chose Caleb, who had gone with him on his first reconnaissance, and Phinehas the priest. They traveled to Jericho disguised as peddlers of pots. Some Sages say that the men did not sell pots (*heres*) but acted as if they were deaf and dumb (*hérésh*) because Joshua feared that if they spoke they might betray themselves by their accents.

⋥ [7] RAHAB: The Lord rewarded Rahab for two other reasons besides the fact that she had hidden and saved Joshua's spies. First, because

וַנִּשְׁמַע וַיִּמַּס לְבָבֵנוּ וְלֹא קָמָה עוֹד רוּחַ בְּאִישׁ מִפְּנֵיכֶם, כִּי יְיָ אֱלֹהֵיכֶם הוּא אֱלֹהִים בַּשָּׁמַיִם מִמַּעַל וְעַל הָאָרֶץ מִתָּחַת.

land, we will deal kindly and truly with you."

Then she let them down by a rope through the window, for her house was part of the city wall. And she said to them: "Go to the mountains; otherwise the pursuers might chance upon you. Hide in the mountain for three days until the pursuers return."

And the men said to her: "When we shall return to the land, you shall tie this line of scarlet thread in the window through which you let us down. And you shall gather into your house your father, your mother, your brothers, your sisters, all your father's household. And it shall be that whoever will go out of the door of your house into the street,

his blood shall be on his head, and we will be guiltless. And if you tell of our errand, we will not be bound by our oath that you made us swear."

She said: "So be it." She sent them away, and she tied the scarlet line in the window.

And the men went into the mountains and waited there for three days, until the pursuers returned. The pursuers searched every road, but found nothing. Then the two men went down the mountain and crossed the Jordan, and came to Joshua. They told him all that had befallen them, and said: "Truly, the Lord has delivered the whole land into our hand. All the inhabitants [8] have lost heart before us."

---

when the spies came to her house, she repented her sins and acknowledged the greatness of the Lord. Second, when Rahab pleaded for mercy she asked for the lives of her parents and family before asking for her own. Therefore God rewarded her.

The Midrash recounts that she confessed her sins: "I have sinned with the wall, the window and the rope. My house is on the wall that surrounds the city. My window faces out on the open country. At night I leave it open with a rope suspended from it. Brigands and thieves climb up the rope into my house to bring me their stolen goods to sell. Now, Lord, I have used all these things with which I did evil to do good—wall, window and rope—to save these two men, so forgive my transgressions."

 و§ [8] ALL THE INHABITANTS: How could Rahab know that all the inhabitants were frightened? The Midrash tells us that there was

נָתַן יְיָ בְּיָדֵנוּ אֶת כָּל הָאָרֶץ וְגַם נָמוֹגוּ כָּל יוֹשְׁבֵי הָאָרֶץ מִפָּנֵינוּ.

JOSHUA COMMANDS THE PEOPLE TO GET READY

JOSHUA COMMANDED the officers of the people: "Pass through the camp and command the people, saying, 'Prepare yourselves with supplies, because within three days you are going to cross the Jordan to enter the land which the Lord God gives you to possess it.'"

ISRAEL CROSSES THE JORDAN

AND JOSHUA awoke early in the morning, and he and all the Children of Israel set out from their camp and reached the Jordan and passed the night there before crossing.

At the end of the three days the officers went through the camp and commanded the people: "When you see the priests and the Levites carrying the Ark of the Covenant [9] of the Lord your God you shall follow it. There should be a space between you and the Ark, about two thousand cubits. Come not nearer to it."

And Joshua said to the people, "Sanctify yourselves, for tomorrow the Lord will do wonders in your midst." And to the priests Joshua said: "Take up the Ark of the Covenant and go ahead of the people."

The Jordan was full at that time, overflowing its banks as always in the time of harvest. And the priests took the Ark of the Covenant and went ahead of the people. The people left their tents and followed. As the feet of the priests who carried the Ark dipped into the edge of the stream the waters flowing down from above stood up and rose up

---

neither an officer nor an official who did not visit Rahab's inn and who did not speak his mind there when drunk.

     [9] THE ARK OF THE COVENANT: When the Israelites left the desert, the manna ceased to rain. Had the manna not ceased, the people would not have eaten the produce of the land and become part of it. And they would have continued to rely on miracles instead of working the land to make it yield.

In the time of Moses, they had been guided by pillars of cloud and fire, but now they would no longer be guided by miracles. Instead, they would be guided by the Ark of the Covenant which would be carried by the priests.

וַיֹּאמֶר יְהוֹשֻׁעַ אֶל הָעָם: הִתְקַדָּשׁוּ, כִּי מָחָר יַעֲשֶׂה יְיָ בְּקִרְבְּכֶם נִפְלָאוֹת.

in one heap; and the waters flowing down toward the sea were wholly cut off. The people crossed the Jordan opposite Jericho. The priests who carried the Ark of the Covenant of the Lord stood on dry ground in the middle of the Jordan until the whole nation crossed the Jordan.

And the men of the tribe of Reuben and the men of the tribe of Gad and the half-tribe of Manasseh crossed over around before the Children of Israel, as Moses spoke to them. About forty thousand armed men crossed over to the plains of Jericho to do battle.

THE TWELVE STONES

AND IT WAS when the entire nation crossed the Jordan, the priests who carried the Ark remained standing in the middle of the Jordan. They stood there until all was finished that the Lord commanded Joshua to speak to the people.

And Joshua called the twelve men whom he had appointed from the Children of Israel, a man from each tribe, and he said to them:

"Go over before the Ark of the Lord your God, in the middle of the Jordan, and every man lift a stone and put it on his shoulder." And they did as Joshua commanded them.

They took twelve stones from the middle of the Jordan, and carried them to the place where they lodged, and laid them down there. Joshua also set up twelve stones in the middle of the Jordan, in the place where the feet of the priests who carried the Ark of the Covenant had stood; and they are there to this day.

And the Lord said to Joshua: "Command the priests who carry the Ark that they come out of the Jordan."

And Joshua commanded the priests, saying: "Come up out of the Jordan."

And it was that as soon as the soles of the feet of the priests touched dry ground, the waters of the Jordan returned to their place and overflowed all its banks as before.

The people crossed the Jordan in the tenth day of the first month, and camped in Gilgal, on the east border of Jericho. And the twelve stones which they took out of the Jordan, Joshua set up in Gilgal. And he said to the Children of Israel: "When the children will ask their fathers in time to come, 'What is the meaning of these stones?' then you shall let your children know that Israel crossed the Jordan on dry land, for the Lord your God dried up the waters of the Jordan before you until you passed over, as the Lord your God did to the Sea of Reeds when we came out of Egypt."

On that day the Lord magnified

וְהוֹדַעְתֶּם אֶת בְּנֵיכֶם לֵאמֹר: בַּיַּבָּשָׁה עָבַר יִשְׂרָאֵל אֶת הַיַּרְדֵּן הַזֶּה.

Joshua in the sight of Israel. They revered him as they revered Moses all the days of his life.

THE PASSOVER

WHEN THE Children of Israel camped at Gilgal they observed the Passover on the evening of the fourteenth day of the month, in the plains of Jericho. They ate of the produce of the land on the day after the Passover, unleavened cakes and parched wheat, and the manna ceased. And the Children of Israel had no more manna but they ate of the produce of the land of Canaan.

AN ANGEL APPEARS TO JOSHUA

NOW JERICHO was shut up tight, because of the Children of Israel. None went out and none came in. And it was when Joshua was near Jericho, that he lifted his eyes and saw a man standing in front of him with a drawn sword in his hand. And Joshua came to him, saying: "Are you for us or for our enemies?" And the man said: "No, I am captain of the host of the Lord."

And Joshua prostrated himself. The captain of the Lord's host said to him: "Take your shoes from off your feet, for the place on which you stand is holy." And Joshua did so.

And the Lord said to Joshua: "See, I have given into your hand Jericho and its king, and all her men of valor. Now, take all your men of war and go around the city once. And seven priests shall carry seven ram's horns. Thus shall you do for six days. On the seventh day you shall go around the city seven times and each time the priests shall blow the *Shofars*. And at the seventh time when you hear the sound of a long blast of the *Shofar*, all the people shall shout with a great shout. The wall of the city shall fall down flat, so that every man can go straight into the city from where he stands.

יָרִיעוּ כָל הָעָם תְּרוּעָה גְדוֹלָה, וְנָפְלָה חוֹמַת הָעִיר תַּחְתֶּיהָ, וְעָלוּ הָעָם אִישׁ נֶגְדּוֹ.

2. JOSHUA [6–10]

THE WALL OF JERICHO FALLS

AND JOSHUA called the priests and said to them: "Take up the Ark of the Covenant and let seven priests carry seven ram's horns before the Ark of the Lord." And to the people he said: "Pass on and go around the city, and the armed troops shall go before the Ark of the Lord. But you shall not shout nor let a word leave your mouth until the day I bid you shout. Only then you shall shout."

And Joshua rose early in the morning and the priests carried the Ark of the Lord. Seven priests, carrying seven ram's horns before the Ark of the Lord, went on sounding the *Shofars* continuously.

The armed men went before them and the rear guard followed the Ark of the Lord. And they went around the city once and returned to the camp. Thus they did for six days.

On the seventh day they arose early, at daybreak, and marched around the city seven times. And it was when the priests blew the *Shofars* the seventh time that Joshua said to the people: "Shout! for the Lord has given you the city. And the city and all that is in it shall be devoted to the Lord. But Rahab shall be spared and all that are in her house, because she hid the messengers that we sent."

And the people shouted a great shout

הָרִיעוּ! כִּי נָתַן יְיָ לָכֶם אֶת הָעִיר.

and the *Shofars* were blown. The walls of the city fell flat, so the people went into the city, each man from the place where he stood; and they captured the city. And the spies went into Rahab's house and brought out Rahab, her father, mother, her brethren, and all her relatives and put them outside the camp of Israel. She has lived among Israel [1] to this day. And they burned the city with fire and all that was in it. Only the silver and gold, and the vessels of brass and iron they put into the treasury of the house of the Lord.

THE CURSE ON JERICHO

AT THAT TIME Joshua charged the people to swear, saying: Cursed be the man before the Lord who undertakes to rebuild the city Jericho. With the loss of his first born shall he lay its foundation, and with the loss of his youngest son shall he erect its gates.

And the Lord was with Joshua so that his fame spread throughout the entire land.

WAR ON AI

AND THE LORD said to Joshua: "Take all the men of war and go up against Ai. I have given into your hand the king of Ai, his people, his city and his land."

Joshua chose thirty thousand of the most valiant warriors and sent them by night, and he commanded them, saying: "See, you are to lie in ambush against the city and be ready. I and all the people with me will approach the city, and when they come out against us, we shall flee from them. And we will flee until we have drawn them away. Then you shall rise up from your ambush and seize the city. And when you have taken the city, you shall set it afire. This have I commanded you."

Then Joshua sent them away, and they went to the ambush.

Joshua rose early in the morning. He inspected the people, and he and the elders went up before the people to Ai. Then men of war who were with him went up and encamped on the north side of the city. When the king of Ai saw this, he hastened the men of the city, and they went out against Israel to do battle. Joshua and his men acted as though they were beaten by them, and fled by way of the wilderness. And all the people who were in the city were summoned together to pursue after

---

ঙ্গ   [1] SHE HAS LIVED AMONG ISRAEL: Rahab dwelt outside the camp of Israel until her conversion to Judaism. It was after that that

אָרוּר הָאִישׁ לִפְנֵי יְיָ אֲשֶׁר יָקוּם וּבָנָה אֶת הָעִיר הַזֹּאת אֶת יְרִיחוֹ. בִּבְכֹרוֹ יְיַסְּדֶנָּה וּבִצְעִירוֹ יַצִּיב דְּלָתֶיהָ.

them. And they pursued after Israel; and there was not a man left in Ai.

And the Lord said to Joshua: "Stretch out the spear in your hand toward Ai, for I will give Ai into your hand." And Joshua signaled with his spear, and the men in ambush rose quickly from their place, and entered the city and took it, and set it on fire. When the people of Ai turned and saw the smoke of the city rising to heaven, they became confused and knew not which way to flee, this way or that.

And when Joshua and all Israel saw that the ambush had taken the city and that the smoke of the city was rising, they turned back. And the others came out of the city, so the people of Ai were in the midst of Israel. And they defeated the people of Ai. Not one remained to escape. And the king of Ai was taken alive and brought to Joshua.

And it was when Israel defeated the inhabitants of Ai on the field of battle, they returned and destroyed the city and raised a great heap of stones over it, that stands to this day.

JOSHUA BUILDS AN ALTAR

THEN JOSHUA built an altar to the Lord the God of Israel on Mount Ebal, an altar of unhewn stones [2] on which no iron tool was lifted, as it is written in the book of the Torah of Moses. And he wrote upon the stones a copy of the Torah of Moses. And all Israel, their elders, officers and their judges, the stranger and the home-born, stood on each side of the Ark, opposite the priests and Levites who carry the Ark of the Covenant of the Lord—half of the people in front of Mount Gerizim and half of them in front of Mount Ebal, as Moses the servant of the Lord commanded to bless the people of Israel.

And he read all the words of the Torah, the blessing and the curse.

THE GIBEONITES

WHEN THE INHABITANTS of Gibeon heard [3] what Joshua did to Jericho and Ai, they acted cunningly. They

---

Joshua gave her land as an inheritance and that she became one with Israel.

–ᶜ [2] UNHEWN STONES: Why did Joshua make this altar without iron? The Rabbis tell us that the altar is the symbol of reconciliation between God and man, between man and man, woman and man,

וְאַחֲרֵי־כֵן קָרָא אֶת כָּל דִּבְרֵי הַתּוֹרָה, הַבְּרָכָה וְהַקְּלָלָה.

took old sacks and put them on their donkeys and wine skins worn, cracked and patched. They put on their feet worn shoes and worn garments on their backs. For their provisions they took dry bread, spotted with mold. And they went to Joshua, to the camp of Gilgal and they said to him and to the men of Israel: "We have come from a far country, and now make a covenant with us."

And Joshua said to them: "Who are you, and where do you come from?"

And they said: "Your servants have come from a far-off country because we heard the name of the Lord your God and all that He did in Egypt to Sihon, king of Heshbon and to Og, king of Bashan. And the elders and all the inhabitants of our country said to us: 'Take provisions on your journey and go to meet them and say to them: We are your servants and now make a covenant with us.' We took for our provisions this bread which you see. When we left, it was hot out of our houses, but now it is dry and moldy. These wine skins were new when we filled them, but now they are dry and cracked. These garments and our shoes are worn out from the very long journey."

And the princes of Israel broke bread with them and Joshua made a covenant of peace with them, and the princes of the congregation swore to observe the Covenant.

Three days after the covenant was

---

nation and nation. Because the sword is a weapon of iron made to kill, iron should not therefore be used on the altar of reconciliation.

[3] THE GIBEONITES HEARD: The sly Gibeonites said: "We will trick the Israelites into making a treaty with us. If they keep their oath and do not make war, they will break their God's commandment to make war on any nation that does not sue for peace immediately after Joshua's proclamation. If they declare war on us, their God will be angry at them for breaking their word. Whichever they do, they incur the wrath of their God." According to law, the Israelites might have broken their solemn oath because the Gibeonites extracted their promise by deceit. But the Israelites kept their bargain so that the nations of Canaan might see that they kept their bargains and remained true to their word even in the face of the duplicity of those with whom they dealt.

מֵאֶרֶץ רְחוֹקָה בָּאנוּ, וְעַתָּה כִּרְתוּ לָנוּ בְרִית.

made, they heard that they were neighbors and were dwelling among them. And the Children of Israel journeyed and came to their cities on the third day. And the whole congregation of Israel murmured against the princes. But all the princes of Israel said to the congregation: "We have sworn to them by the Lord, the God of Israel. Now we cannot touch them. We shall do as we have sworn."

And Joshua called for them and said: "Why did you deceive us by telling us that you live far from us when you dwell among us?"

And they answered Joshua: "Because it was told your servants how the Lord your God commanded His servant Moses to give you all the land and to destroy all the inhabitants of the land. Therefore, we were very much afraid of our lives and so we have done this. And now we are all in your hands. Do to us whatever you think is right and fair."

And he saved them from the hands of the Children of Israel, so they did not slay them. And the princes said: "Let them be hewers of wood and drawers of water to the whole congregation. Let them live."

And Joshua made them that day hewers of wood and drawers of water for the congregation and for the altar of the Lord.

GIBEON IS ATTACKED

WHEN ADONI-ZEDEK, king of Jerusalem, heard that Joshua captured Ai and destroyed it, as he had done to Jericho, and that the inhabitants of Gibeon had made peace with Israel, he became greatly frightened because Gibeon was a great city, one of the royal cities. It was larger than Ai, and all her men were valiant warriors. So Adoni-zedek of Jerusalem sent this message to the king of Hebron, the king of Jarmuth, the king of Lachish and the king of Eglon:

"Come up to me and help me. Let us attack Gibeon and destroy it, because it made peace with Joshua and the Children of Israel." And all the five kings of the Amorites gathered together and then went up with their armies and encamped against Gibeon. And the men of Gibeon sent to Joshua at the camp of Gilgal, saying: "Do not abandon your servants. Come up to us quickly and help us and save us, for all the kings of the Amorites who inhabit the hill country are gathered together against us."

SUN AND MOON STAND STILL!

AND JOSHUA went up from Gilgal, he and all the people with him and all the men of valor. And the Lord said to

וַיַּעַל יְהוֹשֻׁעַ מִן הַגִּלְגָּל, הוּא וְכָל עַם הַמִּלְחָמָה עִמּוֹ וְכל גִּבּוֹרֵי הֶחָיִל.

Joshua: "Fear not, for I have delivered them in your hand; not a man of them shall stand up against you."

And Joshua came upon them suddenly, for he marched from Gilgal all the night. And the Lord threw them into a panic before Israel, and they were defeated in a great battle at Gibeon. And when they fled before Israel the Lord cast down great stones from the sky upon them. There were more who died from hailstones than from the swords of the Children of Israel [but the sun began to set].

Then Joshua called out in the presence of the Children of Israel and said in their sight:

"Sun, stand still [4] upon Gibeon! Moon, in the valley of Aijalon!"

And the sun stood still,
And the moon waited.

Is this not written in the book of Jashar? The sun stayed in the midst of the sky and hastened not to go down about a full day. And there was no day like that before it or after it, a day that the Lord heeded the voice of a man; for the Lord fought for Israel.

And Joshua and all Israel with him returned to the camp at Gilgal.

---

    [4] SUN, STAND STILL: How can the sun stand still when that is against the laws of its nature? God foresaw that Joshua would need a longer day to complete his victory, the Midrash tells us, and arranged it with the sun before the sun was created.

Joshua saw that the battle might be prolonged into the Sabbath so he had the sun stand still to keep the holy day inviolate.

שֶׁמֶשׁ בְּגִבְעוֹן – דּוֹם! וְיָרֵחַ, בְּעֵמֶק אַיָּלוֹן.

3. JOSHUA [10–24]

JOSHUA CONQUERS CANAAN

AND JOSHUA conquered all the land, the hill country, all the south, the lowland, and valleys. Joshua made war a long time with the kings of Canaan. There was not a city that made peace with the Children of Israel, except the Hivites, the inhabitants of Gibeon. At that time Joshua defeated the Anakim, the giants from the hill country of Hebron, and destroyed them and their cities. Joshua conquered the whole land as the Lord spoke to Moses. Joshua was victorious over thirty-one kings, all of them, and possessed their land.

So the land had rest from war.

THE DIVISION OF THE LAND

AND JOSHUA was old, well advanced in years. And the Lord said to him: "Now divide this land as an inheritance to the nine tribes and the half-tribe of Manasseh." And the half-tribe of Manasseh received their inheritance which Moses gave to them, with the tribe of Reuben and the tribe of Gad on the other side of the Jordan.

וַיַּכֶּה יְהוֹשֻׁעַ אֶת כָּל הָאָרֶץ, הָהָר וְהַנֶּגֶב וְהַשְּׁפֵלָה וְהָאֲשֵׁדוֹת.

And the whole congregation of the Children of Israel assembled together at Shiloh, and set up there the Tent of Meeting. And Joshua cast lots for them in Shiloh, before the Lord. And there Joshua divided the land to the Children of Israel.

And the heads of the families of the Levites went up to Eleazar the priest and Joshua there in Shiloh, and they spoke to them: "The Lord commanded through Moses to give us cities to dwell in, with open land for our cattle."

And the Children of Israel gave the Levites some of their own inheritance, cities with open land about them. For the Levites were not given a separate portion in the conquered land, as the Lord commanded Moses.

TRIBES ACROSS THE JORDAN

THEN JOSHUA called the Reubenites and the Gadites and the half-tribe of Manasseh and said to them: "You have observed all that Moses commanded you and have obeyed all that I have commanded you. You have not forsaken your brethren during these many days. Now the Lord your God has given rest to your brethren, as He promised them; therefore, return to your tents, to the land of your possession, which Moses the servant of the Lord gave you across the Jordan. But observe very carefully the Torah that Moses commanded you, to love the Lord your God, to walk in all His ways and to keep His commandments; to serve Him with all your heart and all your soul."

Joshua blessed them and sent them away.

ALTAR BEYOND THE JORDAN

WHEN THE children of Reuben, the children of Gad and the half-tribe of Manasseh came to the region of the Jordan they built there a great altar by the Jordan, facing the land of Canaan.

When they heard of it, the whole congregation of the Children of Israel gathered in Shiloh to go up against them to war.

And the Children of Israel sent to Reuben and to Gad and to the half-tribe of Manasseh, Phinehas, the son of Eleazar the priest, and with him ten princes, a prince from each tribe. They came to these tribes and they spoke to them:

"Thus said the whole congregation of the Lord. You rebelled today against of God of Israel in that you have built you an altar. Because of you tomorrow He will be angry with the whole congregation of Israel. If the land of your possession is unclean, [you will not sanctify it by this rebellion;] it would be better if you were to cross over into the

וְעַתָּה הֵנִיחַ יְיָ אֱלֹהֵיכֶם לַאֲחֵיכֶם כַּאֲשֶׁר דִּבֶּר לָהֶם, וְעַתָּה פְּנוּ וּלְכוּ לָכֶם לְאָהֳלֵיכֶם.

land of the possession of the Lord where the Tabernacle of the Lord is. Do not rebel against the Lord by building another altar."

Then the children of Reuben, of Gad, and the half-tribe of Manasseh answered: "The God, the Lord God knows, and all Israel shall know, that we built the altar because of our fear and anxiety. In time to come your children might say to our children: 'What have you to do with the Lord, the God of Israel? For the Lord made the Jordan a border between us and you. You have no share in the Lord. Your children will prevent our children from fearing the Lord.' Therefore, we said: 'Let us now build us an altar, not for sacrifice; but it shall be a witness between us and you and the generations after us! If your children will say to our children: 'You have no share in the Lord,' they will say: 'Look at the altar of the Lord which our fathers made, not for sacrifice, but as a witness between us

and you.' Far be it from us to rebel against the Lord, and build an altar for sacrificing beside the altar of the Lord that is before His Tabernacle."

When Phinehas the priest [1] and the heads of the tribes of Israel heard the words from the Reubenites, Gadites and the children of Manasseh, it pleased them well, and Phinehas said to them: "Now we know that the Lord is in our midst, for you have not rebelled against the Lord."

JOSHUA WARNS THE PEOPLE

AND IT WAS when the Lord had given rest to Israel from all their enemies, and Joshua was old, that he called all Israel, their elders, their heads, their judges and their officers and said to them: "I am old, well advanced in years, and you have seen [2] all that the Lord has done to all these nations. For the Lord, your God has fought for you. I have allotted to you as inheri-

---

ﻬ [1] PHINEHAS THE PRIEST: Whenever Phinehas' name was mentioned before, it was followed by "the son of Eleazar." Here, for the first time, he is called "the priest" without his father's name appended because, having brought peace between the tribes, he had earned the title in his own right.

ﻬ [2] YOU HAVE SEEN: The generation that had experienced the Exodus was dead. Those who now stood before Joshua were their

רְאוּ אֶת תַּבְנִית מִזְבַּח יְיָ אֲשֶׁר עָשׂוּ אֲבוֹתֵינוּ לֹא לְעוֹלָה וְלֹא לְזֶבַח, כִּי עֵד הוּא בֵּינֵינוּ וּבֵינֵיכֶם.

tance all the land from the Jordan to the great sea at the west, the land of the nations I conquered and the land of the nations that remain. The Lord your God will drive them out and you will possess their land, as the Lord your God has promised you. Therefore, you shall strive to observe and do all that is written in the book of the Torah of Moses. You shall not turn to the right or to the left. You shall not mingle with the nations who remain among you. You shall not mention the names of their gods, nor swear by them. Only to the Lord your God shall you cleave as you have done to this day. The Lord has driven from before you great and mighty nations so that no one has stood against you to this day. One man of you chased a thousand, for the Lord your God, He has fought for you as He promised you. Therefore, take great care that you shall love the Lord your God.

"But if you turn back and attach yourselves to the remnant of the nations that remains among you, and you intermarry with them, then you shall know that the Lord your God will no longer drive these nations from before you. They shall be a snare and a trap to you, a scourge in your sides and thorns in your eyes, until you perish from off this good land that the Lord your God has given you.

"Behold this day I am to go the way of all the earth. But you know with all your heart and with all your soul, that not one thing which the Lord your God has promised you has not been fulfilled. And it shall be that as all the good things which the Lord your God has promised to you became true, so shall the Lord bring upon you all the evil things if you will transgress the covenant of the Lord your God, which He commanded you."

ISRAEL RENEWS THE COVENANT

AND JOSHUA gathered all the tribes of Israel to Shechem, and called the elders of Israel and they presented themselves before God. Then Joshua said to the people:

"When you crossed the Jordan and you came to Jericho the men of Jericho fought against you and seven other na-

---

children or grandchildren. But Deuteronomy tells us: "Not only with you do I make this covenant and this oath; but with him who stands here with us this day before the Lord our God, and also with

וַחֲזַקְתֶּם מְאֹד לִשְׁמֹר וְלַעֲשׂוֹת אֵת כָּל הַכָּתוּב בְּסֵפֶר תּוֹרַת מֹשֶׁה, לְבִלְתִּי סוּר מִמֶּנּוּ יָמִין וּשְׂמֹאל.

tions, and I delivered them into your hand. I sent before you the hornet which drove them out—it was not with your own sword and bow. And I gave you a land for which you have not toiled and cities which you have not built, and you dwell within and you eat of vineyards and olive groves and orchards you did not plant. So fear the Lord and serve Him with sincerity and truth. Now if you do not want to serve the Lord, choose this day whom you will serve, the gods your ancestors worshipped beyond the river or the gods of the Amorites in whose land you now dwell. But as for me and my household, we will serve the Lord."

And the people answered and said: "Far be it from us that we should forsake the Lord to serve other gods, for the Lord is our God."

And Joshua said to the people: "It is not easy to serve the Lord, because He is a holy God and a demanding God. If after you take upon yourself to serve the Lord and then you forsake the Lord and serve other gods, He will turn and do you evil, after having done you good."

And the people answered Joshua: "No, we will serve the Lord."

Then Joshua said to the people: "You are witnesses against yourself that you have chosen to serve the Lord."

And they said: "We are witnesses."

And Joshua made a covenant with the people on that day. He interpreted for them the statutes and the ordinances and wrote all these words in the book of the Torah of God. [3] Then he took a great stone and set it under an oak tree which was by the Sanctuary

---

him who is not here with us this day" (29:13–14). So Exodus, like the Covenant, is not only part of the history of the Jewish people but part of the personal history of every Jew in every epoch.

    [3] THE BOOK OF THE TORAH OF GOD: Rabbi Ḥananiah said that had Israel not sinned, the Lord would have given the people only the Five Books of Moses and the Book of Joshua. These would have sufficed to teach them His ways. But they rebelled and sinned again and again so the Lord, out of His compassion, sent them prophets, books and precepts to continue their instruction, to deepen their understanding, to mature them in the ways of God and of goodness.

וְאָנֹכִי וּבֵיתִי נַעֲבֹד אֶת יְיָ.

of the Lord, and he said to the people: "This stone shall be a witness against you that you may not deny your God."

And Joshua sent the people away, each one to his inheritance.

THE DEATH OF JOSHUA

AFTER ALL these things, Joshua, the son of Nun, the servant of the Lord, died at the age of one hundred and ten years. And they buried him in the bor-

der of his inheritance, in the hill country of Ephraim, on the north of the mountain of Gaash. [4] And Israel served the Lord all the lifetime of Joshua and of the elders who lived after him.

And the bones of Joseph, which the Israelites brought out of Egypt, were buried in Shechem, in the field which Jacob bought for one hundred pieces of money from the sons of Hamor, the father of Shechem.

---

  [4] THE MOUNTAIN OF GAASH: When Canaan was divided among the Israelites, they busied themselves with their fields and vineyards. Prosperity made them wayward and forgetful. They soon forgot Joshua and what he had done for them, and when he died they neither eulogized nor mourned him with feeling. The Lord waxed angry and caused the mountain to quake as a sign of their waywardness and ingratitude. In Hebrew *Gaash* means to quake or tremble.

וַיְהִי אַחֲרֵי הַדְּבָרִים הָאֵלֶּה, וַיָּמָת יְהוֹשֻׁעַ בִּן־נוּן עֶבֶד יְיָ בֶּן מֵאָה וָעֶשֶׂר שָׁנִים.

4. JUDGES [2–5]

THE NEW GENERATION

JOSHUA, THE SON of Nun, the servant of the Lord, died, and his generation died too. Another generation arose who knew nothing of the Lord or the work that He had done for Israel. And the Lord left the Philistines and the other nations and did not drive them out [1] hastily, neither did He deliver them into the hands of Joshua. He left them to test Israel, that the generations to come would be counselled to learn war, which beforetime they did not know.

---

[1] AND DID NOT DRIVE THEM OUT: The Lord permitted the Philistines and Canaanites and Israel's other enemies to remain in the land. And so generations of Israelites were forced to learn to wage war. The Rabbis considered the necessity to learn and to practice war to be a punishment. Even under the most compelling urgency, to make war was considered an affliction.

וַיָּקָם דּוֹר אַחֵר אַחֲרֵיהֶם אֲשֶׁר לֹא יָדְעוּ אֶת יְיָ וְגַם אֶת הַמַּעֲשֶׂה אֲשֶׁר עָשָׂה לְיִשְׂרָאֵל.

They forsook the Lord, [2] the God of their fathers, and they followed other gods, the gods of the peoples around them. They worshiped them and so provoked the Lord. And the anger of the Lord blazed against Israel, and He gave them into the hands of their enemies, and they could no longer withstand their enemies.

They were in sore plight. Then the Lord had compassion [3] on the Israelites because of their groans under the oppressors. He raised up judges who delivered them from the hands of their plunderers. When the Lord raised up a judge, He would be with the judge and save them out of the hands of their enemies all the days of the judge. But when the judge died, they would relapse and behave worse than did their fathers. Again they followed other gods. They served them and bowed to them, and would not give up their practices and their stubborn ways.

ﻉ [2] THEY FORSOOK THE LORD: After Joshua died the people forgot the word of the Lord and His commandments; instead each of them was concerned only about himself and his possessions. The common good and the common purpose were lost. None had time for or interest in the Covenant and the worship of God. And because they had in this way forsaken the Lord they were unable to resist their enemies.

ﻉ [3] THE LORD HAD COMPASSION: A king settled his young bondsmen and bondswomen on a tract of his land. There he raised them as if they were his children. He had houses built for them, planted vines and trees for them, and fed them from his own table. But the children neglected the vines, broke the saplings and left their houses untended. Then the king grew angry and punished them. But he punished them with compassion because he said, "How can I punish them severely? They are only children!"

So it was with the Children of Israel. The Lord gave them fields for which they did not labor, cities which they did not build, vineyards and olive groves which they did not plant. When they strayed, He forgave them their sins as a father forgives his children. And from among them He raised eighteen judges to save Israel from its enemies.

וַיָּקֶם יְיָ שֹׁפְטִים וַיּוֹשִׁיעוּם מִיַּד שֹׁסֵיהֶם.

And the Lord's anger was hot against Israel, and He said: "Because this nation has violated My covenant which I made with their fathers, and they did not listen to My voice, I will no longer drive out before them any of the peoples that Joshua left when he died."

THE JUDGE OTHNIEL

AND THE CHILDREN OF ISRAEL dwelt among the Canaanites, the Hittites, the Amorites, the Perizzites, the Hivites and the Jebusites. They married their daughters and their own daughters they married to their sons, and they served their gods. They forgot the Lord their God, and they served the Baalim and the Asheroth. Then the anger of the Lord was kindled against Israel, and He gave them over into the hand of Cushan-rishathaim, king of Aram-naharaim. And the Israelites served him eight years.

And the Israelites cried to the Lord, and the Lord raised a deliverer for the Children of Israel, Othniel, the son of Kenaz. The spirit of the Lord came upon him and he judged Israel, and went to war, and the Lord delivered Cushan-rishathaim into his hand. And the land had peace for forty years.

THE JUDGE EHUD

AND OTHNIEL died, and the Israelites again did evil in eyes of the Lord. And the Lord made Eglon, king of Moab victorious over Israel. And the Israelites served Eglon for eighteen years.

And the Israelites cried to the Lord, and He raised up for them a deliverer, Ehud, the son of Gera, a Benjamite, a left-handed man.

And the Israelites sent tribute by him to Eglon, the king of Moab. And Ehud made for himself a two-edged sword, a cubit long, and girded it under his cloak upon his right thigh.

Now Eglon was a very fat man. After Ehud had finished delivering the tribute he sent away the people who carried the present. But he himself turned back from the quarries that were near Gilgal. And he said: "I have a secret message for you, O king."

And the king said: "Silence!"

And all his attendants went out. And Ehud approached him as he sat alone in the cool upper chamber, and said: "I have a message from God to you."

And Eglon arose from his seat, [4] and Ehud put out his left hand and

---

⊷§   [4] EGLON AROSE FROM HIS SEAT: Eglon, the king of Moab, was the great-great-grandfather of King David. And Ruth, Eglon's daughter, was David's great-grandmother. Why did Eglon, a tyrant, an idol

וַיִּזְעֲקוּ בְנֵי יִשְׂרָאֵל אֶל יְיָ וַיָּקֶם יְיָ לָהֶם מוֹשִׁיעַ אֶת אֵהוּד בֶּן גֵּרָא.

took the sword from his right thigh and thrust it into Eglon's belly. Then Ehud went out to the porch and shut the doors of the upper chamber and locked them. When he had gone out the servants came. They saw that the doors of the upper chamber were locked, and they said: "He is relieving himself there." After waiting a long time, they took the key and opened the doors. And there was their master, fallen down dead.

While they were waiting Ehud escaped. He passed the quarries and came to Seirah. When he got there, he blew a *Shofar* throughout the hill country of Ephraim. And the Israelites went down with him. He went before them and he said to them: "Follow after me, for the Lord has delivered your enemies, into your hand."

And they followed him down. They seized the fords of the Jordan and they would not allow anyone to cross. They were victorious over the Moabites. So Moab was subdued that day under the hand of Israel. Afterward, the land was at peace for eighty years.

SHAMGAR, THE SON OF ANATH

AFTER HIM CAME Shamgar, [5] the son

worshiper, the scourge of Israel, merit the honor of such offspring? The Rabbis reply that though Eglon was a sinner and was punished for his transgressions by the sword, he was also rewarded for his respect for the Lord. For when Ehud said to him, "I have a message from God to you," Eglon rose from his throne in conscious awe of God's name. Then the Lord declared that because Eglon had risen in reverence for His throne, so would one of Eglon's descendants eventually sit on the throne of Israel.

[5] SHAMGAR: Shamgar was working in the fields when a band of Philistines raided his village. Though he had no weapon Shamgar seized an ox-goad and ran to fight them. Only a man of immense strength could wield such a heavy weapon—an ox-goad was eight to ten feet long with a spike at one end and a chisel-like blade at the other—but with it Shamgar stood against the Philistines. The villagers came to help him and six hundred Philistines perished in the battle. For his courage and simplicity, Shamgar remained in the peo-

וַתִּכָּנַע מוֹאָב בַּיּוֹם הַהוּא תַּחַת יַד יִשְׂרָאֵל, וַתִּשְׁקֹט הָאָרֶץ שְׁמוֹנִים שָׁנָה.

of Anath, who slew six hundred Philistines with an ox-goad. And he also saved Israel.

DEBORAH AND BARAK

EHUD DIED, and the Israelites again did evil in the eyes of the Lord, and the Lord gave them over to the hand of Jabin, the king of Canaan who reigned in Hazor. The captain of his army was Sisera. [6] The Israelites cried to the Lord, for he had nine hundred iron chariots, and he oppressed the Israelites mightily for twenty years.

Now Deborah, a prophetess, [7] the wife of Lappidoth, [8] judged Israel at that time. In the hill country of Ephraim

---

ple's memory and was "written in the register of the House of Israel" (Ezekiel 13:9).

[6] SISERA: Sisera was one of the most ferocious and mighty warriors in history. When he hunted and cried aloud, animals were frozen in fear and could not move. All men feared him and bowed low before him. If they did not, he slew them unmercifully. And when people trembled and bowed before him, Sisera exulted: "Who is like me on the whole earth? Who, indeed, is like me in the heavens above?" Because he was a tyrant and a boaster, God had him brought low by a woman's hand.

[7] THE PROPHETESS DEBORAH: The Rabbis asked: How is it that Deborah, a woman, became a prophet and a judge when Phinehas the son of Eleazar and grandson of Aaron still lived? Was not Phinehas' lineage more illustrious? And the prophet Elijah answered them: "As heaven and earth are my witness, whether Jew or gentile, man or woman, maleservant or maidservant, the spirit of the Lord rests upon him who merits it according to his deeds."

[8] THE WIFE OF LAPPIDOTH: The Rabbis note that Deborah's husband is known by three names. At first he was called Michael. When Deborah went to the academies to search out those who would help her redeem the nation from Sisera, she saw Michael.

בֵּין גּוֹי וּבֵין יִשְׂרָאֵל, בֵּין אִישׁ וּבֵין אִשָּׁה ... הַכֹּל לְפִי מַעֲשָׂיו רוּחַ הַקֹּדֶשׁ שׁוֹרָה עָלָיו.

she sat under the palm tree of Deborah and the Israelites came up to her to be judged.

And she sent for Barak, the son of Abinoam, and said to him: "The Lord, the God of Israel commanded: 'Go toward Mount Tabor and take with you ten thousand men from the tribes of Naphtali and Zebulun. And I will draw Sisera, the captain of Jabin's army with his chariots and his army to the brook Kishon, and I will deliver him into your hand.'"

And Barak said to her: "If you will come with me, [9] then I will go; but if you will not go with me, I will not go myself."

And she said: "I will go with you, but the glory will not be yours; because they will say that the Lord delivered Sisera into the hand of a woman."

Deborah arose and went with Barak to Kedesh. Barak summoned the men of Zebulun and Naphtali to Kedesh. Ten thousand men came up to him.

They told Sisera that Barak had gone up to Mount Tabor. So Sisera gathered together all his nine hundred iron char-

---

He was a fine youth and a brilliant student. The Lord brought them together and they were married. And Deborah, who was very rich, helped to support the academies of study. She sent olive oil and thick wicks for their study lamps. Because it was her husband Michael who brought these gifts, his fellow students called him *Lappidoth*, the flame. But he was also called Barak, which means *lightning*, because his face shone bright as lightning when he served the Lord.

[9] IF YOU WILL COME WITH ME: Barak was a great and brave general. Yet he asked Deborah to go with him to meet Sisera in battle. Our Sages say that Barak did so because he knew the value of morale in the face of numbers. When the Israelites saw the mighty armies and chariots of Sisera and the thirty-one kings with him, they were afraid and ready to take flight. But when they saw the prophetess their spirits lifted. Deborah encouraged them, saying, "Fear not. The Lord goes before you. Take courage. You will defeat your enemies." And the Children of Israel took heart and attacked and defeated Sisera.

וַיֹּאמֶר אֵלֶיהָ בָּרָק: אִם תֵּלְכִי עִמִּי וְהָלָכְתִּי, וְאִם לֹא תֵלְכִי עִמִּי לֹא אֵלֵךְ.

iots and all of the people who were with him.

Then Deborah said to Barak: "Up! This is the day on which the Lord is to deliver Sisera to your hand."

Barak went down from Mount Tabor with the ten thousand men after him. And the Lord routed Sisera and all his chariots and all his men before Barak. And Sisera alighted from his chariot and fled on foot. Barak pursued the chariots and Sisera's army. The whole army of Sisera fell before the sword.

Sisera fled on foot to the tent of Jael, the wife of Heber the Kenite. Jael came out to meet Sisera, and said to him: "Turn, my lord, turn to me. Have no fear." And he turned into her tent, and she covered him with a blanket. And he said to her: "Give me, please, a little water. [10] I am thirsty." So she opened the goat-skin and gave him milk to drink, and covered him. Then he said to her: "Stand at the door of the tent, and if anyone asks you, 'Is there a man here?' You shall say, 'No.'"

And he fell into a deep sleep because he was weary. So Jael took a tent-pin and a hammer in her hand, and went up softly to him, and she drove the pin into his temple, and it pierced through into the ground, and he died.

And Barak pursued Sisera, and Jael came out to meet him, and said: "Come and I will show you the man you are looking for." Barak went inside and saw Sisera lying dead.

THE SONG OF DEBORAH

THEN SANG Deborah and Barak on that day, saying:

"Hear, O kings, give ear, O princes:
To the Lord will I sing;
I will praise the Lord, the God of Israel.

ᥥᥫ [10] A LITTLE WATER: How did Jael, a woman and the wife of a humble Kenite, find the strength to kill the mighty Sisera? Jael gave Sisera milk instead of water to see if his head was clear. When Sisera did not know the difference, Jael understood that he was confused, and knew she could go ahead to kill him. As he slept, the Rabbis tell us, Jael thought of how many women Sisera had widowed, how many children he had orphaned, how many husbands he had killed leaving their tents empty. And she knew he would do more killing if he lived. And then, not with a sword, but with the homely instruments of the tent dweller she slew him.

שִׁמְעוּ מְלָכִים, הַאֲזִינוּ רוֹזְנִים: אָנֹכִי לַיְיָ, אָנֹכִי אָשִׁירָה, אֲזַמֵּר לַיְיָ אֱלֹהֵי יִשְׂרָאֵל.

Lord, when Thou didst go out of
  Seir,
When Thou didst march out of
  the field of Edom,
The earth trembled, the heavens
  also shook;
The clouds, too, dropped water.
The mountains quaked at the
  presence of the Lord,
Like Sinai, at the presence of the
  Lord, the God of Israel.

In the days of Shamgar, the son
  of Anath, the caravans
  disappeared,
The travelers kept to the byways.
There were no open cities in
  Israel, they disappeared,
Until I arose, Deborah,
Until I arose, a mother in Israel.
Then was there war at·the gates.

Awake, awake, Deborah!
Awake, awake, strike up a song!
Arise, Barak,
Take your captives, you son of
  Abinoam!

The kings came, they fought.
Then fought the kings of Canaan.
At Taanach, by the waters of
  Megiddo;
They did not take booty of silver.

The stars fought from heaven,

From their courses they fought
  Sisera.
The brook Kishon swept them
  away,
That ancient brook Kishon.
Tread on them, O my soul, in
  strength!

O how the hoofs of the horses
  stamped,
From the prancings,
The prancings of their mighty
  ones.
Cursed be Meroz, said the angel
  of the Lord.
Curse, curse its inhabitants,
Because they did not come to the
  help of the Lord,
To help the Lord with the heroes.

Blessed above women shall Jael be,
The wife of Heber, the Kenite;
Blessed above the women in the
  tents.
Water he asked: milk she gave
  him.
In a lordly bowl she brought his
  curd.
Her hand she put to the tent-pin.
And her right hand to the
  workmen's hammer.

She hammered Sisera, she smote
  his head,
She pierced through his temples.

עוּרִי, עוּרִי, דְּבוֹרָה! עוּרִי, עוּרִי, דַּבְּרִי שִׁיר!

At her feet he sank, he fell,
  he lay.
He sank, he fell at her feet.
Where he sank, there he fell
  down dead.

Through the window peered the
  mother of Sisera,
Through the lattice, she looked
  and lamented:
  'Why is his chariot so long in
    coming?
  Why is the clatter of his
    chariots so late?'
The wisest of her princesses [11]
  answer her,

Why, she answers herself:
  'Will they not find and divide
    booty?
  A maid, two maids for every
    man.
  To Sisera a spoil of dyed
    garments,
  One dyed robe, two dyed
    embroidered cloths
  For the neck of every spoiler?'

Thus perish all Thy enemies,
  O Lord!
But those who love Him,
May they be as the rising of the
  sun in his might!"

⤜§ [11] THE WISEST OF HER PRINCESSES: Why does Sisera's mother ask
her women for counsel, then answer her own question? Our Sages
remind us that Sisera's mother was anxious because Sisera had not
yet returned from the battle. So she spoke to her wise woman, or
diviner. In a vision the diviner saw two women—Deborah and Jael—
and the color red—Sisera's blood. But the mother misinterprets the
two women in the vision to be Sisera's captives and the scarlet color
the dye of the garments he had taken as booty.

כֵּן יֹאבְדוּ כָל אוֹיְבֶיךָ, יְיָ, וְאוֹהֲבָיו כְּצֵאת הַשֶּׁמֶשׁ בִּגְבוּרָתוֹ.

5. JUDGES [5–8]

THE JUDGE GIDEON

THE LAND was at peace for forty years. Then the Israelites again did evil in the eyes of the Lord, [1] and the Lord delivered them into the hand of Midian for seven years. The hand of Midian lay heavy upon Israel. The Israelites made hiding places in the mountains, [2] in the caves and in strongholds. For when the Israelites had sown, the Midianites, the Amalekites and the Kedemites came up and destroyed the produce of the earth, and did not leave sustenance for

---

[1] EVIL IN THE EYES OF THE LORD: After the death of each Judge, it is written that the people "*again* did evil in the sight of the Lord." But after the death of Deborah the word *again* is left out. The Midrash tells us that after Deborah sang her song of praise for the Lord, He forgave Israel all its previous transgressions. The Israelites then repented truly and prosperity returned to the land. But the people soon found a new and even more grievous sin, the sin of worshiping one's own reflection.

וַיַּעֲשׂוּ בְנֵי־יִשְׂרָאֵל הָרַע בְּעֵינֵי יְיָ, וַיִּתְּנֵם יְיָ בְּיַד מִדְיָן שֶׁבַע שָׁנִים.

Israel, not even for a sheep, an ox, or ass. They would come up with their cattle and their tents, swarming like locusts. Both they and their camels were numberless. And Israel was brought low and cried unto the Lord.

An angel of the Lord [3] came and sat under the terebinth tree which was in Ophrah and belonged to Joash. And his son Gideon was threshing wheat [4] in the winepress, to hide it from the Midianites. And the angel said to him: "The Lord is with you, valiant warrior!"

And Gideon said to him: "Oh, my lord, if the Lord is with us, then why has all this happened to us? Where are all His wonderful deeds which our fathers told us about, saying: Did not the Lord bring us out of Egypt? But now the Lord has cast us off and delivered us into the hand of Midian."

And the Lord turned toward him and said: "Go, and with the strength you have shown you shall save Israel from the hand of Midian. For it is I who send you."

---

    [2] HIDING PLACES IN THE MOUNTAINS: When the Midianites oppressed Israel, they seized everything in their path. When the enemy approached, the Israelites signaled from village to village. Then the people drove their sheep and cattle into caves, and hid their crops in pits, and fled into strongholds they had prepared in the hills for just such emergencies.

    [3] AN ANGEL OF THE LORD: Why does God first send an angel to Gideon and then moments later speak to Gideon Himself? Man must be prepared for his vision of God, the Rabbis tell us. Gideon must know before Whom he stands. So was Moses prepared when he was confronted with the mystery of the burning bush.

    [4] GIDEON WAS THRESHING WHEAT: High among Gideon's merits was that he was a devoted son. When his father was old and the time to thresh the wheat came, Gideon said, "I am young, father. If the Midianites should come upon me I shall be able to defend myself against them. Or if they are too many I shall be swift in my flight. But at your age, you can neither defend yourself strongly nor run swiftly enough to escape them. Therefore, let me be the one to do the threshing."

לֵךְ בְּכֹחֲךָ זֶה וְהוֹשַׁעְתָּ אֶת יִשְׂרָאֵל מִכַּף מִדְיָן, הֲלֹא שְׁלַחְתִּיךָ.

And Gideon said to Him: "Oh, my Lord, how can I save Israel, when my family is the poorest in Manasseh, and I am the youngest in my father's house?"

The Lord answered him: "I will be with you, and you shall defeat the Midianites as one man."

And it was on the same night the angel of the Lord said to him: "Arise and destroy the altar of Baal that your father built and you shall cut down the Asherah beside it. Then build an altar to the Lord your God on the top of this rock, and take your father's bullock [5] and offer it as a burnt offering with the wood of the Asherah which you cut down."

Then Gideon took ten of his servants, and did as the Lord had told him to do. But because he was afraid of his father's household and the men of the city to do it by day, so he did it at night. When the men of the city rose in the morning, they saw that the altar of Baal was torn down and the Asherah around it was cut down, and the bullock had been offered upon the altar which had been built. They said one to another: "Who has done this thing?" They searched and inquired and they found out that it was Gideon. Then the men of the city said to Joash: "Bring out your son. He must die, because he has torn down the altar of the Baal and cut down the Asherah."

And Joash said to those who stood against him: "Are you going to take the Baal's part? Do you intercede for him? If he is a god, let him contend for himself for his broken altar."

So on that day Gideon was called Jerubbaal, meaning: Let Baal contend against him, because he has overthrown his altar.

WAR WITH MIDIAN

THE MIDIANITES, the Amalekites and the Kedemites joined forces, and crossed the Jordan and encamped in the valley of Jezreel. And the spirit of the Lord

---

৵৪ [5] TAKE YOUR FATHER'S BULLOCK: Rabbi Abba bar Kahana noted that the Lord allowed Gideon to commit many infractions of Jewish law in this sacrifice. He used the wood of a pagan idol, an Asherah. He used hewn stones to build the altar. He made his sacrifice at night rather than by day. He was not a priest yet he performed the sacrifice. And he performed the sacrifice on a "high place," which was specifically forbidden. But, Rabbi bar Kahana continues, because Israel was in such desperate need, the offering was accepted.

בִּי אֲדֹנָי, בַּמָּה אוֹשִׁיעַ אֶת יִשְׂרָאֵל? הִנֵּה אַלְפִּי הַדַּל בִּמְנַשֶּׁה וְאָנֹכִי הַצָּעִיר בְּבֵית אָבִי.

rested upon Gideon and he blew the *Shofar,* and the men of Abiezer gathered around him. Then he sent messengers throughout Manasseh, Asher, Zebulun and Naphtali, and they came up to meet him and his men.

And Gideon said to God: "If Thou wilt save Israel by my hand, as Thou hast spoken, look, I will put a fleece of wool on the threshing-floor. If there will be dew only on the fleece and the ground will be dry, then I shall know Thou wilt save Israel by my hand, as Thou hast spoken."

And it was so. He rose up early the next day and squeezed the fleece, and wrung dew from the fleece, a bowlful of water. And Gideon said to God: "Let not Thine anger be kindled against me, and I will speak but this time. Let me have proof, I pray Thee, this time with the fleece. Let the fleece only be dry, and let there be dew only upon all the ground."

And God did so that night. The fleece alone was dry, and there was dew on all the ground.

Then Jerubbaal, who is Gideon, and all the people who were with him, rose up early and encamped in En-harod, and the camp of Midian was on the north side of them, by the hill of Moreh.

And the Lord said to Gideon: "The people who are with you are too many for Me to deliver the Midianites in their hands. Israel might give itself greater glory than Me and say: 'My own power has saved me.' Therefore, proclaim to the people: Whosoever is fearful and trembling should arise early and depart from Mount Gilead." [6] And twenty-two thousand of the people went home, and there remained ten thousand.

And the Lord said to Gideon: "There are still too many people. Bring them down to the water and there I will select them for you." And Gideon brought the people down to the water. And the Lord said to Gideon: "Every one who laps the water with his tongue, as a dog laps, place him to one side. And every one who kneels down to drink [7] on

---

&§ [6] DEPART FROM MOUNT GILEAD: Here Gideon speaks according to the Torah. "If there is a man who is fearful and fainthearted, let him return to his house, lest his brethren's heart melt as does his" (Deuteronomy 20:8). And the Lord told Gideon to send them home early in the morning before the camp was awake so that those who remained would not jeer at those who departed.

מִי יָרֵא וְחָרֵד יָשֹׁב וְיִצְפֹּר מֵהַר הַגִּלְעָד.

the other." There were three hundred men who lapped with their tongues, drawing their hands to their mouths. But all the rest of the people knelt down to drink water. And the Lord said to Gideon: "With the three hundred men [8] who lapped will I save you and deliver the Midianites into your hands. All the rest of the people shall go home." And Gideon sent all the men of Israel home, but kept only the three hundred.

THE DREAM

THE CAMP OF Midian lay below him in the valley. On that same night the Lord said to him: "Go down into the Midianite camp, you and your servant Purah, and you shall hear their talk. Then you will have the courage to attack the camp."

Gideon and his servant Purah went down to the outpost of the armed men who were lying along the valley like a swarm of locusts. Their camels could not be counted, like the sand which is at the seashore. When Gideon arrived there, he heard a man telling a dream to his fellow. He said: "I dreamt that a cake of barley bread [9] tumbled into the camp of Midian. When it reached a tent, it struck so hard that it fell and turned it upside down and it lay flat."

[7] EVERY ONE WHO KNEELS DOWN TO DRINK: First, Gideon eliminates those who are fearful and afraid. Then he eliminates those who worshiped their reflections in the water. Those who kneeled Gideon knew to be reflection worshipers and he sent them away. And so Gideon was left with the righteous and the pious. With those remaining three hundred, the Lord would save Israel.

[8] WITH THE THREE HUNDRED MEN: The Rabbis understood this to mean that God intended that the warrior should not become a hero and an example to Jews. Those who have faith in the Lord will stand fast in His stead. The number of Gideon's host therefore mattered little.

[9] A CAKE OF BARLEY BREAD: The barley loaf is a circular flat cake baked on hot stones. It was the food of the humble and the poor. Eating the barley loaf showed in what dire straits the Israelites were

בִּשְׁלֹשׁ מֵאוֹת הָאִישׁ הַמְלַקְקִים אוֹשִׁיעַ אֶתְכֶם וְנָתַתִּי אֶת מִדְיָן בְּיָדֶךָ.

His fellow answered and said: "This is nothing else but the sword of Gideon, and that God has delivered all Midian into his hand."

As soon as Gideon heard the dream and its interpretation, he bowed in prayer, and he then returned to his camp and said to his men: "Arise! The Lord has delivered into your hand the host of Midian."

Then Gideon divided the three hundred men into three companies, and he placed *Shofars* in the hands of all of them, and empty pitchers, and torches in the pitchers. And he said to them: "Watch me and do likewise. As I come to the outskirts of the camp, I will blow the *Shofar*. You too will blow your *Shofars* and cry out: 'For the Lord and Gideon.'"

And Gideon and the hundred men who were with him came to the outskirts of the camp at the beginning of the middle watch, and they blew the *Shofars* and broke the pitchers that were in their hands. And the three companies blew the *Shofars*, smashed the pitchers; held the torches in their left hands and the *Shofars* to blow in their right hands, and they cried: "The sword for the Lord and Gideon!"

Every man stood in his place around the camp, and they blew the three hundred *Shofars*. And throughout the whole camp the Lord set the Midianites fighting one against another. The entire host fled as far as Tabbath. And the men of Naphtali, Asher and Manasseh gathered and pursued after Midian.

Gideon sent messengers through the hill country of Ephraim saying: "Come down against the Midianites, and seize the waters as far as Beth-barah and the Jordan." So all the men of Ephraim gathered together and seized the streams as far as Beth-barah and the Jordan. And they captured the two princes of Midian, Oreb and Zeeb, and killed both of them.

THE END OF THE WAR

AND THE MEN of Ephraim said to Gideon: "Why did you not call us when you went to fight against Midian?" And they rebuked him sharply.

---

because of their enemies. But the barley cake also was symbolic of the few in Israel who remained true to the simple strong traditions of the Hebrews. The tent is the symbol of the nomadic Midianite invaders. The dream prophesied truly that the barley loaf of Israel would overthrow the tents of Midian.

קוּמוּ! כִּי נָתַן יְיָ בְּיֶדְכֶם אֶת מַחֲנֵה מִדְיָן.

And he answered them: "What have I done in comparison with you? The gleaning of Ephraim [10] is better than the vintage of Abiezer. God has delivered into your hand the two princes of Midian. What is my achievement compared to yours?" When they heard what he said their anger abated.

So Midian was subdued by Israel, and they never raised their head again. And the people of Israel said to Gideon: "Rule over us, you, then your son and also your grandson, for you saved us from the hand of Midian." And Gideon said to them: "I will not rule over you, neither shall my son rule over you. The Lord shall rule over you!"

Gideon returned home, and he had seventy sons, for he had many wives. His concubine in Shechem bore him a son, and he called his name Abimelech. And Gideon died at a good old age and was buried in Ophrah. The country was at peace for forty years.

---

[10] THE CLEANING OF EPHRAIM: The figure of speech means that "the weakest of the Ephraimites is better than the strongest of the Abiezerites." The tribe of Ephraim had grown angry and its leaders thought they had been ignored by Gideon, who came from a poor family of the tribe of Manasseh. To avoid further dispute, Gideon placated the anger of the Ephraimites by magnifying their achievement in war and speaking of his own part as insignificant. Gideon knew that "A soft answer turns away wrath" (Proverbs 15:1) and he wanted to avoid the war of brother against brother.

לֹא אֶמְשֹׁל אֲנִי בָּכֶם וְלֹא יִמְשֹׁל בְּנִי בָּכֶם. יְיָ יִמְשֹׁל בָּכֶם.

6. JUDGES [8–10]

AND IT WAS as soon as Gideon died that the Israelites again went astray after the Baalim, and they made Baalberith their god. The Israelites forgot the Lord their God who had delivered them out of the hand of their enemies. Neither were they kind [1] to the fam-

ily of Jerubbaal, in return for all the good he had rendered to Israel.

Then Abimelech, the son of Jerubbaal, went to Shechem, to his mother's kinsmen, and he spoke to his mother's whole family: "Speak, please, to the men of Shechem: 'Which is better for you, to have seventy men rule over you, all the sons of Jerubbaal, or to have one

---

[1] NEITHER WERE THEY KIND: Why are ingratitude and idolatry spoken of together as if they were the same sin? Because ingratitude and idolatry go together; and only faith in God is proof against both. The Rabbis tell us that Israel's ingratitude to the house of Gideon was like ingratitude to the Lord. This the Israelites did when they

וַיְהִי כַּאֲשֶׁר מֵת גִּדְעוֹן וַיָּשׁוּבוּ בְּנֵי יִשְׂרָאֵל וַיִּזְנוּ אַחֲרֵי הַבְּעָלִים.

man rule over you?' And also, remember, that I am your bone and flesh."

And his mother's kinsmen spoke of him to all the men of Shechem, and their hearts inclined to follow Abimelech, because they said: "He is our brother." So they gave him seventy pieces of silver from the temple of Baalberith. With them Abimelech hired worthless and reckless men who followed him. He went to his father's house in Ophrah, and slew his brothers, the sons of Jerubbaal, seventy of them, upon one stone. Only Jotham, the youngest of Jerubbaal, escaped, because he hid himself.

Then all the people of Shechem and all Beth-millo assembled together and made Abimelech [2] king by the oak of the pillar that was by Shechem.

JOTHAM'S PARABLE

WHEN JOTHAM was told of this, he permitted Abimelech to murder the children of their benefactor Gideon. They refused to remember all Gideon had done in their behalf. To fail to show gratitude to Gideon, therefore, was to deny their history. Our Sages understood this to mean that the Israelites had forgotten what the Lord had done in their behalf in the past ever since He had led them out of Egypt. Ingratitude was thereby idolatry and the Israelites had thus forsaken the ways of the Lord.

[2] ABIMELECH: Abimelech was one of the judges who helped to save Israel. In the three years he ruled, Israel was not oppressed by its enemies. As the son of Gideon, Abimelech had the right to rule and might have ruled for a long time, even established a dynasty, had he not been evil and greedy. He murdered his brothers and unjustly took money from the people. For this he came to an untimely and ignoble death, and was unworthy of being a judge. He was allowed to rule for three years because of the merit of his father, Gideon, who was modest, humble and honest, and when the Israelites offered him the crown, he refused it, saying: *"I will not rule over you, neither shall my son rule over you: the Lord shall rule over you."* Because of this the Lord said: "I do swear that one of your sons will rule for at least three years."

וַיֵּאָסְפוּ כָּל בַּעֲלֵי שְׁכֶם וְכָל בֵּית־מִלּוֹא וַיֵּלְכוּ וַיַּמְלִיכוּ אֶת אֲבִימֶלֶךְ לְמֶלֶךְ ׃

went and stood on the top of Mount Gerizim, and lifting up his voice he called out: "Listen to me, you men of Shechem, so that God may listen to you. The trees once set out to anoint a king over them, and they said to the olive tree: 'Reign over us!' But the olive tree said: 'Should I leave my rich soil with which they honor God and men, to hold sway over the trees?'

"So the trees said to the fig tree: 'Come, rule over us!' But the fig tree said: 'Should I leave my sweetness and good fruit to hold sway over the trees?'

"Then the trees said to the vine: 'Come and reign over us!' But the vine said: 'Should I leave my wine which cheers God and men, to hold sway over the trees?'

"Then the trees said to the bramble: 'Come, rule over us!' And the bramble said to the trees: 'If in truth you anoint me king over you, come and take shelter in my shade. But if not, let fire come out of the bramble and consume the cedars of Lebanon!'

"Now," continued Jotham, "my father fought for you, risked his life and delivered you from the hand of Midian, and you have risen up against my father's family and have slain his sons, seventy upon one stone. Then you made Abimelech, the son of his maidservant, king over you. Now, if you did this thing because he is your kinsman and in good faith, then rejoice in Abimelech and let him rejoice in you. But if not, let fire come out from Abimelech and devour the men of Shechem and Beth-millo, and let fire come out from the men of Shechem and Beth-millo and devour Abimelech."

Jotham ran away, and fled to Beer in fear of his brother Abimelech.

WAR BETWEEN SHECHEM AND ABIMELECH

ABIMELECH RULED over Israel three years. God sent an evil spirit between Abimelech and the men of Shechem, and the men of Shechem revolted against Abimelech, so that the murder of the seventy sons of Gideon might be laid upon Abimelech, who had killed them, and also upon the men of Shechem who aided him in killing his brothers. And Gaal, the son of Ebed, came with his kinsmen to Shechem. The men of Shechem put their trust in him. They went out to the field and gathered their vineyards and trod their grapes and they made joyful feasts. They went into the temple of their god and ate and drank and they cursed Abimelech. And Gaal said to them: "Who is Abimelech, that we should serve him?"

When Zebul, the governor of the city, heard what Gaal said, he sent messengers to Abimelech and told him: "Let

אִם בֶּאֱמֶת אַתֶּם מֹשְׁחִים אוֹתִי לְמֶלֶךְ עֲלֵיכֶם, בֹּאוּ חֲסוּ בְצִלִּי; וְאִם אַיִן, תֵּצֵא אֵשׁ מִן הָאָטָד וְתֹאכַל אֶת אַרְזֵי הַלְּבָנוֹן.

Abimelech gather all his troops and come out to fight."

So Abimelech and all the people with him rose up by night, and lay in wait in four companies. In the morning, Gaal stood at the city gates, and Abimelech and the people with him rose from the lying in wait. When Gaal saw it, he said to Zebul: "Look, there are people coming down from the tops of the mountains." Zebul answered him: "You see the shadows of the mountains as though they were men." And Gaal said again, "But look, there are people coming down from the highest mountain, and another company is coming by way of Elon-meonenim." Then Zebul said: "Where is your mouth now, that you said, 'Who is Abimelech, that we should serve him?' Go out now and fight with him." And Gaal led the men of Shechem and fought against Abimelech. Abimelech defeated Gaal and he fled Shechem before him and many fell slain. And the next day Abimelech fought against the city and captured it. He razed all of the city and sowed it with salt.

THE TOWER OF SHECHEM

WHEN ALL THE men of the Tower of Shechem heard of this, they barricaded themselves in the fortress of the temple of El-berith. So Abimelech and his people went up to Mount Zalmon, and he took an axe in his hand and cut down a branch from a tree, and put it on his shoulder. Then he said to the people who were with him: "Hurry and do just as you saw me do." So all the people likewise cut down branches and followed Abimelech. They put the branches around the tower and set it on fire, and all the people of the Tower of Shechem perished.

THE DEATH OF ABIMELECH

THEN ABIMELECH went to Thebez, besieged it and captured it. There was a strong tower in the city, and all the men and women fled into it. Abimelech came to the tower to attack it. As he reached the doorway of the tower in order to burn it, a woman threw an upper millstone [3] at Abimelech's head and split his skull. Abimelech called hastily to the young man who bore his arms and said to him: "Draw your sword and kill me, lest men say of me, a woman killed him." His young man stabbed him and he died.

When the men of Israel saw that Abimelech was dead, they went each to his home. Thus God requited the wickedness of Abimelech which he had done to his father, killing his seventy brothers. Also the wickedness of the men of Shechem did God requite upon

וַיֹּאמֶר אֵלָיו זְבוּל: אֶת צֵל הֶהָרִים אַתָּה רוֹאֶה כָּאֲנָשִׁים.

their heads so that the curse of Jotham descended upon them.

THE ISRAELITES IN DISTRESS

THE ISRAELITES again did evil in the eyes of the Lord. They served the Baalim, the Ashtaroth and other strange gods. They forsook the Lord and did not serve Him. And the anger of God was kindled against Israel, and He gave them over into the hands of the Philistines and the Ammonites, who oppressed the Israelites for eighteen years. The Israelites cried to the Lord, saying: "We have sinned against Thee, for we have forsaken our God and served the Baalim."

And the Lord said to the Israelites: "Did I not deliver you from the Egyptians and from the Amorites, from the Ammonites and the Philistines? And when the nations oppressed you, you cried to Me and I rescued you from their hand. And yet you forsook Me and served other gods, so I will save you no more. Go, wail to the gods whom you have chosen! Let them rescue you in the time of your trouble!"

And the Israelites said unto the Lord: "We have sinned. Do unto us as Thou dost desire, only rescue us, we pray, this time."

They put away the strange gods from among them, and served the Lord, so He would no longer bear the misery of Israel.

Then the Ammonites gathered together and camped in Gilead and the Israelites in Mizpah. Now the princes of Gilead said one to another: "The man who will lead us in the war against the Ammonites shall be the head of all the inhabitants of Gilead."

&ξ [3] AN UPPER MILLSTONE: Abimelech was punished "measure for measure." Because he had killed his brothers, seventy of them on one stone, so too was he killed by a single stone. Because he was a fierce and bloodthirsty warrior, the unworthy son of a judge, so was he brought low by an ordinary woman's hand and her common household millstone. Because he was a conqueror of great cities, so was he finally defeated by a small town.

מִי הָאִישׁ אֲשֶׁר יָחֵל לְהִלָּחֵם בִּבְנֵי עַמּוֹן יִהְיֶה לְרֹאשׁ לְכֹל יוֹשְׁבֵי גִלְעָד.

7. JUDGES [11–12]

JEPHTHAH

JEPHTHAH, THE Gileadite, was a mighty warrior, but he was the son of a woman of a different tribe. Gilead was the father of Jephthah, but when his wife's sons had grown up they said to Jephthah: "You shall not inherit anything in our father's house, for you are the son of another woman." And Jephthah fled from his brothers, [1] and settled in the land of Tob. And there gathered

---

[1] FLED FROM HIS BROTHERS: Jephthah's mother came from a different tribe than his father. In those days it was considered improper to marry out of one's tribe. Jephthah's father had taken his first wife from his own tribe. When the sons of the first wife grew up they drove Jephthah out, after his father had died, refusing to give him his part of the inheritance. This was contrary to the law of the Torah which decreed that a son is the legitimate heir whether his mother is from the same tribe or not. But the elders of Gilead did

לֹא תִנְחַל בְּבֵית אָבִינוּ כִּי בֶן אִשָּׁה אַחֶרֶת אָתָּה.

around him dispossessed men who followed him.

When the Ammonites made war
against Israel, the elders of Israel went
into the land of Tob, and said to Jephthah: "Come, and be our chief, so that
we may fight the Ammonites."

Jephthah said: "Did you not hate
me [2] and drive me out of my father's
house? Why then have you come to me
now, when you are in trouble?"

The elders said to Jephthah: "[True,
we have wronged you,] but now we turn
to you, that you may be our leader, to
come with us and fight against the
Ammonites."

And Jephthah said: "If you bring me
back home to fight against the Ammonites and the Lord does deliver them
to me, I will remain your leader."

And the elders of Gilead said: "The
Lord shall be witness between us, if we
do not just as you say."

Jephthah went with the elders of
Gilead and the people made him chief
over them, and they made a vow before
the Lord in Mizpah. Then Jephthah
sent messengers to the king of Ammon,
saying: "As I have not sinned against
you, you do me wrong to come to war
against my land. Let the Lord be judge
this day between the children of Israel
and the children of Ammon!"

But the king of the Ammonites would
not listen to his words. Then the spirit
of the Lord came upon Jephthah, so he
crossed to Gilead [and collected troops],
and he came to Mizpah. He made a
vow to the Lord, saying: "If You will
indeed deliver the Ammonites into my

---

not right the wrong done to Jephthah. Thus, when war broke out
and they came to seek his help, Jephthah refused them because of
the wrong done him. But when the people chose him to be chief
over them, Jephthah relented.

ـعۏ [2] DID YOU NOT HATE ME?: Why did Jephthah rebuff the elders
who came to ask him to be their leader? Rabbi Jonah of Gerona
explains that if a man wrongs his fellow man and then, when he is
in trouble, comes and apologizes, humbles himself because he needs
the man he has wronged, then the wronged man will find that an
even greater insult and more painful wrong has been done him than
before. As Jephthah said, "Why did you come to me when you are
in distress?"

הֲלֹא אַתֶּם שְׂנֵאתֶם אוֹתִי וַתְּגָרְשׁוּנִי מִבֵּית אָבִי, וּמַדּוּעַ בָּאתֶם אֵלַי עַתָּה כַּאֲשֶׁר
צַר לָכֶם?

hand, [3] then whatsoever comes from the doors of my house to meet me shall be the Lord's." [4]

And Jephthah crossed over to the Ammonites to fight against them, and the Lord delivered them into his hand. Thus were the Ammonites subdued by the Israelites.

JEPHTHAH'S DAUGHTER

THEN JEPHTHAH went home to Mizpah, and his daughter came out to meet him with timbrels and with dances. She was his only child. When he saw her, he tore his clothes and cried out: "Alas, my daughter, you have struck me down and brought calamity upon me! For I made a vow to the Lord."

And she said: "My father, do to me according to that which has come out of your mouth, since the Lord has given you vengeance on your enemies. But, let me wander [5] for two months upon the mountains and bewail my maidenhood, I and my companions."

And he said: "Go!" And he sent her away for two months. And she and her

---

⋙ [3] JEPHTHAH'S VOW: The Rabbis declare that the Lord neither wished Abraham to sacrifice Isaac, nor Jephthah to sacrifice his daughter. The Lord does not need or want human sacrifices. Because Jephthah's vow was so rash, calamity befell him. Even more repugnant than his vow was his willingness to sacrifice his daughter. The Rabbis protested that Jephthah's vow and sacrifice were against the teaching of the Torah. Jephthah's actions are the result of over-zealousness and stubborn pride.

⋙ [4] SHALL BE THE LORD'S: Which is more important, the Rabbis asked, a good heart or knowledge of the Torah? And they answered that even if a man try to be righteous, if he is not learned in the Torah, he may actually destroy life. Though Jephthah was full of zeal for the Lord, he had been an outcast and he did not know the Torah and the story of Abraham and Isaac.

⋙ [5] LET ME WANDER: Jephthah's daughter tried to reason with her father. She said: "It is written in the Torah that if a man wishes to

אָבִי, עֲשֵׂה לִי כַּאֲשֶׁר יָצָא מִפִּיךָ, אַחֲרֵי אֲשֶׁר עָשָׂה לְךָ יְיָ נְקָמוֹת מֵאוֹיְבֶיךָ, מִבְּנֵי עַמּוֹן.

companions went to bewail her maidenhood on the mountains. Then she returned to her father, and he did to her
as he had vowed. [6] She never married.

And it became a custom in Israel for
the maidens of Israel to lament the
daughter of Jephthah for four days in
the year. [7]

CIVIL WAR

THE MEN OF Ephraim gathered together,
went northward, and said to Jephthah:
"Why did you go to fight against the
Ammonites and did not call us to go
with you? We will burn your house
down on you."

---

make a sacrifice, then he should take from his herds or flocks."

Jephthah answered, "My daughter, I did swear!"

"Remember Jacob," she said. "He promised to give the Lord a
tenth of all he should gain. He had twelve sons but did not attempt
to sacrifice one of them." But Jephthah would not heed her.

The *Zayit Raanan* declares: No Sanhedrin would have allowed
Jephthah's vow to stand. What if his whole family had come forth
to greet him? Would he have sacrificed them all, mother and child,
servants and relatives?

    [6] AS HE HAD VOWED: The Midrash tells us that Phinehas, the
High Priest, could have absolved Jephthah from his oath so that
Jephthah's daughter would go free. But both men stood on their
pride. Jephthah said, "I am a judge and a general. I have saved
Israel. Let Phinehas come before me." And Phinehas said, "I am the
High Priest, the son of the High Priest. This man is a common
upstart. Let him come before me." And so between their two prides
the maiden perished.

    [7] FOUR DAYS IN THE YEAR: Some of our Sages say that Jephthah
did not sacrifice his daughter but only sent her into seclusion. She
was kept from a normal woman's life and devoted to the service of
the Lord. And, therefore, every year the daughters of Israel came
for four days to comfort her.

וַתְּהִי חֹק בְּיִשְׂרָאֵל: מִיָּמִים יָמִימָה תֵּלַכְנָה בְּנוֹת יִשְׂרָאֵל לְתַנּוֹת לְבַת יִפְתָּח
הַגִּלְעָדִי אַרְבַּעַת יָמִים בַּשָּׁנָה.

Jephthah said: "I and my people were in a great war with the Ammonites. I called on you, but you did not come [8] to help me. When I saw that you did not come, I risked my life and crossed over against the Ammonites, and the Lord delivered them in my hand. Why then do you come to make war against me?"

The Ephraimites answered: "You Gileadites are no more than the deserters of the tribes of Ephraim and Manasseh."

And Jephthah gathered together all the men of Gilead, and fought with Ephraim and defeated them. Then the Gileadites seized the fords of the Jordan. When any of the fugitive of Ephraim said, "Let me cross over," the Gileadites said to him: "Are you an Ephraimite?" If he said, "No," they said to him: "Say now 'Shibboleth.'" He would say "Sibboleth," for he could not pronounce it correctly. Then they seized him and slew him at the fords of the Jordan.

Jephthah judged Israel for six years. He died, and was buried in one of the cities of Gilead.

ᴇᴊ [8] YOU DID NOT COME: The same pride and stubbornness Phinehas and Jephthah showed in dealing with Jephthah's vow to sacrifice his daughter, they both displayed in dealing with Ephraim. When the Ephraimites threatened to burn Jephthah's house down over his head, Phinehas, the High Priest, should have rebuked the proud Ephraimites and said, "You did not intercede in behalf of Jephthah's daughter, but you are ready to go to war for an imagined affront."

וַיֹּאמְרוּ לוֹ: אֱמָר־נָא שִׁבֹּלֶת. וַיֹּאמֶר: סִבֹּלֶת, וְלֹא יָכִין לְדַבֵּר כֵּן.

8. JUDGES [13-15]

THE BIRTH OF SAMSON

AND THE ISRAELITES again did evil in the eyes of the Lord. And the Lord delivered them into the hand of the Philistines for forty years.

And there was a man in Zorah, of the family of the tribe of Dan, whose name was Manoah. His wife was barren and childless. And an angel of the Lord appeared to the woman and said to her: "You are barren and childless; [1] but

---

[1] YOU ARE BARREN AND CHILDLESS: Our Rabbis said that for the sake of peace, one may use a deceptive utterance. Thus, when the angel spoke to Zelalponit, he said to her: "You are barren and childless." But when he spoke to her husband the angel did not say that his wife was barren because this might destroy their domestic peace. Instead the angel told him, "Let the woman abstain from everything I said." That meant that though Manoah's wife had borne him no children she was not barren. There were means to cure her.

מֻתָּר לוֹ לְאָדָם לְשַׁנּוֹת בְּדָבָר מִפְּנֵי הַשָּׁלוֹם.

you shall conceive and bear a son. Therefore, be careful not to drink wine or any strong drink, nor eat any unclean thing. When the son is born, no razor shall be used on his head, for the child shall be a Nazirite to God from his birth. And he shall begin to deliver Israel from the Philistines."

Then the woman came to her husband and said to him: "A man of God came to me, and his appearance was like an angel of the Lord, great and awful. I did not ask him where he came from, neither did he tell me his name."

Then Manoah prayed to the Lord, and said: "Hear me, O Lord, let the man of God whom Thou didst send come to us again, and teach us to what to do for the boy that shall be born."

And God heeded Manoah. And the angel of God came again to the woman as she sat in the field. And she ran and told her husband that the man appeared to her again. And Manoah arose and went after his wife, and came to the man and said, "When your words are fulfilled, how shall we act toward the child?"

And the angel of the Lord said: "The woman must abstain from everything of which I spoke to her. She shall not drink any wine or strong drink, nor eat any unclean thing."

And Manoah said: "Let us detain you, that we may prepare a lamb for you to eat."

And the angel said: "Though you detain me, I will not eat [2] of your food; and if you prepare a burnt-offering, you must offer it to the Lord!"

Manoah did not know that the man was an angel of the Lord, and he said:

---

[2] I WILL NOT EAT: When the angels appear to Abraham to announce the birth of Isaac, they accept the food which Abraham himself set before them. The Rabbis said that this was because Abraham's hospitality was being put to the test. The angels appear to him as wayfarers and impart their message to him only after he has proved his welcome. The angel Pahadiel who appears to Manoah was immediately recognized as divine and had no need to accept food. Moreover, if the angel should now accept food, it would seem to be in compensation for the prophecy which he had brought to Manoah and therefore he declines. A prophet is not to be paid for his prophecy.

כִּי נְזִיר אֱלֹהִים יִהְיֶה הַנַּעַר מִן הַבֶּטֶן, וְהוּא יָחֵל לְהוֹשִׁיעַ אֶת יִשְׂרָאֵל מִיַּד פְּלִשְׁתִּים.

"What is your name, so that we may honor you when your words are fulfilled?"

And the angel said: "Why do you ask my name? For it is hidden." [3]

So Manoah took the lamb and the meal-offering, and offered them upon the rock to the Lord. Then flame came out of the rock, and the flame went up toward heaven, and the angel ascended in the flame.

When Manoah and his wife saw it, they fell upon their faces to the ground. And Manoah said to his wife: "We will surely die because we have seen God."

But his wife said: "If the Lord meant to kill us, He would not have told us such things as these."

And the woman gave birth to a son and called him Samson. The boy grew and the Lord blessed him. And the spirit of the Lord [4] began to move him, between Zorah and Eshtaol.

SAMSON WEDS A PHILISTINE WOMAN

AND SAMSON went down to Timnah and there he saw a woman, a daughter of the Philistines. He came back and said to his father and mother: "I have seen a woman in Timnah, a Philistine. Now, get her for me as a wife."

And his father and mother said: "Is there no woman among the daughters of our kinsmen, or among all our people, that you must take a wife from the Philistines?"

And Samson said to his father: "Get her for me, for she is the one that pleases me." And his father and mother did not know that it was at the instigation of the Lord that Samson should have occasion to quarrel [5] with the Philistines. At that time the Philistines ruled over Israel.

Then Samson and his father and

᜕ [3] FOR IT IS HIDDEN: The angel said to Manoah: My name is without meaning to you. The Lord's messengers are embodied in different forms, as wind or fire, or any living thing according to the Lord's desire and as the occasion requires.

᜕ [4] THE SPIRIT OF THE LORD: When the spirit of the Lord filled Samson, he ran so fast that his hair sang in the wind and could be heard from a great distance. It was then too that Samson uprooted the mountains between Zorah and Eshtaol and ground them to

וַתָּחֶל רוּחַ יְיָ לְפַעֲמוֹ בְּמַחֲנֵה דָן, בֵּין צָרְעָה וּבֵין אֶשְׁתָּאֹל.

mother went down to Timnah. As they came to the vineyards there, a young lion came roaring toward him. And the spirit of the Lord came upon Samson and he tore the lion as one would have torn a lamb. He had nothing in his hand, and he did not tell [6] his father and mother what he had done. And he went down and talked with the woman, and she pleased Samson well.

After a while, Samson returned with his father and mother to marry and turned aside to see the carcass of the lion. There was a swarm of bees and honey inside the body of the lion. So he scraped it out in his hand, and ate it as he went. He went to his father and mother and he gave them some to eat, but he did not tell them whence it came.

---

powder one against the other. And, the Rabbis tell us, lest you wonder at such feats, remember that the width of Samson's shoulders was the width of the gates of Gaza. When the Lord was with him, Samsons's strength was beyond compare.

[5] OCCASION TO QUARREL: In Samson's time the Israelites were not strong enough to make war against the Philistines. Samson therefore sought an occasion to attack them for a personal affront but not as a representative of Israel. He did that so that when he afflicted the Philistines, he would not bring reprisals down on the heads of his people. In that way Samson protected Israel in his generation.

[6] HE DID NOT TELL: How can Samson be accompanied by his parents without their knowing that he slew the lion? Samson and his parents walked together until they came to the vineyards of Timnah. Manoah and his wife wanted to take the shortest route through the vineyards but Samson would not. He was a Nazirite and therefore expressly forbidden in the vineyards. The Nazirite is cautioned: "Keep away, go round about, approach not the vineyard" (Y'vamot 46a), and also, "Take a circuitous route, O Nazirite, but do not approach the vineyard" (Shabbat 13a). Therefore Samson walked around the vineyards and was then confronted by the lion while his parents went directly through the vineyards.

וַתִּצְלַח עָלָיו רוּחַ יְיָ וַיְשַׁסְּעֵהוּ כְּשַׁסַּע הַגְּדִי, וּמְאוּמָה אֵין בְּיָדוֹ.

And Samson made a feast, for so the bridegrooms used to do. And the bride's family brought thirty companions to be with him. And Samson said: "Let me now ask you a riddle. If you will tell me the answer within the seven days of the feast, I will give you thirty linen robes and thirty festal garments, but if you are unable to tell me the solution, then you must give me thirty linen robes and thirty festal garments."

And they said: "Propose your riddle so we may hear it."

And he said: "Out of the eater came forth food; out of the strong came forth sweetness."

They could not solve the riddle in three days. They said to Samson's wife: "Persuade your husband to tell you the meaning of the riddle, or we will burn you and your father's house with fire. Did you invite us here to impoverish us altogether?"

And Samson's wife wept before him, and said: "You do not love me at all. You proposed a riddle to my people, and you did not tell me the solution."

And he said: "I have not told my father and mother; shall I tell you?"

And she wept before him the remainder of the seven days of the feast. On the seventh day because she pressed him hard he told it to her. And she told the riddle to her people. And on the seventh day, before the sun went down,

the men of the city said to him: "What is sweeter than honey? And what is stronger than a lion?"

And he answered them: "If you had not plowed with my heifer, you would not have found out my riddle."

And the spirit of the Lord came upon him, and he went to Ashkelon and smote thirty of the Philistines; and he took their garments and gave the garments to those who solved the riddle. Then he went up to his father's house in great anger. And Samson's wife was given to one of his companions.

SAMSON TAKES REVENGE

AT THE TIME of the wheat harvest Samson went to visit his wife, with a present, a kid. And he said: "I want to go in to my wife, in her chamber." But her father would not let him go in. Her father said: "I thought you hated her, so I gave her to one of your companions. Now, is not her younger sister more beautiful than she? Take her instead."

And Samson said: "This time will I surely be innocent of sin if I do harm to the Philistines." And Samson went and caught three hundred foxes. And he tied them tail to tail and he put torches between each two tails. Then he set the torches on fire, and let the foxes loose in the standing grain of the Philistines. It burnt up both the shocks

וַיֹּאמֶר לָהֶם: מֵהָאוֹכֵל יָצָא מַאֲכָל, וּמֵעַז יָצָא מָתוֹק.

and the standing grain, and also the oliveyards.

The Philistines asked: "Who has done this?" And they said: "Samson, the son-in-law of the Timnite, because he took his wife and gave her to his companion." And the Philistines came and burnt her and the house of her father.

And Samson said to them: "If this is the manner in which you act, I will take my revenge on you." He smote them hip and thigh with great slaughter, and he went down and dwelt in the cleft of the rock of Etam.

Then the Philistines went up and camped in Judah, and they spread themselves around Lehi. And the men of Judah said: "Why have you come against us?" And they said: "To bind Samson, to do to him as he has done to us."

Then three thousand men of Judah went down to the cleft of the rock, and they said to Samson: "Do you not know that the Philistines are rulers over us?

What have you done unto us?" And he said: "As they did to me, so I have done to them."

And they said to him: "We have come down to bind you, to deliver you into the hand of the Philistines."

And Samson said: "Swear to me that you yourselves will not assail me. And they said to him: "We will only bind you fast, and deliver you into their hand." And they bound him with two new ropes, and brought him up from the rock.

When they brought him to Lehi, the Philistines shouted. And the spirit of the Lord came upon him, and the ropes upon his arms became as flax that has caught fire; and his bonds melted from his hands. And he found a fresh jawbone of an ass. He took it and felled a thousand men. Then Samson said:

"With the jawbone of an ass, heaps upon heaps,
With the jawbone of an ass I have felled a thousand men."

בִּלְחִי הַחֲמוֹר, חֲמוֹר חֲמֹרָתָיִם, בִּלְחִי הַחֲמוֹר הִכֵּיתִי אֶלֶף אִישׁ.

9. JUDGES [16]

THE GATES OF GAZA

AND SAMSON went to Gaza and saw there a woman, an innkeeper, and he went to her. And it was told to the Gazites: "Samson has come here." They lay in wait for him at the gate of the city, and they whispered to each other. "We will wait till the morning light. Then we will kill him."

And Samson lay till midnight. Then he arose and took hold of the doors of the gate of the city and the two posts; pulled them up, bar and all, and put them upon his shoulders, and carried them to the top of the mountain that faces Hebron.

SAMSON AND DELILAH

AND IT WAS after this that he loved a woman of the valley of Sorek whose name was Delilah. And the lords of the Philistines came and said to her: "Entice him and find out wherein his great strength [1] lies, and how we can over-

---

[1] HIS GREAT STRENGTH: If Samson's great strength came from the Lord, why did he fall prey to Delilah? Samson had used Philistine

וַיִּסָּעֵם עִם הַבְּרִיחַ וַיָּשֶׂם עַל כְּתֵפָיו, וַיַּעֲלֵם אֶל רֹאשׁ הָהָר אֲשֶׁר עַל פְּנֵי חֶבְרוֹן.

power him, bind him and subdue him. We will give you, every one of us, eleven hundred pieces of silver."

And Delilah said to Samson: "Tell me wherein lies your great strength, and with what can you be bound to subdue you?"

And Samson answered: "If they bind me with seven fresh bowstrings that were not dried, then I shall become weak and be as any other man."

And the lords of the Philistines brought up to her seven fresh bowstrings which had not been dried, and she bound him with them. And she had men lying in wait in the chamber. And she said: "The Philistines are upon you, Samson!" And he broke the bowstrings as a string of tow snaps when it touches fire. So the source of his strength was not discovered.

And Delilah said: "You have mocked me and told me lies. Now do tell me with what can you be bound?" And he said: "If you bind me with new ropes with which no work has been done,

then I shall become weak like any other man." And Delilah took new ropes and bound him with them. The men were lying in wait in the next chamber. And she said to Samson: "The Philistines are upon you, Samson!" And he broke the new ropes off his arms like thread.

And Delilah said to Samson: "Up till now you have mocked me and told me lies. Tell me with what you can be bound?" And he said: "If you weave the seven locks of my head into the web and you fasten it with the pin." So when he was asleep she wove the seven locks of his head into the web and fastened it with the pin, and she said: "The Philistines are upon you, Samson!" And he awoke out of his sleep and pulled out the pin of the loom and the web.

And she said: "How can you say that you love me when your heart is not with me? You have mocked me three times and you did not tell me wherein lies your great strength."

She pressed him daily with her words

---

women as the pretext to attack the Philistines, but his passions blinded him to his purpose. He let his passion for Delilah cause him to betray his trust as a judge and as a Nazirite. Because of that Delilah was able to bind him and betray him to his enemies. As Samson had used the Philistine women as a trap, now he was in turn trapped by a Philistine woman.

וַתֹּאמֶר דְּלִילָה אֶל שִׁמְשׁוֹן׃ הַגִּידָה־נָּא לִי בַּמֶּה כֹּחֲךָ גָדוֹל וּבַמֶּה תֵּאָסֵר לְעַנּוֹתֶךָ׃

and urged him, until he was wearied to death. He told her his heart and said to her: "A razor has never been used upon my head, for I have been a Nazirite to God from my birth. If I were to be shaven, then my strength would go from me, and I would become weak, and be like any other man."

When Delilah saw that he had told her the truth, she called for the lords of the Philistines, saying: "Come up, this once, for he has told me the truth." [2] So the lords of Philistines came to her and brought the money in their hands.

Then Delilah made Samson sleep upon her knees, and she called for a man, and had the seven locks of his head shaven off and his strength left him. Then she said: "The Philistines are upon you, Samson." He awoke from his sleep and he said to himself, "I will go as I did before and shake myself free." But he did not know that the Lord departed from him. Then the Philistines seized him and put out his eyes, and brought him down to Gaza. They bound him with brass chains and made him grind corn in the prison house.

LET ME DIE WITH THE PHILISTINES

AND THE HAIR on Samson's head began to grow again. The lords of the Philistines gathered to offer a great sacrifice to Dagon, their god, and rejoiced; for they said: "Our god has delivered Samson, our enemy, into our hand."

And it was when the people became merry they said: "Call for Samson, that he may be a laughing stock for us." They called Samson out of the prison and he was a laughing stock for them. Then they put him between the pillars.

And Samson said to the lad who held his hand: "Let me feel the pillars on which the house is supported, that I may lean upon them." And the house was full of men and women, and the lords of Philistines were there. There were upon the roof about three thousand men and women, looking on while Samson was a laughing stock.

✦ [2] HE HAS TOLD ME THE TRUTH: How did Delilah know that Samson was now telling her the truth about his great strength? Had he not lied to her before and laughed at her discomfiture? This time Samson spoke the Name of the Lord and Delilah knew that he would not take the Name of God in vain.

וַיְהִי כִּי טוֹב לִבָּם וַיֹּאמְרוּ׃ קִרְאוּ לְשִׁמְשׁוֹן וִישַׂחֶק־לָנוּ.

And Samson called to the Lord: "Lord, God, remember me and give me strength just this once, O God, so that I may be avenged of the Philistines for my two eyes." And Samson grasped the two middle pillars on which the house was supported. And Samson said: "Let me die with the Philistines!" And he pushed with all his might. The house fell upon the lords and all the people who were in it. So those he killed at his death were more than those he killed during his life.

Then his kinsmen and all his father's household came down and took him and brought him up, and buried him in the burying-place of Manoah, his father. And he judged Israel twenty years. [3]

&ε [3] AND HE JUDGED ISRAEL TWENTY YEARS: The Rabbis asked why these words were repeated for did not Scripture say earlier that Samson had judged Israel for twenty years (15:20)? The Rabbis explained by saying that Samson judged Israel twenty years while he was alive and for a full twenty years after his death Samson's influence remained. The Philistines still feared him and dared not oppress Israel until twenty years had passed.

וַיֹּאמֶר שִׁמְשׁוֹן : תָּמוֹת נַפְשִׁי עִם פְּלִשְׁתִּים.

10. I SAMUEL [1–4]

THE PARENTS OF SAMUEL

THERE WAS a man of Ramah, in the hill country of Ephraim, and his name was Elkanah. He had two wives. The name of one was Hannah and the other Peninnah. Peninnah had children but Hannah had none.

And this man used to go [1] from his city from time to time to worship and sacrifice to the Lord in Shiloh. There the sons of Eli, Hophni and Phinehas

---

[1] AND THIS MAN USED TO GO: Elkanah was a man of great merit and his name was known in all Israel because of his pilgrimages. Four times a year Elkanah went up to the Tabernacle of Shiloh, three times as prescribed by the Torah, and once a year to fulfill his vow to sacrifice to the Lord. Each time he went he took a different route and stopped in different towns. He did this deliberately to bring more people to the service of the Lord.

On his pilgrimages Elkanah took his wives, children and relatives, all of his household. No quarters were large enough to accommodate

וְלוֹ שְׁתֵּי נָשִׁים, שֵׁם אַחַת חַנָּה וְשֵׁם הַשֵּׁנִית פְּנִנָּה. וַיְהִי לִפְנִנָּה יְלָדִים וּלְחַנָּה אֵין יְלָדִים.

were priests to the Lord. On the day
that Elkanah sacrificed he gave portions
to Peninnah his wife and all her sons
and daughters, and to Hannah he gave

a double portion, for he loved her, [2]
though she was childless.

And when Elkanah went up to sacrifice, her rival taunted her, so that she

---

such a large retinue so they lodged in tents in the town squares.
There the people gathered to watch, asking: "Whither do you
journey?" And Elkanah always answered: "To the Sanctuary in
Shiloh from whence goes forth the Torah of the Lord and where
we are taught to observe the Law and to perform the *mitzvot*. Join
us so that you too will merit God's grace." Because Elkanah was
sincere and persuasive, many people responded and followed him to
the Tabernacle at Shiloh.

Soon Israel observed the three pilgrimages as prescribed by the
Torah. They abandoned the worship of idols and began to cleave
to the Lord. Then the Lord said: "Elkanah has turned the heart of
My people away from idol worship and brought them near to Me.
He merits to be the father of a son who will make the hearts of all
Israel yearn for the Lord."

[2] HE LOVED HER: Hannah was one of the seven prophetesses of
Israel. She had been married to Elkanah for ten years but bore him
no children. Because she wanted her beloved husband to have an
heir, she insisted that Elkanah take a second wife, as was the custom
in those times. Elkanah then took Peninnah who bore him a child
every year. In time Peninnah began to look on the barren Hannah
with disdain and often she taunted and mocked her.

Hannah's heart was heavy and full of sorrow and she poured out
her heart in prayer before God. In her great grief she spoke rebel-
liously to the Lord, saying, "Lord of the universe, You are like a
king who has made a sumptuous banquet for hundreds of people.
A poor and hungry man came and stood at the door asking for a
crust of bread but the servants turned him away. The poor man then
approached the king and said, 'Your Majesty, your tables are laden

וּלְחַנָּה יִתֵּן מָנָה אַחַת אַפָּיִם כִּי אֶת חַנָּה אָהֵב, וַיָי סָגַר רַחְמָהּ.

wept and could not eat. Then her husband Elkanah said to her: "Hannah, why do you weep and not eat? Why is your heart so sad? Am I not better to you than ten sons?"

And after they ate and drank, Hannah arose and stood before the Lord and prayed. She wept bitterly and vowed, "O Lord of hosts, if Thou wilt indeed look upon the affliction of Thy handmaiden, and remember me, and give me a son, then I will give him to the Lord all the days of his life, and no razor shall come on his head."

And Eli, the priest, was sitting upon his seat by the doorposts of the temple of the Lord, and he watched her mouth. She prayed for a long time, speaking to herself. Only her lips moved, but her voice could not be heard. And Eli thought that she was drunk, and he said: "How long will you display yourself drunken? Put away your wine [and depart from the presence of the Lord]."

And Hannah answered: "Do not take me for a worthless woman. I have drunk neither wine nor strong drink. I have poured out my heart before the Lord because I am a very unhappy woman."

And Eli answered her: "Go in peace, and may the God of Israel grant your petition."

So Hannah went her way, and she was not sad any longer. They rose early the next morning, and they worshiped before the Lord and returned to their home.

THE BIRTH OF SAMUEL

AT THE TURN of the year Hannah bore a son, and she called him Samuel. Elkanah and all his house went up to offer to the Lord the yearly sacrifice, but Hannah did not go up, for she said to Elkanah: "When the child is weaned, then I shall bring him before the Lord, and he will remain there forever."

And Elkanah said to her: "Do what seems best to you."

Hannah waited and nursed her son until she weaned him. Then she took him up with her, along with a three-year-old bullock and an ephah of meal, and a skin of wine, and she brought him to the Lord's house in Shiloh. And the boy was a real boy. After the bullock had been sacrificed, she brought the child to Eli, and said: "O my lord, I am the woman who stood here in your pres-

---

with food, will you not spare a crust for a hungry man?' So, Lord, look! Hosts come to Your Tabernacle; multitudes come up to Your Sanctuary in Shiloh. Cannot You spare a child also for me?"

וּזְכַרְתַּנִי וְלֹא תִשְׁכַּח אֶת אֲמָתֶךָ, וְנָתַתָּה לַאֲמָתְךָ זֶרַע אֲנָשִׁים, וּנְתַתִּיו לַיָ כָּל יְמֵי חַיָּיו.

ence praying to the Lord. For this child I prayed, and the Lord granted my petition. So I have lent him to the Lord; as long as he lives he is set apart to the Lord."

HANNAH'S SONG OF THANKS

AND HANNAH prayed and said:

"My heart is joyful with the Lord
There is none so holy as the Lord,
For there is none besides Thee;
Neither is there a Rock like our
   God.
Do not boast so proudly!
Let no arrogance escape your
   mouth,
For the Lord is a God of
   knowledge,
And deeds are weighed by Him.
The bows of mighty men are
   broken,
And they that stumble are braced
   with strength.
And they that were hungry have
   ceased to hunger,
The barren has borne seven,
She that had many is bereaved.

The Lord puts to death and gives
   life;
He brings down to the grave and
   brings up.
The Lord makes poor and makes
   rich

He humbles and exalts;
He lifts up the needy from the
   refuse heap
To make them sit with the noble
And inherit the throne of glory.

He guards the feet of His pious
   ones,
And the wicked He puts to
   silence in darkness;
For not by might shall men prevail.
They that contend with the Lord
   shall be broken;
Against them will He thunder in
   Heaven.
The Lord judges to the very ends
   of the earth.

Elkanah went to Ramah, to his house. And the Lord blessed Hannah and she became pregnant. She bore three sons and two daughters. And the boy Samuel grew in the service of the Lord.

THE WICKEDNESS OF ELI'S SONS

THE SONS OF Eli were base men. They cared not for the Lord, [nor the priests' due from the people]. Whenever a man offered a sacrifice, the priest's attendant would come with a three-pronged fork in his hand, and he would thrust it into the pot. All that the fork brought up would be taken for the priest. If the man said: "Let the fat be burned first, then take as much as you desire," the

אֵין קָדוֹשׁ כַּיְיָ כִּי אֵין בִּלְתֶּךָ, וְאֵין צוּר כֵּאלֹהֵינוּ.

servant would say: "No, give it to me now, or I will take it by force." The sons also abused the women who assembled to pray at the door of the Sanctuary of the House of the Lord.

Eli was very old and he heard all that his sons did to Israel, and he said to them: "Why do you do such things? I hear evil reports concerning you from all this people. If a man sins against another, God shall judge him. But if a man sins against the Lord, who shall entreat for him?" But his sons would not listen to their father.

THE YOUNG SAMUEL

SAMUEL MINISTERED before the Lord, girded with a linen ephod. His mother used to make a little robe which she brought to him year after year, when she came up with her husband to offer the yearly sacrifice. The boy grew older and found favor with the Lord and with the Lord's people.

THE CALL

AND THE LAD Samuel ministered to the Lord before Eli. The word of the Lord was rare in those days: there was no frequent vision. Eli's eyes became so dim that he could not see. And it happened that Eli lay down in his place, and the lamp of God had not yet gone out, and Samuel lay down to sleep in the Sanctuary of the Lord, where the Ark of God was. And the Lord called [3] to Samuel. And he said: "Here I am," and he ran to Eli and said, "Here I am, for you called me."

And he said: "I did not call; lie down

⭕ [3] THE LORD CALLED: When the Lord first revealed Himself to Samuel in the Sanctuary at Shiloh, Samuel was young and innocent, like a "naive calf." Samuel thought the Lord revealed Himself only in thunder and lightning, in storm and earthquake. When Samuel heard an ordinary voice, he did not suspect it was the Lord who spoke to him. Even after Eli had implied that it was the Lord calling him and had instructed him how to reply: "Speak, Lord, for Thy servant hears," Samuel did not believe it. When he did hear the voice again, therefore, Samuel said, "Speak, for Thy servant hears," but he omitted the word, "Lord." Only later when he was older and more mature did Samuel come to understand that the prophet may hear the voice of the Lord in plain speech.

וַיִּקְרָא יְיָ אֶל שְׁמוּאֵל, וַיֹּאמֶר: הִנֵּנִי. וַיָּרָץ אֶל עֵלִי וַיֹּאמֶר: הִנְנִי כִּי קָרָאתָ לִּי.

again." And Samuel went and lay down.

Then the Lord called once again Samuel. Samuel arose and went to Eli, and said to him: "Here I am, for you called me."

And he answered: "I did not call you, my son. Lie down again."

The word of the Lord was not yet revealed to Samuel. When the Lord called Samuel the third time, he rose and went to Eli, and said: "Here I am. You called me."

Now Eli perceived that the Lord was calling the lad. He said to Samuel: "Go, lie down and if you are called, you shall say: 'Speak, Lord, for Thy servant hears!'" Samuel went and lay down in his place.

Then the Lord came [4] and stood and called as the other times: "Samuel! Samuel!" And he said: "Speak, for Thy servant hears."

And the Lord said to Samuel: "I am about to do a thing in Israel that will make the ears of every one who hears it tingle. I will punish the house of Eli forever for the iniquity, for his sons blasphemed, and he rebuked them not. Therefore I have sworn that the sins of Eli's house will not be expiated by sacrifice and offering."

Samuel lay until the morning. Then he opened the doors of the house of the Lord. But he feared to tell Eli his vision. Then Eli called Samuel, and said: "Samuel, my son, what is the thing that He has spoken to you? I beg you, hide it not from me." Samuel told him. He hid nothing from him. Eli said: "Let Him do what seems good to Him."

And Samuel grew and the Lord was with him, and all Israel from Dan to Beer-sheba knew that Samuel was chosen to be a prophet of the Lord.

  ✈ [4] THE LORD CAME: When the Lord wanted to speak to Moses He would call him into the Tabernacle. But when God wanted to speak to Samuel He Himself would come to the prophet. Why, our Rabbis ask, this extra honor for Samuel?

The Lord said: "I do come to My people with justice and righteousness. Moses sat in one place and whoever had a matter for him came to him, and he judged between man and his neighbor (Exodus 18:16). But Samuel respected and honored My people. He went in a circuit to Beth-el, Gilgal and Mizpah; and he judged Israel in all those places (I Samuel 7:16). Therefore he deserved extra honor. As he went to My people whenever they had a matter and he judged

הִנֵּה אָנֹכִי עֹשֶׂה דָבָר בְּיִשְׂרָאֵל אֲשֶׁר כָּל שֹׁמְעוֹ תְּצִלֶּינָה שְׁתֵּי אָזְנָיו.

WAR WITH THE PHILISTINES

AND THE PHILISTINES gathered to war against Israel. Then Israel went out against them in battle, and encamped at Eben-ezer and the Philistines encamped in Aphek. When the battle was joined, Israel was defeated by the Philistines who slew about four thousand men. When the people returned to camp, the elders of Israel said: "Why has the Lord routed us today before the Philistines? Let us bring the Ark of the Covenant of the Lord out of Shiloh, that He may come among us, and save us from our enemies."

The people sent to Shiloh and brought from there the Ark of the Covenant of the Lord, and the two sons of Eli, Hophni and Phinehas were with the Ark. When the Ark was brought into the camp, all Israel raised a great shout so that the earth rang. When the Philistines heard the noise of the shout they knew that the Ark of the Lord had come into the camp. The Philistines were afraid, and [some of them] said: "God has come to the camp. Woe unto us! [5] Nothing like this has happened before." [Then the others said:] "Now, O Philistines, be brave and be men, lest you become slaves to the Israelites as they have been to you. Be men and fight."

So the Philistines fought, and Israel was defeated. And they fled, every man to his tent. There was a great slaughter, for there fell of Israel thirty thousand men and the Ark of God was captured

---

between man and his neighbor, so will I go to him whenever he wants and needs My word."

&S [5] WOE UNTO US: Two groups of Philistines are here involved in an argument. One says, "Woe unto us! Who will deliver us from the hands of these mighty gods? The gods of Israel delivered them from Egypt and performed many miracles for them. They will perform a miracle for them now too." The other group replied: "The God of the Israelites is only one God. All He had was ten plagues. He punished the Egyptians with them and He has not a single plague left for His adversaries. So be brave and real men and fight!" Then the Lord said to them: "You say I have no plagues left, but I will bring upon you a plague which you never heard of."

שְׁמוּאֵל שֶׁהָלַךְ אֵצֶל יִשְׂרָאֵל בָּעֲיָרוֹת וְדָן אוֹתָם – אֲנִי הוֹלֵךְ וּמְדַבֵּר עִמּוֹ.

[6] and the two sons of Eli were killed.

A Benjamite ran from the battle line and came to Shiloh on the same day. His clothes were torn and earth was on his head. When the man came to the city and told the tidings, all the city cried out. Eli was sitting on his seat by the wayside, watching, for his heart trembled for the Ark of God. When Eli heard the noise of the crying, he said: "What is the meaning of the noise of this tumult?" Eli was then ninety-eight years old and his eyes were so dim that he was blind. The man said to Eli: "I am he who came today out of the battle."

Eli asked: "How did things go, my son?" And he answered: "Israel fled be-

---

⮑ [6] AND THE ARK OF GOD WAS CAPTURED: Why did the Ark of the Lord bring victory to Joshua when he marched around Jericho with it and the Israelites shouted with a great shout (Joshua 6:20) but did not when the sons of Eli brought the Ark of the Lord into the camp of the battlefield? Then too the Israelites shouted a great shout (I Samuel 4:5) yet the army was defeated and the Holy Ark was captured by the Philistines. Because, the Rabbis explain, in the time of the sons of Eli, the hearts of the people of Israel were far from the Lord. For years a divine voice was heard crying in the Tabernacle in Shiloh: "Begone, you sons of Eli, who defile the Sanctuary" (P'saḥim 57a), but no one paid the voices any attention. The people did not reprove the sons of Eli but instead more and more followed the priest-leaders in their wicked ways.

When the Israelites were first defeated by the Philistines, the elders did not realize that it was because Israel had sinned. "Why has the Lord routed us before the Philistines?" they asked. And they decided to bring the Holy Ark into their camp so that the Lord might dwell among them.

Then the Lord replied: "You did not consider the Holy Ark when the sons of Eli provoked Me with their transgressions. Now, in your distress, you remember it. This is repentance without deeds." Because the people of Israel had not understood that the Holy Ark was only the symbol of God's holiness and Israel's righteousness, the Ark brought Israel no victory and was captured by the Philistines.

וְהִנֵּה עֵלִי יוֹשֵׁב עַל הַכִּסֵּא יַד דֶּרֶךְ מְצַפֶּה, כִּי הָיָה לִבּוֹ חָרֵד עַל אֲרוֹן הָאֱלֹהִים.

fore the Philistines, and there was a great slaughter among the people. Your two sons are dead, and the Ark of God is taken." And when the man mentioned the Ark of God, Eli fell from his seat backward and his neck was broken, and he died.

ICHABOD

HIS DAUGHTER-IN-LAW, Phinehas' wife, was pregnant when she heard that her husband and her father-in-law were dead, and the Ark of God was captured. Her pains came suddenly upon her and she gave birth to a boy. The women who stood by said to her: "Fear not, for you have borne a son." But she did not answer. Then she named the child Ichabod, saying: "The glory is departed from Israel, because the Ark of God has been taken." And she died.

וַתִּקְרָא לַנַּעַר אִי כָבוֹד לֵאמֹר: גָּלָה כָבוֹד מִיִּשְׂרָאֵל, אֶל הִלָּקַח אֲרוֹן הָאֱלֹהִים.

11. I SAMUEL [5–10]

THE PHILISTINES AND THE ARK

THE PHILISTINES took the Ark and brought it to the house of Dagon, in Ashdod, and put it by Dagon. The next day, when the people of Ashdod rose, they found Dagon prostrate on his face before the Ark of the Lord. They raised Dagon and sat him in his place again. But when the men of Ashdod arose early next morning, there was Dagon fallen, the head and both palms of the hands lay cut off upon the threshold. Only the trunk of Dagon was left to him.

The hand of the Lord was heavy upon the people of Ashdod. He brought upon them a plague of boils. When the people of Ashdod saw this, they said: "The Ark of the God of Israel shall not remain with us, for His hand is severe upon us and upon Dagon our god." So they sent the Ark to Ekron. The Ekronites cried out, "They brought the Ark of the God of Israel to kill us all." So they gathered together all the lords of the Philistines and said: "Send away the Ark of the God of Israel and let it return to its own place, and not kill us."

The men of Kiriath-jearim came and took up the Ark, and brought it to the house of Abinadab and sanctified Elea-

וַיַּשְׁכִּמוּ אַשְׁדּוֹדִים מִמָּחֳרָת וְהִנֵּה דָגוֹן נוֹפֵל לְפָנָיו אַרְצָה לִפְנֵי אֲרוֹן יְיָ.

zar his son to take charge of the Ark of the Lord.

Lord." Samuel became judge of the Children of Israel in Mizpah.

SAMUEL BECOMES A JUDGE

TWENTY YEARS passed from the day that the Ark was brought to Kiriath-jearim, and all the house of Israel yearned after the Lord. Then Samuel spoke to all the house of Israel, saying: "If you do return to the Lord with all your heart, then put away the foreign gods from among you and direct your hearts to the Lord, and serve only Him. Then He will deliver you out of the hand of the Philistines." The Children of Israel did put away the Baalim and the Ashtaroth, and served the Lord only. So Samuel said: "Gather all Israel together, and I will pray for you to the Lord."

They gathered together in Mizpah, and drew water [1] and poured it before the Lord. They fasted on that day, and said: "We have sinned against the

VICTORY OVER THE PHILISTINES

WHEN THE PHILISTINES heard that the Israelites were gathered together, the lords of the Philistines went up against Israel to make war. When the Israelites heard it, they were terrified of the Philistines, and said to Samuel: "Do not cease crying to the Lord our God for us, that He may save us from the hand of the Philistines." Samuel cried out to the Lord of Israel and the Lord answered him. As Samuel brought up the burnt-offering, the Philistines drew near to do battle against Israel; but the Lord thundered with a great voice upon the Philistines, and routed them. Then the men of Israel went out of Mizpah, and pursued the Philistines and harassed them.

Samuel judged Israel [2] all the days

ᴇᏚ   [1] THEY DREW WATER: Drawing the water and pouring it before the Lord was a symbolic act. The people poured out their hearts in repentance like water, saying: "Our hearts are as humble as is this water which is poured out before You." Then Samuel stood in prayer and spoke to the Lord: "Your people now admit that they have sinned. Lord of the universe, You judge people only when they do not acknowledge their sins. But look at your people now!"

ᴇᏚ   [2] SAMUEL JUDGED ISRAEL: Israel took the defeat by the Philistines

אַל תַּחֲרֵשׁ מִמֶּנּוּ מִזְּעֹק אֶל יְיָ אֱלֹהֵינוּ וְיוֹשִׁעֵנוּ מִיַּד פְּלִשְׁתִּים.

of his life. He went on a circuit every year to Beth-el, Gilgal and Mizpah, and he judged Israel in these places. Then he returned to Ramah, for there was his home, [3] and there he judged Israel and built an altar to the Lord.

THE ISRAELITES DEMAND A KING

WHEN SAMUEL became old he made his two sons Joel and Abijah judges over Israel. But the sons walked not in his ways. [4] They took bribes and perverted justice.

Then the elders of Israel gathered together and came to Samuel in Ramah and said: "You are old, and your sons do not follow your ways. Appoint us a king [5] to judge us like all the nations." It displeased Samuel when they said, "Give us a king to judge us," and

---

as a double omen: first, that the Lord had rejected them; and second that the Philistine gods were more powerful than the God of Israel. Samuel went to the villages teaching the people that neither of these was true. "The Lord will not forsake His people, for His great name's sake; because it has pleased the Lord to make you a people unto Himself (I Samuel 12:22)." He reassured the Israelites that though the Philistines had temporarily triumphed, there was nothing to fear from their gods. "For they cannot profit and they cannot deliver" (12:21). Samuel emphasized that the Covenant between the Lord and His people was eternal and that if Israel returned to the Lord with all its heart, it would be united and overcome its enemies. After twenty years of such intense activity the Israelites were not only repentant, but "All the house of Israel yearned after the Lord." It was then that Samuel called an assembly in Mizpah and told the people that if "Israel served the Lord only," it could stand against the Philistines and conquer them.

᠊ᢀᢀ [3] TO RAMAH, FOR THERE WAS HIS HOME: Our Rabbis ask: "It is written: he returned home to Ramah, for there was his home. Do we not know that Ramah was his home?" But the Sages answer that this teaches us that wherever Samuel traveled—Beth-el, Gilgal, Mizpah— he took his "home" with him. He was careful not to use any of the things from the people he judged; instead, he brought his own needs,

הִנֵּה אַתָּה זָקַנְתָּ וּבָנֶיךָ לֹא הָלְכוּ בִּדְרָכֶיךָ. עַתָּה שִׂימָה לָּנוּ מֶלֶךְ לְשָׁפְטֵנוּ כְּכָל הַגּוֹיִם.

he prayed to the Lord. The Lord said to Samuel: "Listen to the voice of the people, for it is not you whom they have rejected, but they have rejected Me from being king over them. But forewarn them and tell them how the king shall behave who shall rule over them."

---

from kitchen utensils to food. In Rashi, the Hebrew reads: *shelo lehenot min ha'aḥérim,* that is, Samuel did not partake of anything from a stranger.

    [4] HIS SONS WALKED NOT IN HIS WAYS: The verse, "They took bribes and perverted justice," should not be taken literally. The sons of Samuel were not like Hophni and Phinehas, Eli's sons. Our Rabbis tell us that the verse means that the sons fell short of their father's integrity. Samuel journeyed the entire circuit of the country to dispense justice, but his sons made the people from all parts of the country come to them in Beer-sheba. This system required a bureaucracy of officials, secretaries and clerks all of whom had to be paid from the public treasury. So the verse means that compared to Samuel's frugal dispensation of justice, it was as if they had taken bribes and perverted justice.

Other Sages say that the sons of Samuel were partners with many businessmen so that they had conflicting interests and could not render true and just decisions in lawsuits.

Still another tradition has it that the sons of Samuel were themselves in business. Judges cannot be businessmen; judges must devote their entire lives to considering and rendering justice.

    [5] APPOINT US A KING: Why was Samuel displeased when the Israelites asked for a king? The Torah states explicitly, "When you came to the land which the Lord, your God gives you, you shall set a king over you" (Deuteronomy 17:14–15). Why then did Samuel say: "Your wickedness is great, which you have done in the sight of the Lord, in asking for yourself a king" (12:17)? The Rabbis say that two groups, the elders and the people asked for a king. The

שְׁמַע בְּקוֹל הָעָם, כִּי לֹא אוֹתְךָ מָאָסוּ כִּי אוֹתִי מָאֲסוּ מִמְּלֹךְ עֲלֵיהֶם.

THE KING'S WAYS

THEN SAMUEL told the words of the Lord to the people who asked for a king: "This will be the manner of the king who shall reign over you: He will take your sons for his chariots and to be his horsemen, and to run before his chariots. They will be his commanders of thousands and captains of fifties. They will plow his fields and reap his harvest; make his instruments of war and equipment for his chariot. He will take your daughters to be perfumers, to be cooks and to be bakers. He will take your best fields and your vineyards and oliveyards, and give them to his servants. He will take a tenth of your grain crops and of your vineyards, and give it to his officers and servants. He will take your manservants and maidservants and your donkeys and put them to his work. He will take a tenth of your flocks, and you shall be his servants. Then you will cry on that day because of your king, but the Lord will not answer you."

But the people refused to listen to Samuel, and said: "No, there shall be a king over us, that we also may be like the other nations; that our king may judge us and fight our battles." [6]

---

elders said, properly, "Appoint us a king." But the wicked said, "To judge us like all the nations." They wanted the king to judge them according to the pagan laws of the nations around them. They wanted to invalidate the Torah and that was why it was a sin.

Some Rabbis say that Samuel was dejected when the people asked him to appoint them a king because he felt it as a rebuke. He had judged Israel honestly and fairly, and led the Israelites well all his life, and now they wanted a king. Then the Lord spoke to Samuel, saying, "They want a king 'to judge them like all the nations.' It means that they do not want to be judged by My laws, but by pagan laws. They have not rejected you, Samuel; they have rejected Me."

᳙ [6] FIGHT OUR BATTLES: A king would be able to gather all the people together behind him, whereas until then only those tribes who were attacked had fought. The rest of the tribes had often not come to the help of those in danger or under attack.

זֶה יִהְיֶה מִשְׁפַּט הַמֶּלֶךְ אֲשֶׁר יִמְלֹךְ עֲלֵיכֶם: אֶת בְּנֵיכֶם יִקַּח וְשָׂם לוֹ בְּמֶרְכַּבְתּוֹ וּבְפָרָשָׁיו וְרָצוּ לִפְנֵי מֶרְכַּבְתּוֹ.

Samuel repeated this in the presence of the Lord. Then the Lord said to Samuel: "Listen to their voice and make them a king."

SAMUEL MEETS SAUL

THERE WAS a man of Benjamin whose name was Kish, and he had a son whose name was Saul, [7] a handsome young man. There was not a man among all the Israelites more handsome than he. From his shoulders and upward he was taller than any of the people. Now, the donkeys of Kish were lost. Kish said to Saul: "Take one of the servants with you, and go and search for the donkeys." So he went, and they passed through the hill country of Ephraim, but they found them not.

When they reached the land of Zuph, Saul said to his servant: "Come, let us return lest my father cease to care about the donkeys and become anxious for us." And he answered: "There is in the city a man of God. Whatever he says comes surely to pass. Let us go to him. Perhaps he can tell us concerning our journey."

Saul said to his servant: "Well said, let us go."

As they went up the path to the city,

---

[7] SAUL: Why did Saul merit the kingdom? Because, the Rabbis tell us, of his heroism and his modesty and his considerateness; and also because of the good deeds of his grandfather. Saul distinguished himself in the battle against the Philistines in Eli's time by wresting the Tables of the Law from the hands of Goliath and returning them to the sanctuary in Shiloh. He showed his modesty after he was anointed and Samuel called a national assembly to proclaim him king; then Saul hid himself. He still believed himself unworthy of being king of Israel. Saul accepted only after he was told that the Lord had chosen him. His decency and humility were demonstrated when he and his servant were searching for the donkeys and he said, "My father will become anxious for us," showing that he considered the servant and himself equally.

Saul's grandfather was Ner (I Chronicles 8:33), which in Hebrew means *candle* or *lamp*. Ner was called that because he lit the streets at night so people might walk safely to the houses of worship and study.

וְאֵין אִישׁ מִבְּנֵי יִשְׂרָאֵל טוֹב מִמֶּנּוּ. מִשִּׁכְמוֹ וָמַעְלָה־גָּבוֹהַּ מִכָּל הָעָם.

they met young maidens [8] going to draw water. And they said: "Is the seer here?"

And they answered: "He is here. Make haste for he came today to the city, for the people have a sacrifice today in the high place. As soon as you come into the city you shall find him before he goes to the high place to eat. The people will not eat until he comes, because he blesses the sacrifice. Now therefore go, for at this time you will find him." They went up to the city. As they entered, Samuel came toward them.

Now a day before Saul came, the Lord revealed to Samuel, saying: "Tomorrow, about this time, I will send you a man out of the land of Benjamin, and you shall anoint him to be prince over My people Israel, and he shall save them out of the hand of the Philistines."

When Samuel saw Saul, the Lord spoke to him: "This is the man of whom I said to you: 'He shall have rule over My people.'" When Saul came near Samuel in the gate, he said: "Tell me please, where is the seer's house?"

Samuel answered: "I am the seer. Come with me to the high place, for you shall eat with me today. As for your donkeys that were lost three days ago, do not worry. They are found. And to whom is all that is desirable in Israel? Is it not for you and all your father's house?"

And Saul answered: "Am I not a Benjamite, of the smallest of the tribes of Israel? And my family is the least of all the families of the tribe of Benjamin. Why do you speak to me in this manner?"

SAMUEL ANOINTS SAUL

SAMUEL BROUGHT Saul and his servant into the chamber and made them sit at the head of the guests. Samuel said to the cook: "Bring the portion which I told you to put aside." The cook took it and put it before Saul. So Saul ate with Samuel that day.

In the morning Samuel came and said to Saul: "Arise, I will escort you." They went out in the street, and when they were at the edge of the city, Samuel said to Saul: "Tell the servant to go ahead, but you stand here so that I may

---

[8] YOUNG MAIDENS: When Saul asked the maidens the brief, "Is the seer here?" the girls replied with a long speech. They engaged in this long disquisition because Saul was very handsome and they wanted to enjoy his beauty.

הִנֵּה הָאִישׁ אֲשֶׁר אָמַרְתִּי אֵלֶיךָ: זֶה יַעְצֹר בְּעַמִּי.

make known to you the word of God."

Then Samuel took the vial of oil and poured it on Saul's head, kissed him, and said: "The Lord has anointed you to be a prince over His inheritance."

And it was when Saul turned to go from Samuel, God gave him another heart. When he came to the hill a band of prophets met him. The spirit of God came upon him, and he prophesied among them. The people who knew him said one to another: "Is Saul also among the prophets?" Therefore, it became a proverb: "Is Saul also among the prophets?"

He ceased prophesying and went home. And Saul's uncle said to him: "Where have you been?" And he answered: "We went to seek the donkeys. When we saw that we could not find them, we went to Samuel."

The uncle said: "What did Samuel say to you?" Saul answered: "He told me the donkeys were found." But Saul did not mention the kingdom of which Samuel had spoken.

SAUL ELECTED KING

SAMUEL CALLED all the people together to the Lord in Mizpah. He said to the Israelites: "Thus said the Lord, the God of Israel: 'I brought up Israel out of Egypt, and I delivered you from the hand of the Egyptians, and from the hand of all the kingdoms that oppressed you. But you have this day rejected your God who Himself saved you from your calamities. You said to Him: "But set a king over us." Therefore, now take your stand before the Lord by your tribes and your clans [and we will see whom the Lord will select by lot].' "

When Samuel brought the tribes of Israel near, the tribe of Benjamin was selected by lot. He brought the tribe of Benjamin near by their families, and the family of the Matrites was taken. He made the family of the Matrites approach man by man, and Saul the son of Kish was taken. But when they looked for him, he could not be found. They inquired of the Lord again: "Did the man come here?" And the Lord answered: "He hid himself among the supplies." [9] They ran and brought him from there. He stood among the people and he was a head and shoulders taller than any of the people.

So Samuel said to all the people: "Look whom the Lord has chosen. There is none like him among all the

---

⤷ [9] HE HID HIMSELF AMONG THE SUPPLIES: Saul was modest and humble. Even after he was anointed, he refused to accept the regal

עַל כֵּן הָיְתָה לְמָשָׁל: הֲגַם שָׁאוּל בַּנְּבִיאִים?

people." Then all the people shouted: "Long live the king!"

Samuel recited before the people the custom of the kingdom, and wrote it in a book and laid it up before the Lord. Thereupon Samuel sent all the people away, every man to his home. Saul also went to his home at Gibeah. There went with him brave men whose hearts God had touched. But there were some base fellows who said: "How shall this man save us?" They despised him and brought him no presents. But he ignored them and held his peace. [10]

---

dignities until they were forced on him. Yet when he was king and transgressed, when Samuel rebuked him and told him the Lord was departed from him, Saul was ready to kill David to keep his throne.

Rabbi Joshua said: "At first when they told me to ascend, I was ready to tie the hands and feet of those who nominated me and cast them to the lions. But now, after the honor has been bestowed upon me, whoever will say to me: 'Descend!' I am ready to scald with boiling water." .

[10] AND HELD HIS PEACE: Our Sages say that Saul's dynasty did not last because he forgave too easily those who insulted him. In thus disregarding the honor and dignity of his office, he weakened his ability to rule. When the base fellows scoffed and said, "How shall this man save us?" Saul kept his peace. After the victory over Nahash, when the people wanted to punish those men, Saul would not permit it. That proved that Saul was too unworldly to govern, Rabbi Ashi said. It is indicated in the Torah that people not only should respect and honor him, but have fear for him, or else he could not reign.

וַיָּרִיעוּ כָל הָעָם וַיֹּאמְרוּ: יְחִי הַמֶּלֶךְ!

12. I SAMUEL [11–15]

THE INVASION OF NAHASH

NAHASH, THE AMMONITE, came and besieged Jabesh-gilead. All the men of Jabesh said to Nahash: "Make terms with us that we may serve you." Nahash said to them: "On this condition will I make a covenant with you: I shall gouge out your right eyes and thereby will I put a reproach upon all Israel."

The elders of Jabesh said to him: "Give us seven days' respite, that we may send messengers through all the territory of Israel. Then if there will be none to save us, we will come out and surrender to you."

The messengers came to Gibeah of Saul and told the people about Nahash, and all the people wept aloud. Just then Saul came from following the oxen in the field. He asked: "What troubles the people that they are weeping?" And they told him the words of the men of Jabesh. When he heard them, the spirit of God came upon him, and he became very angry. He took a yoke of oxen and cut them to pieces, and sent them throughout all the territory of Israel, saying: "Whoever does not come forth after Saul and after Samuel, so shall it be done to his oxen."

The terror of the Lord fell upon the

אֲשֶׁר אֵינֶנּוּ יוֹצֵא אַחֲרֵי שָׁאוּל וְאַחַר שְׁמוּאֵל כֹּה יֵעָשֶׂה לִבְקָרוֹ.

people, and they came out as one man. He numbered them in Bezek. The Israelites were three hundred thousand, and the men of Judah thirty thousand. Then Saul said to the messengers: "Thus shall you say to the elders of Jabesh-gilead: 'Tomorrow you will have deliverance by the time the sun is hot.'"

The men of Jabesh said to Nahash: "Tomorrow we will come out to you, and you may do to us whatever you please."

SAUL IS PROCLAIMED KING

ON THE FOLLOWING day Saul divided the people into three companies. They came in the midst of the camp in the morning watch, and they routed the Ammonites by the time the sun was hot. The Ammonites scattered so that not two of them were left together. Then the people said to Samuel: "Where are those who said: 'Shall Saul reign over us?' Bring the men here so we may put them to death!"

But Saul said: "There shall not be a man put to death today, for today the Lord has brought deliverance to Israel."

Then Samuel said: "Let us go to Gilgal, and there renew the kingdom." So all the people went to Gilgal and there they proclaimed Saul king before the Lord. All the people and Saul rejoiced greatly.

SAMUEL'S FAREWELL ADDRESS

AND SAMUEL said to Israel: "I have listened to you and made a king over you. Now the king walks before you, and I am old and gray, and my sons are among you. And I have walked before you from my youth to this day. Here I am. Testify before the Lord and before His anointed; whose ox have I taken, or whose donkey have I taken? Whom have I defrauded, or whom have I oppressed? From whose hand have I taken a bribe to blind my eyes? Testify against me and I will restore it to you."

And the people answered: "You have not defrauded us, nor oppressed us; neither have you taken anything from any man's hand."

He said to them: "The Lord is witness and His anointed is witness that you have not found anything in my hand."

And they said: "He is witness."

Then Samuel said: "Here is the king you have chosen and you have asked for. The Lord set a king over you. But you shall know that your wickedness is great in the sight of the Lord in asking for a king."

Then all the people said to Samuel: "Pray for us to the Lord your God in behalf of your servants. We have added to all our sins [1] the wickedness of asking for a king."

אֶת שׁוֹר מִי לָקַחְתִּי, וַחֲמוֹר מִי לָקַחְתִּי; וְאֶת מִי עָשַׁקְתִּי, אֶת מִי רַצּוֹתִי?

Samuel answered: "Fear not. Indeed, you have done all this evil, but turn not aside after vain things which cannot profit nor deliver. But serve the Lord. If you serve Him and listen to His voice and do not rebel against the commandments of the Lord, it will be well for both—for you and the king who reigns over you. But if you persist in doing evil you shall be swept away, you and your king. But the Lord will not forsake His people for His great name's sake. It pleases the Lord to make you a people for Himself. Far be it from me that I should sin against the Lord in not praying for you."

WAR WITH THE PHILISTINES

WHEN SAUL had reigned [two] years,

[2] in the second year of his reign over Israel, Saul chose three thousand men of Israel. Two thousand were with him in Michmas, and a thousand with Jonathan in Gibeah. Then Jonathan attacked the garrison of the Philistines in Geba, and overcame it. The Philistines heard of it.

Saul blew the *Shofar* throughout Israel, and all Israel heard that Saul had smitten the garrison of the Philistines. So the people gathered together after Saul in Gilgal, and the Philistines assembled to fight Israel. They mustered against Israel thirty thousand chariots, and six thousand horsemen, and people as the sand which is on the seashore.

Now, there was not a blacksmith found throughout all the Land of Israel,

---

⋙ [1] WE HAVE ADDED TO ALL OUR SINS: When the Israelites confessed to Samuel that they had sinned and wanted to repent, Samuel replied, "Fear not. Far be it from me that I should sin against the Lord in not praying for you." Samuel had rebuked the people severely but when they admitted their sins, he was reconciled and willing to pray for them.

Our Sages say that this teaches us that if a man wrongs someone, repents and asks forgiveness, then the wronged man should promptly forgive him. If he does not, he is to be considered cruel and brutal.

⋙ [2] SAUL HAD REIGNED: Why does the Bible say that Saul was only one year old when he came to the throne? Was he really only an infant? Rabbi Huna explains that Saul was as innocent as an infant of a year who has not yet tasted the sins of men.

כִּי לֹא יִטֹּשׁ יְיָ אֶת עַמּוֹ בַּעֲבוּר שְׁמוֹ הַגָּדוֹל, כִּי הוֹאִיל יְיָ לַעֲשׂוֹת אֶתְכֶם לוֹ לְעָם.

for the Philistines said: "Lest the Hebrews make sword or spear." So neither
sword nor spear was found in the hands
of any of the people of Israel; only Saul
and Jonathan had them.

JONATHAN'S HEROISM

ONE DAY JONATHAN, the son of Saul,
said to the youth who was his armor-
bearer: "Come, let us go over to the
garrison of the Philistines that is on the
other side of that crag. It may be that
the Lord will give us deliverance for
the Lord has no difficulty in delivering
by many or by few." And the armor-
bearer said to him: "Do whatever is in
your heart. I am with you."

At the first attack which Jonathan
and his armor-bearer made they killed
about twenty men. Terror spread in the
camp of the Philistines and in the field
and in the whole garrison. The earth
quaked and it became a mighty panic.

The watchmen of Saul in Gibeah
looked and they saw the camp of the
Philistines melted away. Saul said:
"Search and see who is gone from us."
They investigated and they saw that
Jonathan and his armor-bearer were not
there. While Saul was talking with the
priest the tumult in the camp of the
Philistines increased, so Saul and the
people with him gathered together and

came to the battlefield. They saw that
every man's sword was against his fellow's, and there was wild confusion.
The Philistines fled. When all Israel
heard it they pursued them hard in the
battle.

Saul charged the people, saying:
"Cursed be the man who will eat any
food until evening, that I be avenged
on my enemies." All the people came
into the forest and there was honey
on the ground, but no man put his
hand to his mouth, for the people feared
the oath. But Jonathan did not hear
when his father charged the people with
the oath, so he put forth the end of the
rod that was in his hand and dipped it
in the honeycomb, and put his hand to
his mouth, his eyes brightened. Then
the people said: "Your father strictly
charged the people and he said, 'Cursed
be the man who eats any food until
evening.'" Then Jonathan said: "My
father brought trouble on the people.
Look, my eyes brightened because I
tasted a little honey. How much greater
would have been the defeat of the Philistines if the people had eaten freely
today of the spoils of the enemy which
they found."

[It became known to Saul what Jonathan did] and he said: "Jonathan, you
shall surely die." And the people said
to Saul: "Shall Jonathan die, he who

וַיֹּאמֶר הָעָם אֶל שָׁאוּל: הֲיוֹנָתָן יָמוּת, אֲשֶׁר...

has brought this great deliverance to Israel? Far from it! As the Lord lives, not one hair of [3] his head shall fall to the ground." The people ransomed Jonathan and he did not die.

So Saul established his kingdom firmly, and fought against Israel's enemies on every side, against Moab, and against the children of Ammon, and against Edom, and against the kings of Zobah, and against the Philistines; and whichever way he turned, he put them to the worse. And he did valiantly, and smote the Amalekites, and delivered Israel out of the hands of them that spoiled them. The fighting with the Philistines was severe throughout all his reign. And whenever Saul saw a mighty man or a valiant man, he took him for himself.

WAR WITH AMALEK

SAMUEL SAID to Saul: "The Lord sent me to anoint you to be king over His people Israel. Now, therefore, listen to the voice of the Lord. Thus says the Lord of hosts: 'I remember that which Amalek did to Israel when he came out of Egypt. Now go and attack Amalek.

❧ [3] NOT ONE HAIR: Why did Jonathan accept without protest Saul's verdict that he would surely die? According to law, Jonathan was not guilty of any transgression. He was not present when his father charged the people not to eat and had therefore not heard Saul's charge. Second, he had only tasted some honey which is considered neither eating nor drinking.

Medieval commentators interpreted this story as follows. Most of the soldiers could not know that Jonathan had not heard Saul's command. They were also not legalists who knew that tasting honey is not considered eating or drinking. Therefore, if Saul had not punished him they would have thought that Saul was showing favoritism because Jonathan was his son. Saul proclaimed him guilty and Jonathan accepted the judgment for the morale of the army.

The soldiers who were with Jonathan knew that he could not have heard Saul's command and it was they who demanded the judgment be revoked. Investigation was begun and Jonathan was cleared at a public hearing.

...עָשָׂה הַיְשׁוּעָה הַגְּדוֹלָה הַזֹּאת בְּיִשְׂרָאֵל؟ חָלִילָה, חַי יְיָ אִם יִפֹּל מִשַּׂעֲרַת רֹאשׁוֹ אַרְצָה.

[4] Destroy all they have [5] and spare him not.'"

Saul summoned the people and he numbered them in Telaim; [6] two hundred thousand foot-men, and ten thousand men of Judah. He came to the encampment of Amalek and lay in wait in the valley. And Saul said to the Kenites: "Go, depart from among the Amalekites, for you showed kindness to

---

✛ [4] NOW GO AND ATTACK AMALEK: When Saul was told to attack Amalek, he asked: "How is it that the Lord told me to make war? He has told us that if a man is found slain in the field and it is not known who killed him, we must expiate the unsolved murder by the ceremony of a heifer. The elders must publicly declare: 'Our hands have not shed this blood' (Deuteronomy 21:7). Now the Lord tells me to make war. Many will be killed, both young and old, and the innocent as well."

Then a voice from heaven called: "Be not overmuch righteous. Whoever is compassionate when and where he must be severe and merciless will turn out to be merciless and brutal when he should be compassionate."

✛ [5] DESTROY ALL THEY HAVE: How had the cattle given offense? Samuel told Saul to destroy even the cattle lest the other nations say that the Israelites had made war for spoils and plunder. Only in this way could it be made clear that this was a war not of aggrandizement but to safeguard Israel.

✛ [6] HE NUMBERED THEM IN TELAIM: All ancient people hated to be counted because they thought that it tempted fate. To circumvent this superstition, leaders had each man deposit a stone or a pottery shard in a pile and then they counted the pile. So, the Midrash tells us, we have two censuses here: Telaim means lambs and Bezek (11:8) means pottery. In the beginning of Saul's reign Israel was so poor that each man who joined the army brought only a shard of pottery with him. When Israel prospered Saul ordered each soldier to bring a lamb to be counted.

אַל תְּהִי צַדִּיק הַרְבֵּה.

the Israelites when they came out of Egypt." And the Kenites departed.

Saul defeated the Amalekites, and captured Agag, their king, alive. But Saul and the people spared the best of the sheep and of the oxen, and all that was good they did not destroy. Only that which was of no account and feeble they destroyed.

THE REJECTION OF SAUL

THEN THE WORD of the Lord came to Samuel, saying: "I repent that I have set up Saul as king, for he turned back from following Me and did not carry out My command." Samuel was grieved, and prayed to the Lord all night. [7]

Samuel rose early to meet Saul in the morning and he was told: "Saul came down to Carmel and set up a monument, and he has gone down to Gilgal."

When Samuel met Saul, Saul said to him: "May the Lord bless you. I have performed the commandment of the Lord."

Then Samuel said: "What is the bleating of the sheep in my ears, and the lowing of the oxen which I hear?"

And Saul said: "The people spared the best of the sheep and the oxen to sacrifice to the Lord your God. The rest we have utterly destroyed."

Then Samuel said: "Be silent! Let me tell you what the Lord said to me last night."

Saul said, "Speak!"

Samuel said: "Though you are little in your eyes, but are you not the head of the tribes of Israel? The Lord anointed you king over Israel. The Lord sent you on a mission and said: 'Go and wipe out the sinners, the Amalekites.' Why did you not listen to the voice of the

---

ς [7] AND HE PRAYED TO THE LORD ALL NIGHT: Rabbi Johanan said: "Old age came prematurely to Samuel when the Lord said: 'I regret that I have made Saul king.'" And Samuel complained, "Sovereign of the universe, You have made me equal to Moses and Aaron. The work of their hands did not come to naught in their lifetimes. So, too, let not the work of my hands come to naught in mine." Then the Lord replied: "The time has come for David to reign and no reign may encroach on another even by a hairsbreadth."

Then Samuel mourned for Saul and was not comforted. His hair turned gray overnight and he died seven months before Saul was killed at Gilboa.

וַיֹּאמֶר שְׁמוּאֵל: וּמֶה קוֹל הַצֹּאן הַזֶּה בְּאָזְנָי, וְקוֹל הַבָּקָר אֲשֶׁר אָנֹכִי שׁוֹמֵעַ?

Lord, but you did fly upon the spoil to do evil in the eyes of the Lord?"

THE PROPHET'S REBUKE

SAUL SAID to Samuel: "Yes, I have listened to the voice of the Lord, I have gone the way the Lord sent me. I have brought Agag, the king of Amalek, and I have utterly destroyed the Amalekites. But the people took some of the spoil, sheep and oxen, the best of the devoted things to sacrifice to the Lord [8] your God in Gilgal."

Samuel answered:

"Does the Lord delight in burnt-
        offerings and sacrifices
As much as in listening to the
        voice of the Lord?

No, to obey is better than
        sacrifices
And to hearken, than the fat of
        rams.
Rebellion is as the sin of
        witchcraft
And stubbornness is as idolatry
        of teraphim.
Because you have rejected the
        word of the Lord,
He has also rejected you from
        being king."

And Saul said to Samuel: "I have sinned. [9] For I have transgressed the commandment of the Lord, because I feared the people [10] and listened to their voice. Now, therefore, I beg you to pardon my sin and turn back

---

᚛᚛ [8] TO SACRIFICE TO THE LORD: Saul tried to justify sparing the best of the cattle by saying he wanted to offer them as sacrifices to the Lord. Samuel rebuked him saying that God has no need for sacrifice but for obedience. When a man wishes to bring a sacrifice, it signifies that he seeks God's nearness. The root of the word *korban* (sacrifice) is *karov*, or nearness. True sacrifice, therefore, is that which brings man nearer to God and His ways. The Lord does not delight in burnt-offerings; He delights in the man who would draw near to Him with his whole heart.

᚛᚛ [9] I HAVE SINNED: Why was Saul's repentance unacceptable? Three requirements are necessary for true repentance: (1) the sinner must know he has sinned; (2) he must not excuse himself for his sin; (3) his repentance must be entirely for love of God and goodness, not for the sake of gain. Saul's repentance lacked these

הַחֵפֶץ לַיָי בְּעוֹלוֹת וּזְבָחִים כִּשְׁמֹעַ בְּקוֹל יְיָ? הִנֵּה שְׁמֹעַ מִזֶּבַח טוֹב, לְהַקְשִׁיב —
מֵחֵלֶב אֵילִים.

with me so that I may worship the Lord."

Samuel answered: "I will not return with you, for you have rejected the word of the Lord, and the Lord has rejected you from being king over Israel."

---

three elements for even when he confessed he laid the blame on the people. Only when Saul says simply, "I have sinned," does Samuel consent to return with him.

[10] BECAUSE I FEARED THE PEOPLE: The Sages asked: "David sinned far more grievously than did Saul. Why, then, was David forgiven and Saul punished and the kingdom taken from him?"

Because, the Rabbis tell us, David repented at once. When the prophet Nathan rebuked him, David replied immediately: "I have sinned against the Lord."

But when Samuel rebuked Saul, Saul was brazen. He said he had fulfilled God's command and killed the cattle when Samuel could hear the bleating sheep and the lowing herd. "Whoever confesses will find mercy," the Sages said. But Saul neither confessed, nor repented, and therefore he was punished.

Saul also justified himself by saying that the people had spared the best cattle to sacrifice to the Lord. Samuel responded: "Dare you forget that you are an anointed king, consecrated by the Lord? You are to lead the people and to teach them the Lord's commandments. You hearkened unto the people's lust for booty because your own eyes darted greedily after the spoils."

Finally, when Samuel rebuked Saul for his transgression, Saul gave the excuse: "I have transgressed the commandment of the Lord, and your word, because I feared the people." A king who fears his people cannot rule and Samuel turned away from him.

When Saul tore his garment, Samuel saw it as an omen. The Rabbis said that Samuel then told Saul: "Whoever cuts off a piece of your garment will reign after you." When later David cut off the hem of Saul's robe and showed it to him (24:21), Saul said, "Now I know that you will surely rule in my stead."

כִּי מָאַסְתָּה אֶת דְּבַר יְיָ, וַיִּמְאָסְךָ יְיָ מִהְיוֹת מֶלֶךְ עַל יִשְׂרָאֵל.

As Samuel turned about to go, Saul caught the skirt of Samuel's robe, and it tore. Samuel said to him: "The Lord has torn the kingdom of Israel from you and given it to one better than you. Moreover the Glory of Israel will not lie nor repent; for He is not a man that He should repent."

And Saul said: "I have sinned, yet honor me now before the elders of my people and before Israel. Return with me that I may worship the Lord, your God."

So Samuel turned back after Saul, and Saul worshiped the Lord.

Samuel went to Ramah, but Saul went up to his house, to Gibeah. Samuel mourned for Saul, and the·Lord repented that He made Saul king over Israel.

קָרַע יְיָ אֶת מַמְלְכוּת יִשְׂרָאֵל מֵעָלֶיךָ הַיּוֹם וּנְתָנָהּ לְרֵעֲךָ הַטּוֹב מִמֶּךָ.

13. I SAMUEL [16-19]

SAMUEL ANOINTS DAVID KING

THE LORD SAID to Samuel: "How long will you mourn [1] for Saul, when I have rejected him from being king over Israel? Fill your horn with oil and go to Jesse, the Beth-lehemite, for I have found Me a king [2] among his sons."

Samuel said: "How can I go? Saul will hear of it and kill me." [3]

And the Lord said: "Take a heifer with you and you will say to the peo-

---

[1] HOW LONG WILL YOU MOURN: The Lord said to Samuel: "I rejected him and it is not proper or suitable to grieve over him for too long a time." Jewish law is very specific about grief for the dead. Our Sages say: "Whoever grieves too much and too long over the dead is a fool; but whoever does not mourn properly is a brute."

The Midrash also tells us that if a man mourns too long, the Holy One, Blessed Be He, rebukes him, saying: "Are you more compassionate toward the departed one than I?"

מַלֵּא קַרְנְךָ שֶׁמֶן וְלֵךְ אֶשְׁלָחֲךָ אֶל יִשַׁי בֵּית־הַלַּחְמִי, כִּי רָאִיתִי בְּבָנָיו לִי מֶלֶךְ.

ple: 'I have come to sacrifice to the Lord.' Call Jesse to the sacrifice, and you shall anoint to Me him whom I name."

Samuel did that which the Lord spoke. When he came to Beth-lehem, the elders of the city trembling came to meet Samuel, and they said, "Do you come in peace?"

He answered: "Peace! I have come to sacrifice to the Lord. Sanctify yourself, and come with me to the sacrifice." Then he himself went to sanctify Jesse and his sons, and called them to the sacrifice. When they came before him and he saw Eliab, [4] Samuel said to himself: "Surely he is the Lord's anointed."

But the Lord said to him: "Do not look at his appearance, his height or his stature. I rejected him. The Lord does not see as a man sees, for man looks at the outward appearance, but the Lord looks at the heart." Then Jesse made seven of his sons to pass before Samuel and Samuel said to him: "The Lord has not chosen these. Are these all your sons?"

Jesse said: "There is still the youngest, and he keeps the sheep."

Samuel said to Jesse: "Send for him." Jesse sent and brought him in. Now, he was ruddy with beautiful eyes and good to look upon. The Lord said to Samuel: "Arise and anoint him, for this is he." Samuel took the oil and anointed him in the midst of his brothers. Then Samuel arose and went to Ramah. The spirit of the Lord came upon David from that day onward.

DAVID IN SAUL'S COURT

THE SPIRIT OF the Lord departed from Saul, and an evil spirit from the Lord terrified him. Saul's servants said to him: "Now, an evil spirit from God

---

[2] I HAVE FOUND ME A KING: The Lord did not say, "I have found a king for Israel," but instead, "I have found Me a king," a king who will obey Me and will listen to My commandments. Not like Saul who would not obey.

[3] SAUL WILL KILL ME: We know that whoever goes to do a good deed, a *mitzvah*, is protected by the Lord from injury or damage. Why, then, was Samuel afraid? The answer of the Rabbis was that when there is a clear and present danger this does not apply. The Lord recognized the truth of Samuel's plea and told Samuel to disguise his mission and that He would protect him.

כִּי הָאָדָם יִרְאֶה לַעֵינַיִם וַיְיָ יִרְאֶה לַלֵּבָב.

terrifies you. Let our lord command your servants to seek out a man who is a skillful player on the harp. Then, whenever the evil spirit from God comes upon you, he shall play for you, and you shall be well."

Saul said to his servants: "Find me a man who can play well, and bring him to me." Then answered a young man: "I have seen a son of Jesse in Beth-lehem, a skillful player, a man of valor, and a man of war, prudent and a comely person, and the Lord is with him."

Saul sent messengers to Jesse, and said: "Send me David your son who is with the sheep." So Jesse loaded a donkey with some bread, a skin of wine and a kid and sent them with his son David to Saul. David came to Saul, and stood before him. Saul loved him and made him his armor-bearer. Whenever the evil spirit from God came upon Saul, David took his harp and played. Saul was relieved and felt well, for the evil spirit departed from him.

Now David went to and from Saul to feed his father's sheep at Beth-lehem.

DAVID AND GOLIATH

THE PHILISTINES gathered together their armies for war, and Saul and the men of Israel were gathered together and arrayed for battle. The Philistines stood on the mountain on the one side and the Israelites stood on the mountain on the other side, and between them was a valley.

There came out a champion from the camp of the Philistines, named Goliath of Gath. [5] He was nine feet six inches tall; a brass helmet on his head and

---

&ᷱ [4] HE SAW ELIAB: When Saul asked Samuel, "Where is the seer's house?" Samuel replied, "I am the seer." The Lord thought this immodest and when Samuel went to anoint Saul's successor, the Lord left him to his own devices as a reminder of how the prophetic vision descended upon him from the Lord.

When Samuel arrived at Jesse's house, he saw the tall, handsome Eliab and said to himself, "Surely he is the Lord's anointed."

Then God told him: "You are mistaken. You are only human and look at the outward appearance, but the Lord sees into the heart. Eliab is not fit to be king because his anger is too swift."

&ᷱ [5] GOLIATH OF GATH: Goliath was challenging Saul, the king of the Israelites, who stood head and shoulders above any man in Israel.

הִנֵּה רָאִיתִי בֵּן לְיִשַׁי בֵּית הַלַּחְמִי; יוֹדֵעַ נַגֵּן, וְגִבּוֹר חַיִל, וְאִישׁ מִלְחָמָה, וּנְבוֹן דָּבָר, וְאִישׁ תֹּאַר וַיְיָ עִמּוֹ.

dressed in coat of mail. The weight of the coat was about two hundred and twenty pounds. He had greaves of brass upon his legs, and a brass javelin between his shoulders. He stood and cried out to the armies of Israel: "Why did you draw up in battle array? Choose for yourself a man, and let him come down to me. If he will overcome me and kill me, then we will be your servant. But if I overcome him and kill him, then you shall be our servants and serve us."

The Philistine champion came forward for forty days, morning and evening, saying: "I taunt the armies of Israel. Give me a man, that we may fight together." When Saul and all Israel heard the words of the Philistine they were dismayed and terrified.

Then David said to Saul: "Let no man be frightened [6] because of him. Your servant will go and fight this Philistine."

Saul said to David: "You are not able to go and fight this Philistine, for you are but a youth and he is a man of war from his youth."

David said to Saul: "Your servant kept his father's sheep, and when a lion,

---

The Philistine giant intended to humiliate Saul who years before at the battle of Shiloh had wrested the Tablets of the Law from his hands. Goliath bellowed: "Why are you people of Israel gathered to make war against us Philistines? You are nothing but slaves to Saul. But I, Goliath of Gath, have killed your two priests, Hophni and Phinehas. I captured the Ark of the Covenant of your God and brought it to the temple of Dagon. I have fought in every campaign of our armies, killed and trampled on as many people as there is sand upon the shores of the sea. What did your King Saul do? What prowess did he show? Yet you made him king. If he is strong and brave, let him come forth and fight with me."

ᔃ [6] LET NO MAN BE FRIGHTENED: David lost his fear of Goliath when he heard the Philistine giant say, "If your Israelites have no brave men among you, then send me your God, who is supposed to be a great warrior. Your Moses said:

The Lord is a man of war,
The Lord is His name (Exodus 15:3)."

אַל יִפֹּל לֵב אָדָם עָלָיו; עַבְדְּךָ יֵלֵךְ וְנִלְחַם עִם הַפְּלִשְׁתִּי הַזֶּה.

or a bear came and took a lamb from the flock, I went after him, smote him and saved it from his mouth. If he rose up against me, I caught him by the beard and killed him. Both lion and bear I killed, and this Philistine shall be as one of them, for he taunted the armies of the living God. The Lord who delivered me from the lion and the bear, He will deliver me out of the hand of this Philistine."

Saul said to David: "Go, and the Lord shall be with you." Then Saul clad David with his apparel, and put a helmet of brass upon his head, and clad him with a coat of mail. David girded his sword over the apparel and attempted to walk, but he could not. David said to Saul: "I cannot go with these, [7] for I am not used to them." So David took them off. He took his staff in his hand, chose five smooth stones out of the brook, and put them in his shepherd's bag. With the sling in his hand, he advanced toward the Philistine.

David saw how huge Goliath was, how heavily armed. Goliath carried a sword, a spear and a javelin. "Any one of those weapons should have been enough," David thought. "But I can overcome him because he has no fear of God, he blasphemes, and he does not understand the spirit in man. This giant is nothing—his shadow has departed from him." Then David called out: "You come to me with a sword, a spear and a javelin, but I come to you in the name of the Lord." Thus our Sages remind us that size and physical might do not necessarily bring victory; spirit and dedication do.

[7] I CANNOT GO WITH THESE: Because Saul's armor did fit David the boy looked kingly in the royal armor. Since he was head and shoulders taller than any man in Israel Saul wondered how this boy should wear his armor and he jealously considered whether David was destined to rule in his place. As he did so a look of hatred crossed his face.

David saw Saul's look and at once said: "This armor is too heavy for me. I cannot wear it." David said to Saul: "Your servant has been guarding his father's sheep and killed the lion and the bear. Am I so important and esteemed to be granted such prowess by the

גַּם אֶת הָאֲרִי גַּם אֶת הַדֹּב הִכָּה הִכָּה עַבְדֶּךָ, וְהָיָה הַפְּלִשְׁתִּי הַזֶּה כְּאַחַד מֵהֶם, כִּי חֵרֵף מַעַרְכוֹת אֱלֹהִים חַיִּים.

When the Philistine looked about and saw David, he despised him [8] for he was a youth, ruddy and handsome, and he said to David: "Am I a dog that you came to me with sticks?" Goliath cursed David by his god.

Then he said to David: "Come to me, and I will give your flesh to the birds of the air and to the cattle of the field."

And David said to the Philistine: "You come to me with a sword, a spear and javelin, but I come to you in the name of the Lord, the God of the armies of Israel, whom you have taunted. This day the Lord will deliver you into my hand, that I may smite you and take your head off. And I will give the carcasses of the Philistine host to the birds of the air and the wild beasts of the earth. Then all the earth will know that there is a God in Israel."

The Philistine rose and as he came to meet David, David hastened and ran to meet him. Then David put his hand into his bag, and took from it a stone,

---

Lord to overcome powerful beasts? The Lord gave me strength and valor as an omen, an indication that Israel will be saved by such powers." Then David went out and found five white stones in the brook. With them he advanced against Goliath. The giant was immense and David thought, "How can any man stand before such a monster?" But when Goliath began to mock Israel and curse God David knew that he could stand against him. "I can defeat Goliath because I fight for the Lord and He will give me strength."

ews [8] HE DESPISED HIM: When Goliath saw David he was so astonished by the youth that he remained rooted to the ground. Used to facing hardened warriors and expecting a seasoned fighter, Goliath saw only a stripling and was taken aback. So confused was he that he scarcely knew what he was saying. "I will give your flesh to . . . the cattle of the field," he threatened. Do cattle eat flesh? At that David knew that the giant was doomed and replied, "I will give your carcass to the birds of the air." When Goliath heard David speak of "birds of the air" he raised his eyes skyward, lifting his visor so that he could see and the stone aimed by David struck his unprotected forehead and killed him.

אַתָּה בָּא אֵלַי בְּחֶרֶב וּבַחֲנִית וּבְכִידוֹן, וְאָנֹכִי בָא אֵלֶיךָ בְּשֵׁם יְיָ צְבָאוֹת, אֱלֹהֵי מַעַרְכוֹת יִשְׂרָאֵל אֲשֶׁר חֵרַפְתָּ.

put it in his sling and slung it. The stone struck the Philistine on his forehead. It sank into his forehead, and he fell upon his face [9] to the ground. David ran to the fallen Philistine, drew out the Philistine's sword from its sheath, and killed him. When the Philistines saw that their champion was dead, they fled. The man of Israel and of Judah pursued the Philistines as far as the gates of Gath and Ekron.

Saul took David that day into his service and did not let him go home to his father's house.

SAUL'S JEALOUSY OF DAVID

SAUL PUT DAVID over the men of war, and it pleased all the people and the servants of Saul. When Saul and David returned from fighting the Philistines the women from all the cities of Israel came out, singing and dancing to meet them, with tambourines, with joy and with three-stringed instruments. The women sang:

> "Saul has slain his thousands [10]
> But David his ten thousands."

Then Saul became very angry, for their saying displeased him. He said: "They have ascribed to David the ten thousands, and to me the thousands. All he lacks is the kingdom!" From that day onward Saul eyed David.

On the next day the evil spirit of God came upon Saul, and he raved within the house, while David played

---

⇜ [9] GOLIATH FELL ON HIS FACE: Why did Goliath fall on his face? Would it not have been more natural for a man struck in the forehead to fall backward? Because Goliath had blasphemed with his mouth and because he bore the image of his idol Dagon on his breastplate, God wanted to humble both. When Goliath fell, his mouth was in the dust and so was his breastplate, thus fulfilling the verse (Leviticus 26:30) "I will . . . cast your carcasses upon the carcasses of your idols."

⇜ [10] SAUL HAS SLAIN: David had just saved the kingdom and Saul's own life. Why was Saul so angry? Should he not have rejoiced with the women for Israel's redemption from the enemy? Because of his jealousy of David Saul thought that the women had praised David more highly than him, had elevated David above him. They had

הִכָּה שָׁאוּל בַּאֲלָפָיו וְדָוִד בְּרִבְבוֹתָיו.

for him as usual. Saul had his spear in his hand and he said: "I will pin David to the wall." He threw the spear at him, and David stepped aside and evaded him twice. Saul became afraid of David because the Lord was with him, and had departed from Saul. So Saul removed him from him, and made him captain over a thousand. <u>David had great success in all his ways, and the Lord was with him.</u> When Saul saw that he had great success, he stood in dread of him, but all Israel and Judah loved David.

DAVID MARRIES MICHAL

MICHAL, SAUL'S daughter loved David. When they told it to Saul, the thing pleased him. He said: "I will give her to him to imperil him, that the hand of the Philistines may be upon him." He said to his servants: "Thus shall you say to David: 'The king does not desire any dowry, but to take vengeance on the king's enemies. Let him bring proof that he has killed in battle a hundred of the Philistines.'" Now Saul thought to make David fall by the hand of the Philistines.

The servants of Saul told these words to David, and it pleased David to become the king's son-in-law. So David arose and went with his men and two hundred Philistines were killed. Saul gave him Michal, [11] his daughter, as wife. Michal, Saul's daughter loved David. Saul saw and knew that the

---

spoken of Saul without giving him his title of king, so making him the equal of the young shepherd. "He is already called my equal and even my superior," Saul mused, "all he lacks now is my throne."

⁓ [11] SAUL GAVE HIM MICHAL: When the Philistines heard that David had married Michal they rejoiced. "Now we can war against Israel and win for it is written in their Torah, 'A bridegroom shall not go out to battle until a year has passed' (Deuteronomy 24:5)." When David heard what the Philistines had said he laughed, because they did not know that the law expounded: "That is true only of wars beyond the borders of Israel. When we are attacked every man must fight, even the groom from under his canopy." The Philistines did attack and David, leading Saul's forces, met and defeated them.

וַיְהִי דָוִד לְכָל דְּרָכָיו מַשְׂכִּיל, וַיְיָ עִמּוֹ.

Lord was with David, so he was yet more afraid of him.

JONATHAN AND DAVID

JONATHAN LOVED David. The soul of Jonathan was knit with the soul of David. He made a pact with David because he loved him as his own soul. Jonathan stripped himself of his robe and gave it to David. Then he gave him his apparel, even his sword, his bow and his belt.

Saul spoke to Jonathan, his son and all his servants to slay David. But Jonathan, Saul's son, who delighted in David told him: "Saul, my father, is plotting to slay you. Now, hide yourself, and I will speak about you to my father, and whatever I will find out I will tell you."

Jonathan spoke favorably of David [12] to his father. He said to him: "Let the king not sin against his servant David, because he has not sinned against you. He risked his life and killed the Philistine, and the Lord brought a great victory for all Israel. You saw it and rejoiced, why then will you sin and shed innocent blood, to kill David without cause?" Saul listened to what Jonathan said, and swore: "As the Lord lives, he shall not be put to death." Jonathan brought David to Saul, and David remained in his presence as he had before.

MICHAL SAVES DAVID'S LIFE

THERE WAS war again, and David went out and fought the Philistines, and defeated them with heavy losses, and they fled before him. Then the evil spirit from the Lord was upon Saul. He sat in his house with the spear in his hand, and David was playing on the harp. Saul tried to pin David to the wall with his spear, but David slipped away. So

---

⤳ [12] JONATHAN SPOKE FAVORABLY OF DAVID: Until this point Jonathan's name in Hebrew had been spelled in the brief fashion, *Yonathan*. But when Jonathan speaks to Saul in defense of David, his rival for the throne, the text gives his name as *Y'Honathan*, the first two letters forming the name of the Lord. The Rabbis explained that Jonathan's firm display of affection for David despite his father's hatred and David's threat to his own succession to the throne grew out of Jonathan's profound spiritual attachment to David and thus merited the name of the Lord attached to his.

רָאִיתָ וַתִּשְׂמָח, וְלָמָּה תֶחֱטָא בְדָם נָקִי לְהָמִית אֶת דָּוִד חִנָּם.

he drove the spear into the wall, and David fled [13] and escaped.

That night Saul sent messengers to David's house to watch him, so as to kill him in the morning. Michal said to David: "If you do not save your life tonight, you will be killed tomorrow." So Michal let David down through the window, and he fled. Michal took the teraphim and laid it on the bed. She put a quilt of goat's hair at the head of the bed, and covered it with a cloth.

When Saul sent the messengers to take David, she said to them: "He is sick." Then Saul sent the messengers again with the command: "Bring him up to me in the bed, so that I may kill him." The messengers brought it, and behold, the teraphim were in the bed. And Saul said to Michal: "Why have you deceived me? You let my enemy escape."

Michal said to Saul: "He said to me: 'Let me go. Why should I kill you?'"

David fled and came to Samuel at Ramah, and told him all that Saul had done to him. Then he and Samuel went and stayed in Naioth.

---

 [13] AND DAVID FLED: Our Sages tell us that when the hour behaves impudently toward you, do not try to force it to do your bidding. Give it time and wait. Whosoever has the patience and endurance will find that the hour will eventually fall into his hand. When Nimrod was angry with Abraham and wanted to kill him, Abraham fled—and lived to become father of a great nation. Esau wanted to murder Jacob and Jacob fled until the time came for him to become Israel. So when Saul wanted to kill David, David too fled until the hour when Saul conceded that David would surely reign.

אִם אֵינְךָ מְמַלֵּט אֶת נַפְשְׁךָ הַלַּיְלָה, מָחָר אַתָּה מוּמָת.

14. I SAMUEL [20–25]

DAVID CONSULTS JONATHAN

DAVID FLED from Naioth and he went and met Jonathan and he said to him: "What have I done? What is my guilt? What wrong have I done to your father that he seeks my life?" Jonathan answered: "Far from it! My father does no thing great or small without letting me know. So why should my father hide this thing from me? No, it is not so!" David said: "Your father knows well that I have found favor in your eyes, so he said to himself: 'Jonathan must not know this because he will be grieved.' But truly, as the Lord lives, there is but a step between me and death."

Jonathan said to him: "What do you wish me to do for you?" David said: "Tomorrow is the festival of the New Moon, when I should sit with the king to eat. So let me go, that I may hide myself until the third day at evening. If your father will miss me, then say: 'David asked leave of me that he might run to Beth-lehem, his city, for it is the yearly sacrifice for the whole family.' If he says, 'Good,' then it will be well with your servant. But if he becomes angry, then you will know that he is determined to harm me." Jonathan said: "If I shall see that my father is determined to harm you, then I shall come and tell it to you." Then David said:

מֶה עָשִׂיתִי, מֶה עֲוֹנִי וּמֶה חַטָּאתִי לִפְנֵי אָבִיךָ, כִּי מְבַקֵּשׁ אֶת נַפְשִׁי?

"How will you let me know your father's determination?"

Jonathan said: "You hide yourself at the stone Ezel. Tomorrow at the festival of the New Moon your seat will be empty. On the third day I will come to the place where you hide yourself and I will shoot three arrows, as though I shot at a mark. I will send the boy who will be with me, and if I say to the boy, 'Look, the arrows are on this side of you, get them,' then come forward, for all is well with you—there is nothing to fear as the Lord lives. But if I say to the boy, 'The arrows are beyond you,' then go, for the Lord sends you away."

David hid himself in the field.

JONATHAN'S PLAN

IT WAS AT the New Moon festival. The king sat down to the meal, and David's place was empty. Nevertheless, Saul did not say anything on that day, for he thought: "Something has befallen David that he could not come." But on the next day, when he saw that David's place was empty again, Saul said to Jonathan: "Why has not come the son of Jesse to the meal; neither yesterday nor today?" Jonathan answered: "David asked leave of me to go to Beth-lehem. He said to me, 'Let me go, for our family has a sacrifice in the city.' Therefore, he did not come to the king's table."

Saul's anger blazed against Jonathan and he said: "Rebellious son, do I not know that you have chosen the son of Jesse to your shame and the disgrace of your mother? For as long as the son of Jesse lives upon the earth you shall not be established, nor your kingdom. Now go! Fetch him, for he deserves death." Jonathan answered Saul, his father: "Why should he be put to death? What has he done?" Saul raised his spear, ready to strike him, so Jonathan knew that his father was determined to put David to death. He rose and left the table in anger, and he did not eat bread on the second day of the month, for he grieved for David.

JONATHAN KEEPS HIS PROMISE

IT WAS MORNING. Jonathan went out into the field at the time appointed with David, and a little boy was with him. He said to the boy: "Run now and find the arrows which I shoot." As the boy ran, Jonathan shot an arrow beyond him. When the boy came to the place of the arrow which Jonathan shot, Jonathan cried after the boy and said: "Is not the arrow beyond you? Quickly, run, do not stop." The boy gathered the arrows and brought them to his master. Jonathan gave his weapons to the boy and said to him: "Go, carry them to the city." As soon as the boy was gone,

וַיַּעַן יְהוֹנָתָן אֶת שָׁאוּל אָבִיו וַיֹּאמֶר לוֹ: לָמָּה יוּמַת, מֶה עָשָׂה?

David came out from his hiding and fell on his face to the ground and bowed down three times to Jonathan. They kissed one another and wept. Jonathan said to David: "Go in peace. Remember! We two have sworn in the name of the Lord, saying: 'The Lord shall be a witness between me and you and between my descendants and your descendants forever.'"

David arose and departed. Jonathan went into the city.

DAVID AND THE PRIEST AHIMELECH

THEN DAVID came to the city of Nob, to Ahimelech, the priest. When Ahimelech saw him, he came eagerly to meet him, and said: "Why are you alone, without attendants?" David said to Ahimelech: "The king has commanded me to do something and he told me: 'Let no man know anything about the business on which I send you.' The young men who attend me I told to wait in such and such a place. Now, what have you at your hand? Five loaves of bread? Give them to me, or whatever you have."

The priest answered David: "I have no common bread, only the holy bread, [1] the showbread." So the priest gave to David the showbread, the holy bread. Now, one of the servants of Saul was there that day, detained before the Lord; his name was Doeg, the Edomite, [2] the chief of Saul's shepherds.

And David said: "Is there a spear here, or a sword?"

And the priest said: "The sword of

⫷§ [1] HOLY BREAD: The holy bread or "showbread" consisted of twelve loaves placed on a golden table in the Sanctuary every Sabbath. The loaves were baked on Friday and tradition holds that they were kept miraculously fresh and warm for the entire week. When the week was up, the loaves were replaced on the following Sabbath, and then divided among the priests and eaten.

⫷§ [2] DOEG, THE EDOMITE: Doeg and David were officers of the same rank in Saul's army. As David advanced rapidly, Doeg became jealous. When he reported David's visit to the Sanctuary at Nob, he made it seem that the priests there had been deliberately contemptuous of Saul.

יְיָ יִהְיֶה בֵּינִי וּבֵינֶךָ וּבֵין זַרְעִי וּבֵין זַרְעֲךָ עַד עוֹלָם.

Goliath, the Philistine, whom you slew, is here wrapped in a cloth."

And David said: "There is none like it; give it to me!"

DAVID FEIGNS MADNESS

DAVID FLED that day in fear of Saul and went to the king of Gath, [which is in the land of the Philistines. When he presented himself to the king,] the servants of Achish, the king of Gath, said to him: "Why, is this not David, the hero of the land? Was it not of him that they sang:

Saul has slain his thousands
But David his ten thousands?"

When David heard it he was frightened of Achish, the king of Gath. So he pretended to be insane: He ran to and fro. He scribbled on the doors of the gate and let his spittle run down his beard. Achish looked at him and said: "Behold, that man is mad! Do I lack madmen here? Who brought him here? He shall not be allowed to come into my house."

DAVID IN ADULLAM

DAVID FLED from there and escaped to the cave of Adullam. When his brothers and all his father's house heard it, they went down there to him. And every one who was oppressed or in debt, and every one who was discontented, gathered themselves to him, and he became their captain. There were with him about four hundred men.

Then David went to the king of Moab, and said: "I beg of you, let my father and mother stay with you until I know what God will do for me." And they remained with the king of Moab, all the time that David was in the stronghold. After that, David went to the forest of Hereth.

Doeg called David not by his name but "the son of Jesse" to point out that David was descended from Ruth the Moabitess and thus not truly an Israelite. Doeg himself was the son of an Edomite mother and what he wanted to stress was that Moabites had been declared ineligible to be accepted into the congregation of Israel.

Tradition has it that a voice was heard saying: "How long will you sin and repeat your false accusations of a taint in David's lineage? All Israelites are of equal lineage in My eyes. The born Israelite and the righteous proselyte, neither is better."

וַיִּתְקַבְּצוּ אֵלָיו כָּל אִישׁ מָצוֹק וְכָל אִישׁ אֲשֶׁר לוֹ נוֹשֶׁא וְכָל אִישׁ מַר נֶפֶשׁ, וַיְהִי עֲלֵיהֶם לְשָׂר.

SAUL KILLS THE PRIESTS OF NOB

THEN SAUL heard that David became the captain of a band. Saul was sitting under the tamarisk tree in Gibeah on a hill, his spear in his hand, and all his servants were standing around him. And Saul said to his servants: "Hear you, Benjamites! Will the son of Jesse give every one of you fields and vineyards? Will he make you all captains? Why did you all conspire against me, and there was none who disclosed it to me when my son made a pact with the son of Jesse? Is there not one of you who feels compassion for me? Has my son incited all my servants against me?"

Then Doeg, the Edomite, said: "I saw the son of Jesse coming to Nob, and Ahimelech inquired of the Lord for him; and gave him food, and the sword of Goliath."

The king sent and called Ahimelech, the priest, and all his father's house, all the priests of Nob. They came to him, and the king said to Ahimelech: "Why did you conspire against me, that you have given the son of Jesse food and a sword? You have inquired of God for him, and risen against me as an enemy!"

Ahimelech answered the king: "But who among all your servants is so trusted as David, who is the king's son-in-law? Is it the first time I inquired of God for him? Your servant knew nothing at all about this."

The king said: "You shall surely die, you and your father's house." He said to the guards who stood about him: "Turn and kill the priests of the Lord. They were in league with David. They knew that he was fleeing, and they did not tell me."

But the guards would not lift their hand [3] to fall upon the priests of the

---

◆§ [3] WOULD NOT LIFT THEIR HAND: The Law clearly states that a king must be obeyed by all men. "Anyone who scorns your orders and does not obey you in all you command him, he shall be put to death" (Joshua 1:18). Our Rabbis say that this edict applied not only to Joshua but to all the kings (Sanhedrin 49a). Yet when Saul commanded the guards to kill the priests of Nob, the guards refused and Saul did not have them killed. Was that not open treason and rebellion?

Abner and Amasa were the two commanders and they refused to

וְלֹא אָבוּ עַבְדֵי הַמֶּלֶךְ לִשְׁלֹחַ אֶת יָדָם לִפְגֹּעַ בְּכֹהֲנֵי יְיָ.

Lord. Then the king said to Doeg, the Edomite: "You turn and fall upon the priests."

Doeg fell upon the priests and killed on that day eighty-five men.

And one of the sons of Ahimelech, Abiathar, escaped and fled after David. He told David that Saul killed the Lord's priests. David said: "I am to blame for the death of all your father's house. When I saw Doeg there, I knew that he would tell Saul. Stay with me and fear not. Whoever seeks your life seeks my life."

DAVID, NABAL AND ABIGAIL

THERE WAS a man in Maon who was very rich. He had three thousand sheep and a thousand goats. The name of the man was Nabal, [4] and the name of his wife was Abigail. The woman had good sense and was beautiful; but the man was rough and evil.

David was then in the wilderness of Maon. He heard that Nabal was shearing his sheep. He called ten young men, and said: "Get you up to Carmel, and go to Nabal and greet him in my name: 'Peace be unto you and your house. I have heard that you have men shearing. Now, your shepherds have been with us, and we did not insult them, and nothing of theirs was missing all the while they were in Carmel. Ask your young men and they will tell you. Therefore, let my young men find favor in your eyes, and give whatever you

order the troops to kill the priests. They said: "We cannot execute your order because it is contrary to God's Law. You bestowed upon us insignias of authority and gave us honors. We hereby return them all to you and we will follow the command of the Lord." Even had they done so, the soldiers would not have obeyed because the Torah forbids obeying an unjust order, even from a king. The command to obey the king on punishment of death applies only when the king's command does not transgress the Law of the Torah.

[4] NABAL: Nabal means *churl*. Why would any parent name a child a churl? Nabal was a stingy man who begrudged even the members of his household food, let alone charity for the poor. His miserliness was so well-known that soon his real name was forgotten and all knew him as Nabal.

וְהָאִשָּׁה טוֹבַת שֶׂכֶל וִיפַת תֹּאַר, וְהָאִישׁ קָשֶׁה וְרַע מַעֲלָלִים.

have on hand to your servants and to your son David.' "

David's young men spoke all this to Nabal in the name of David. Nabal answered: "Who is David? And who is the son of Jesse? There are many slaves nowadays who break away from their masters. Shall I then take my bread and my water, the meat I have slaughtered for my shearers, and give it to the men of whom I know not?" .

David's young men left, and returned and told him all this. Then David said: "Let every man gird on his sword." About four hundred men followed David, while two hundred men remained with the baggage. Then David said: "In vain I guarded all that this man has in the wilderness. May God do so to David's enemies if I leave by morning a single male of all that belongs to Nabal."

One of the young men told Abigail: "David sent messengers from the wilderness to greet our master and he flew at them. His men were good to us. We have not missed anything when we were in the fields. All the while we were tending the sheep, David's men were a wall about us, both by night and by day. Now, therefore, consider what you should do, for there is evil brewing against our master and his house."

Then Abigail hastened and took two hundred loaves of bread; two skins of wine, five dressed sheep, five measures of parched grain, a hundred clusters of raisins, and two hundred cakes of figs. She loaded them on donkeys, and said to her young men: "You go on before me." But she did not tell her husband.

As she was riding her donkey, and came down the side of the mountain, she met David and his men coming toward her. She hastened and alighted from her donkey; bowed herself to the ground before David, and said: "Let your handmaid speak. Let my lord not take seriously this worthless fellow, Nabal, for he is like his name. Churl' is his name, and churlishness is with him. Your handmaid did not see the young men of my lord whom you sent. Now, here is the present which your servant has brought to my lord. May it be given to the young men who follow my lord. The Lord will certainly appoint you prince over Israel. Then my lord will not reproach himself for needless bloodshed. Then you shall remember your handmaid."

David said to Abigail: "Blessed be the Lord, the God of Israel, who sent you this day to meet me. Blessed be you, who has kept me this day from bloodshed."

David accepted the present Abigail brought him, and he said: "Go up to your house in peace."

בָּרוּךְ יְיָ אֱלֹהֵי יִשְׂרָאֵל אֲשֶׁר שְׁלָחֵךְ הַיּוֹם הַזֶּה לִקְרָאתִי, וּבָרוּךְ טַעְמֵךְ וּבְרוּכָה
אַתְּ אֲשֶׁר כְּלִיתִנִי הַיּוֹם הַזֶּה מִבּוֹא בְדָמִים.

When Abigail came to Nabal, he was holding a feast in his house like the feast of a king, and he was very drunk. She told him nothing until the morning. But in the morning, when the wine was gone out of Nabal, she told him all this. His heart died within him, and he became like a stone. About ten days later he died.

When David heard that Nabal was dead, he said: "Blessed be the Lord who has avenged my insult [5] from the hand of Nabal, and kept back His servant from evil."

Then he sent messengers to Abigail, and they said: "David sent us to ask you to be his wife." She arose and bowed, and answered: "Your humble handmaid is ready to wash the feet of my lord's servants." She hastened and mounted a donkey, and five of her maidens followed her. She went after the messengers of David, and became his wife.

◀§ [5] AVENGED MY INSULT: David's young men came to Nabal on the day after Samuel's funeral. All Israel still mourned but Nabal gave a party, saying, "God's prophet and still he dies!" Nabal laughed and drank more wine. When David's young men told how they had protected his flocks, Nabal mocked them: "Tell David that Samuel is dead and the oil he poured over David's head is as forgotten as Samuel's life."

When David was told of Nabal's insults he came down with his four hundred armed men, but Abigail and her maidens, bearing gifts, intercepted him. She bowed before David and said: "Forgive the drunken man who prattles in his wine." But David refused, saying: "Nabal denied my anointing and my kingship. By custom, then, he who rebels is denied a trial."

"You are right, my lord," Abigail replied, "but think. When you are king a poor man will ask a rich man for bread. When the rich man refuses him, the poor man will slay him. The rich man's sons will then try to kill the poor man out of revenge and the poor man will come to you for protection. You will say: 'You were wrong to slay the rich man.' The poor man will answer: 'But your Majesty, is that not what you did to Nabal?'"

David hearkened to the wisdom of her words.

בָּרוּךְ יְיָ אֲשֶׁר רָב אֶת רִיב חֶרְפָּתִי מִיַּד נָבָל וְאֶת עַבְדּוֹ חָשַׂךְ מֵרָעָה.

15. I SAMUEL [23–31]

DAVID AND JONATHAN'S COVENANT

IT WAS TOLD Saul that David was come to Keilah. And Saul said: "God has delivered him into my hand; for he is shut in, by entering into a town that has gates and bars." Saul called all the people to go down to Keilah, to besiege David and his men. David knew that Saul devised mischief against him, and he said: "O Lord, God of Israel, Thy servant has heard that Saul will destroy the city for my sake. O Lord, will the men of Keilah deliver me up into Saul's hand?" And the Lord said: "They will deliver you up." Then David and his men arose and departed and went wherever they could go.

David abode in the wilderness in the strongholds, and remained in the hill country in the wilderness of Ziph. And Saul sought him every day, but God delivered him not into his hand. Then Jonathan, Saul's son, arose, and went to David into the wood, and strengthened his hand in God. And he said to him: "Fear not; for the hand of Saul, my father, shall not find you; and you shall be king over Israel, and I shall be next to you; and that also my father knows." And they two made a covenant before the Lord.

אַל תִּירָא כִּי לֹא תִמְצָאֲךָ יַד שָׁאוּל אָבִי וְאַתָּה תִּמְלֹךְ עַל יִשְׂרָאֵל וְאָנֹכִי אֶהְיֶה לְךָ לְמִשְׁנֶה, וְגַם שָׁאוּל אָבִי יֹדֵעַ כֵּן.

following [1] David and went against
the Philistines.

SAUL SPARES DAVID

THE ZIPHITES came to Saul at Gibeah,
and said, "David hides himself in the
hill of Hachilah." So Saul and his men
went to seek David, and they pursued
him in the wilderness of Maon. Saul
went on this side of the mountain, and
David and his men on that side; and
David hastened to escape from fear of
Saul. Saul and his men surrounded
David and his men and were about to
take them. But there came a messenger
to Saul, saying: "Make haste, and come;
for the Philistines have made a raid
upon the land." So Saul returned from

DAVID SPARES SAUL

WHEN SAUL returned from fighting the
Philistines, it was told him, "David is
in the wilderness of En-gedi." Then
Saul took three thousand chosen men
with him to seek David and his men
upon the rocks of the wild goats. He
came to the caves which served as shelter for the sheep in bad weather and
entered one of the caves to anoint his
feet. David and his men were hidden
in the innermost parts of the cave.
Then David's men said to him: "Here

 [1] SAUL RETURNED FROM FOLLOWING: When Saul had David surrounded, a messenger arrived and reported that the Philistines were
raiding the land. Saul's officers were divided as to whether to abandon the pursuit of David. Some said, "At last we have David at our
mercy. He cannot escape. Let us seize him and once and for all be
done with this rebel." But the others replied: "Let us not tarry. The
country is in danger and the defense of the land comes first. Eventually David will fall in our hands."

Saul had to decide which course to follow. He was tempted to rid
himself of David but he thought: "I am the anointed of the Lord,
king of Israel, a shepherd of the Lord's flock. When the flock is in
danger does not the shepherd overlook his own needs and desires?
Now, I must accept my responsibility for my flock, this people and
this land." Again, Saul showed that neither hatred nor revenge would
stay him from his kingly duties, and then "Saul returned from following David and went against the Philistines."

מַהֲרָה וָלֵכָה כִּי פָשְׁטוּ פְלִשְׁתִּים עַל הָאָרֶץ.

is the day on which the Lord has delivered your enemy into your hand." David said to his men: "The Lord forbid that I do this thing to my lord, the Lord's anointed." He checked his men with these words and did not let them attack Saul. But David arose quickly and cut off the hem of Saul's robe.

Saul left the cave and went on his way. David left the cave and called out to Saul: "My lord, the king!" Saul looked behind him and David bowed his face to the ground and prostrated himself. Then David said to Saul:

"Why did you listen to the words of the men who said that David seeks your life? You can see that this day the Lord has delivered you into my hand in the cave, but I refused to kill you. Because I said, I will not lift my hand against my lord, for he is the Lord's anointed. Yes, my father, look and see the hem of your robe in my hand. Let the Lord judge between me and you. My hand shall not be against you."

When David had finished speaking Saul said to him: "Is this your voice, my son, David?" Saul wept and said to David: "You are more righteous than I, for you have done good to me and I have done evil to you. When the Lord delivered me into your hand, you did not kill me. Now I know that you shall surely be king and the kingdom of Israel shall be established in your hand.

So now swear to me by the Lord that you will not kill my children when I am gone and will not destroy my name out of my father's house." And David swore to Saul. And Saul went home and David and his men went up to the stronghold.

DAVID AGAIN SPARES SAUL

THE ZIPHITES came once more to Saul at Gibeah, and said "David hides himself in the hill of Hachilah." Then Saul arose, and went down to the wilderness of Ziph. He took three thousand chosen men with him to seek David. Saul encamped on the hill of Hachilah. David remained in the wilderness. When he saw that Saul came after him in the wilderness, he sent spies, and discovered where Saul was encamped. David arose and came and he saw Saul was lying inside the entrenchment. Abner, the captain of the armies, and all the people lay round about Saul.

Then David said to Ahimelech, the Hittite, and to Abishai, the son of Zeruiah: "Who will go down with me to Saul, to the camp?"

Abishai answered: "I will go down with you." So David and Abishai made their way to the camp by night, and there was Saul, lying asleep within the entrenchment, his spear thrust in the earth at his head.

הֲקוֹלְךָ זֶה, בְּנִי דָוִד? ... צַדִּיק אַתָּה מִמֶּנִּי כִּי אַתָּה גְּמַלְתַּנִי הַטּוֹבָה וַאֲנִי גְּמַלְתִּיךָ הָרָעָה.

Abishai said to David: "God has delivered your enemy into your hand. Let me pin him to the ground with the spear and I will not strike him again!"

David said to Abishai: "Destroy him not. [2] Who can lay his hands on the Lord's anointed and be guiltless? His day will come to die or he will be swept away in battle. The Lord forbid that I should raise my hand against the Lord's anointed. But take the spear that is at his head, and the jug of water."

Then David went over to the other side, and stood on the top of the mountain, and cried out, saying: "Abner, will you not answer?"

Abner answered: "Who are you that cries to waken the king?"

David said to Abner: "You are a valiant man. There is none like you in all Israel. Why then have you not guarded the lord, your king? As the Lord lives, you deserve to die, because you have not kept watch over your lord. See now, where is the king's spear, and the jug of water that was at his head?"

Saul recognized David's voice, and said: "Is it your voice, my son David?" David answered: "It is my voice, my lord, O king." He continued: "Why does my lord pursue after his servant? What have I done? Of which evil am I guilty? Now therefore, I pray you, let my lord, the king, hear the words of his servant. If it be the Lord that has stirred you up against me, let the Lord accept an offering; but if it be the children of men, cursed be they before the Lord; for they have driven me out this day that I should not cleave unto the inheritance of the Lord, saying: Go, serve other gods. [3] Now therefore, let not my blood fall to the earth away from the presence of the Lord; for the king of Israel is come out like a partridge to hunt a single flea in the mountains."

꧁   [2] DESTROY HIM NOT: Twice David had chances to kill Saul and did not. The first time was when Saul came alone to the cave and David was so close that he was able to cut off a part of Saul's cloak. The second time David stole into Saul's encampment while the king and his guards slept and stole Saul's spear and waterskin. Both times David's followers wanted to kill Saul. They said: "The law is on your side. The law says clearly: 'If one comes to kill you, forestall him by killing him first.'" The second time, David's lieutenant Abishai actually raised his spear to strike Saul but David warned him: "If you kill him, your blood will be mingled with his."

כִּי יָצָא מֶלֶךְ יִשְׂרָאֵל לְבַקֵּשׁ אֶת פַּרְעֹשׁ אֶחָד כַּאֲשֶׁר יִרְדֹּף הַקּוֹרֵא בֶּהָרִים.

Saul answered: "I have sinned. Return, my son David. I will do you no harm, [4] for my life was precious in your eyes this day. I have acted foolishly and erred."

David answered: "Here is the king's spear! Let one of the young men come and fetch it."

Then Saul said to David: "Blessed be you, my son David. You shall certainly succeed in whatever you undertake."

DAVID IN GATH

THEN DAVID said to himself: "Some day I shall be captured by Saul. I had better escape into the land of the Philistines."

David arose and went over, he and the six hundred men who were with him, to Achish, king of Gath. When Saul was told that David had fled to Gath, he finally gave up his search for him.

SAUL AND THE WITCH OF EN-DOR

SAMUEL DIED, and all Israel mourned for him and buried him in Ramah, his own city.

Saul had put out of the land those that divined by ghost and the wizards. The Philistines gathered themselves together and came and encamped in Shunem. And Saul gathered all Israel

---

&⁊ [3] GO, SERVE OTHER GODS: Did David worship idols? No. What David meant was that he who leaves the Land of Israel and goes elsewhere it is as if he worshiped idols. David also said that he who is buried in a land other than the Holy Land it is as if he were buried in Babylonia (where the wicked generation inundated by the Flood lived). But he who is buried in the Land of Israel, it is as if he were buried under the altar, for the whole land is worthy of being the site of the Temple; and he who is buried there it is as if he were buried under the Throne of Glory.

&⁊ [4] I WILL DO YOU NO HARM: Twice solemnly Saul swore he would not pursue David. But David knew he could not depend on Saul's oath. Not only was Saul by temperament unreliable but Abner, the commander of Saul's army, hated David and intrigued against him. When David showed the piece of cloth he had cut from Saul's robe, Abner said: "David lies. The piece of garment was probably torn off

וַיֻּגַּד לְשָׁאוּל כִּי בָרַח דָּוִד גַּת, וְלֹא יָסַף עוֹד לְבַקְשׁוֹ.

together, and they encamped in Gilboa. When Saul saw the hosts of the Philistines, he was afraid and his heart trembled greatly. Saul inquired of the Lord, but the Lord did not answer him, neither by dreams nor by the prophets. Then Saul said to his servants: "Seek for me a woman who divines by ghost, that I may go to her to inquire of her."

The servants said: "There is a woman in En-dor that divines."

Saul disguised himself, [5] and went, he and two men with him, and came to the woman by night. He said to her: "Divine me, I beg of you, by ghost. Bring up the ghost of him I shall name to you."

The woman answered: "You know that Saul has driven the diviners out of the country. Why then are you laying a snare for my life, to cause me to die?"

Saul swore to her, saying: "As the Lord lives, there shall no punishment happen to you for this thing."

The woman said: "Whom shall I bring up to you?" He said: "Bring me up Samuel."

When the woman saw Samuel, she cried out with a loud voice: "Why have you deceived me, for you are Saul!"

The king said to her: "Be not afraid, but what do you see?"

And the woman said: "I see a god-like being coming up out of the earth."

---

when you marched through the thorn bushes. And even if what David says is true, he did not dare kill you in the cave because we would have come in after him and torn him to pieces." The second time David said, "I have the king's waterskin and spear here. Did Saul also lose these in the thorn bushes?" Abner could say nothing and Saul vowed once more not to pursue him.

[5] SAUL DISGUISED HIMSELF: Tradition tells us that when he went to the sorceress, Saul dressed as a commoner. When he asked the sorceress to divine for him by ghost, the woman was afraid because she knew that Saul had forbidden witchcraft and made it punishable by death. But Saul swore to her by the Lord that no harm would come to her. The Rabbis comment on this inconsistency: Saul, involved in a superstitious practice which was tantamount to denial of the Lord, swears by the Lord's name that nothing will happen to the witch who helps him.

וַתֹּאמֶר הָאִשָּׁה אֶל שָׁאוּל: אֱלֹהִים רָאִיתִי עוֹלִים מִן הָאָרֶץ.

And he said to her: "What does he look like?"

She said: "An old man is coming up, and he is covered with a mantle." Saul knew that it was Samuel, and bowed with his face to the earth.

Samuel said to Saul: "Why have you disturbed me, [6] to bring me up?"

Saul answered: "I am in grave trouble. The Philistines make war against me, and God has departed from me. He answers me no more, by prophets or by

---

≈§ [6] WHY HAVE YOU DISTURBED ME: The dialogue between Samuel and Saul, according to tradition, went like this:

Samuel: "Why have you disturbed me and brought me up? Was it not enough for you to anger the Lord by calling up the dead, which is the same as worshiping a graven image, must you make me into idol?"

Saul: "The Lord has departed from me and does not answer me by prophets or by dreams. I called you up to tell me what to do."

Samuel: "You have given yourself your answer. The Lord has departed from you and become your adversary. I told you that the Lord had resolved to take the kingdom from you and give it to David."

Saul: "When you were alive, you did not mention David's name. Why do you speak of him now?"

Samuel: "When I was in the world of deceptions (*olam ha-sheker*) I did not tell you the truth exactly because I feared your wrath. You might have killed me or David. But now that I am in the world of truth (*olam ha-emet*) I can tell you the truth because you can do me no harm. What the Lord has done to you, and what He will do, you have deserved. You killed the priests of Nob. Tomorrow a great calamity will befall you."

Saul: "Tell me. Do not spare me."

Samuel: "The verdict is signed and sealed. Tomorrow the army of Israel will be defeated and you and your sons will be with me."

Saul: "Can I save myself?"

Samuel: "Yes, by fleeing. If you flee, the army will be defeated but you and your sons will be saved. You must choose."

וַיֹּאמֶר שְׁמוּאֵל אֶל שָׁאוּל: לָמָה הִרְגַּזְתַּנִי לְהַעֲלוֹת אוֹתִי?

dreams. [7] Therefore, I have called you, to tell me what I should do."

Samuel said: "Why do you ask me, when the Lord has departed from you? The Lord has done to you as He spoke by me. The Lord has torn the kingdom from your hand, and has given it to David. The Lord will also deliver Israel with you into the hand of the Philistines. Tomorrow you and your sons shall be with me." [8]

Then Saul fell full length upon the earth. He was very frightened because of what Samuel told him. There was no strength in him, for he had not eaten food all the day, nor all the night.

When the woman saw that he was terrified, she said: "Your handmaid has done what you asked. Now therefore, let me set before you a bit of food. Eat, so that you may have strength when you go your way."

Out of fear and hunger Saul stretched full-length on the ground and fainted. The woman revived him and gave him food and drink. When he had eaten, Abner and Amasa, his two chief officers, who he had brought with him, asked what Samuel had prophesied, and Saul answered: "He told me that the army would be victorious and my sons covered with glory."

৩৪ [7] NEITHER BY PROPHETS NOR BY DREAMS: When Samuel asked Saul angrily why Saul had called him back, Saul replied that it was because he had got no response from either prophets or dreams. Why did he not mention that the priestly Urim had also not spoken to him? Our Rabbis tell us that Saul dared not refer to them because he had slain the priests of Nob and still felt remorse for this grievous sin and crime.

৩৪ [8] BE WITH ME: Why did Saul go out to battle when he knew it would bring him defeat and death? He might have fled and lived. But Saul did not flee because the disgrace would have been worse than death itself. When Samuel said that, "Tomorrow you and your sons shall be with me," he was not cursing Saul, but comforting him, said Rabbi Johanan. Saul's death would atone for his sins and thus Saul will be in paradise with Samuel.

וַיִּקְרַע יְיָ אֶת הַמַּמְלָכָה מִיָּדֶךָ, וַיִּתְּנָהּ לְרֵעֲךָ לְדָוִד.

He refused. But his servants, together with the woman, urged him until he yielded. He arose from the ground, and sat upon the bed. The woman hastily killed a fatted calf that she had. She took flour, kneaded it and baked unleavened bread. She brought it before Saul and before his servants. They ate and they arose, and went away that same night.

THE DEATH OF SAUL

THE PHILISTINES fought against Israel, [9] and the men of Israel fled before the Philistines, and they fell down wounded and slain on the Mount of Gilboa. The Philistines overtook Saul and his sons, and they killed Jonathan, Abinadab and Malchishua, the sons of Saul. The fighting pressed hard upon Saul. The archers got him in range, and he was badly wounded. Then Saul said to his armor-bearer: "Draw your sword and run me through with it, lest the Philistines come and make sport of me." His armor-bearer refused, because he was much afraid. So Saul took his sword, and fell upon it. When his armor-bearer saw that Saul was dead, he likewise fell upon his sword, and died with him.

So Saul and his three sons and his armor-bearer died together. When the men of Israel saw that Saul and his sons were dead, they forsook the cities on

---

At the moment that Saul spoke so to Abner and Amasa, the Lord summoned His angels and said: "Did you recognize the bravery and nobility of this mortal? He might have saved his life by fleeing but he chose instead to go into battle with his army, knowing that he would lose not only his own life, but the lives of his three sons. Saul has determined to do this because he knows that without his leadership the army would suffer even more."

[9] THE PHILISTINES FOUGHT: When Saul and his sons drew the Israelite forces into battle array and attacked the Philistines, Moses in heaven cried out: "O Lord, see the bravery of these men! They know they will be defeated and die, yet they march out. Lord, have mercy on them and preserve them."

And the Lord replied: "It is not I who decreed their death. It is the priests of Nob who stand before Me in silent accusation."

שְׁלֹף חַרְבְּךָ וְדָקְרֵנִי בָה, פֶּן יָבוֹאוּ הָעֲרֵלִים הָאֵלֶּה וּדְקָרוּנִי וְהִתְעַלְּלוּ בִי.

the side of the valley and beyond the Jordan, and they fled. The Philistines came and occupied them.

On the next day, when the Philistines came to strip the slain, they found Saul and his three sons fallen on Mount Gilboa. They cut off his head, and stripped off his armor, and they put it in the house of Ashtaroth, and fastened his body to the wall of Beth-shan.

When the inhabitants of Jabesh-gilead heard what the Philistines had done to Saul, all the valiant men arose and marched all night, and took the bodies of Saul and his sons from the wall of Beth-shan, and brought them to Jabesh and they burned them. And they took their bones, and buried them under the tamarisk tree in Jabesh. And they fasted seven days.

וַיָּקוּמוּ כָּל אִישׁ חַיִל וַיֵּלְכוּ כָל הַלַּיְלָה וַיִּקְחוּ אֶת גְּוִיַּת שָׁאוּל וְאֶת גְּוִיֹּת בָּנָיו מֵחוֹמַת בֵּית שָׁן.

16. II SAMUEL [1–5]

SAUL AND JONATHAN'S DEATH

DAVID DWELLED in Ziklag. On the third day a man came from Saul's camp with his clothes torn and earth upon his head. When he approached David he fell to the ground and prostrated himself. David said: "Where do you come from?"

He answered: "I have escaped from the camp of Israel." Then David said to him: "Tell me, what happened?"

And he answered: "The people have fled from the battle and many of them have fallen, and also Saul and Jonathan, his son, are dead."

David said to the man: "How do you know that Saul and Jonathan are dead?" And the man answered: "I happened, by chance, to be on Mount Gilboa, and there was Saul leaning upon his spear, the chariots and the horsemen pressing hard upon him. He looked behind and saw me and he called out to me and said: 'I beg you kill me, because I am in agony of death. I am going to die, but I am afraid to fall into the hands of the Philistines.' So I killed him, because I was sure that he could not live after he had fallen [upon his sword]. I took the crown that was on his head and the bracelet that was on his arm and I brought them to you, my lord."

נָס הָעָם מִן הַמִּלְחָמָה וְגַם הַרְבֵּה נָפַל מִן הָעָם וַיָּמוּתוּ, וְגַם שָׁאוּל וִיהוֹנָתָן בְּנוֹ מֵתוּ.

David said to him: "Where do you come from?" And he answered: "I am a son of an Amalekite who lives in Israel." And David said to him: "Why were you not afraid to destroy the Lord's anointed? You are guilty of murder. [1] Your own mouth testified against you." Then David called one of his men and said to him: "Strike him down."

Then David took hold of his clothes and tore them, and so did all the men who were with him. They wept and lamented and fasted until evening for Saul and his son Jonathan and the people of the Lord, because they had fallen by the sword.

DAVID'S LAMENT

AND DAVID lamented for Saul and for Jonathan, his son.

"Your beauty, O Israel, upon your
   heights is slain;
How are the mighty fallen!

Tell it not in Gath,
Proclaim it not in the streets of
   Ashkelon,
Lest the daughters of the
   Philistines rejoice.

You mountains of Gilboa,
Let there be no dew nor rain
   upon you;
You fields of death,
For there the shields of the mighty
   were defiled.

Saul and Jonathan, the lovely and
   the pleasant,
In their lives and in their death
   they were not separated.
They were swifter than eagles
They were stronger than lions.
You daughters of Israel, weep over
   Saul
Who clothed you in scarlet, with
   other delights,
Who put ornaments of gold upon
   your apparel.

❧ [1] YOU ARE GUILTY OF MURDER: The Amalekite was deemed guilty of murder though he reported that Saul had begged him to kill him. Our Rabbis explain that the law states clearly: "If a man asks his fellow man: 'Cut off my hand, gouge out my eye, and I will not hold you responsible for the act,' the man who obeys him remains responsible." That man is guilty of a crime and must pay damages. The law clearly forbids injury to anyone. The prohibition is a commandment of the Lord which cannot be countermanded.

הַצְּבִי יִשְׂרָאֵל, עַל בָּמוֹתֶיךָ חָלָל, אֵיךְ נָפְלוּ גִבּוֹרִים!

How are the mighty fallen in the
  midst of the battle!

Jonathan upon your heights is
  slain!
I am distressed for you, my brother
  Jonathan,
Most pleasant you have been to
  me;
Wonderful was your love for me.
How are the mighty fallen,
And the weapons of war perished!"

DAVID MADE KING OF JUDAH

AFTER THIS David inquired of the Lord: "Shall I go up into any of the cities of Judah?" The Lord said: "Go up." Then David asked: "Whither shall I go?" And He answered: "To Hebron." So David went up there with his wives, and he also took the men who were with him, every man with his household, and they settled in the cities around Hebron. The men of Judah came and they anointed David king [2] over Judah.

WAR BETWEEN ISRAEL AND JUDAH

NOW ABNER, the son of Ner, captain of Saul's army, took Ish-bosheth, the son of Saul, to Mahanaim and made him king over all Israel. But the house of Judah followed David. Ish-bosheth was forty years old when he was made king over Israel, and he reigned two years.

Abner and the followers of Ish-bosheth went out from Mahanaim to Gibeon. And Joab and the followers of David went out from Hebron and met them at the pool of Gibeon. And there was a bitterly fought battle that day. Abner and his followers were beaten by David's followers. [The followers of Ish-bosheth fled before Joab and his men.]

And the three sons of Zeruiah were there: Joab, Abishai and Asahel. Asahel was as swift of foot as a gazelle of the field. He pursued Abner and followed him closely. Abner looked behind him and said: "Is it you, Asahel?" He answered: "It is I."

And Abner said: "Turn aside, and seize one of the young men and take his armor for yourself." But Asahel would not turn from following.

Abner said again: "Turn aside. Why should I be forced to smite you to the earth? How could I look your brother Joab in the face?" Still Asahel refused

---

⌇ [2] THEY ANOINTED DAVID KING: David wanted to be crowned king in Hebron because from ancient times the city had been hallowed to Jews. In the Cave of Machpelah were buried the Patriarchs and

צַר לִי עָלֶיךָ, אָחִי יְהוֹנָתָן, נָעַמְתָּ לִי מְאֹד, נִפְלְאַתָה אַהֲבָתְךָ לִי.

to turn. Wherefore Abner struck him with a backward thrust of the spear, and Asahel fell dead.

A TRUCE BETWEEN THE ARMIES

JOAB AND ABISHAI pursued Abner. When the sun went down they came to the hill of Ammah. The Benjamites gathered around Abner, and they stood on the top of the hill. Abner called to Joab and said: "Shall the sword devour for ever? Do you not know the end will be bitter? Command your people to stop following their brethren." Joab said: "As God lives, had you not spoken, not one of the men would have stopped pursuing his brethren till morning."

Joab blew the *Shofar* and all the people halted and stopped pursuing Israel.

ABNER NEGOTIATES WITH DAVID

THE WAR BETWEEN the house of Saul and the house of David continued for a long time. David became stronger and stronger, but the house of Saul became weaker and weaker. And it was in this prolonged war that Abner strengthened himself in the house of Saul. Then Abner sent messengers to David, saying: "Make a covenant with me and I will bring all Israel to you." And he said: "Good. I will make a pact with you, but one thing I require: You shall bring me Michal, the daughter of Saul."

David sent messengers to Ish-bosheth, saying: "Deliver to me my wife [3] Michal whom I married." Then Ish-bosheth sent Abner and she was taken from Paltiel, her husband. Her husband went with her, weeping as he followed her to Bahurim. Then Abner said to him: "Go, return." So he returned.

Now Abner came to the elders of Israel and said: "You have long wanted David to be king over you. Now then, do it. For the Lord had promised: 'By the hand of My servant David I will save Israel, My people, from the hand

their wives: Abraham and Sarah, Isaac and Rebekah, Jacob and Leah. To be anointed king there would carry the great weight of tradition with the people.

⊷ [3] DELIVER TO ME MY WIFE: Why is Palti abruptly called Paltiel (in I Samuel 25:44 he is called Palti), which includes the name of God? Because, our Sages explain, Palti showed such strength and sensitivity that he deserved to bear the name of God. Michal was

וַיִּקְרָא אַבְנֵר אֶל יוֹאָב וַיֹּאמֶר: הֲלָנֶצַח תֹּאכַל חֶרֶב?

of the Philistines and from the hand of all their enemies.'" And Abner also went to speak in the ears of David in Hebron. He came and there were twenty men with him. David made a feast for Abner and his men. Then Abner said: "I will go and gather all Israel to my lord and king, so that they will make a covenant with you, and you shall rule over all of them as you desire." David sent Abner away, and he went away in peace.

THE MURDER OF ABNER

JUST THEN the followers of David and Joab came from a raid. Joab was told: "Abner came to the king, but he sent him off in peace." Then Joab came to David and said: "What have you done? Abner came to see you; why did you send him off? Do you not know Abner, that he came to deceive you, to learn your going and coming?"

When Joab left David, he sent messengers after Abner. They brought him back from Bor-sirah, but David did not know it. When he came to Hebron Joab took him aside at the town gate to speak with him quietly, and stabbed him in the groin, and he died.

When David heard it, he said: "I and my kingdom are guiltless before the Lord of the blood of Abner. Let it fall upon the head of Joab."

Then David said to Joab and to all the people who were with him: "Rend your clothes, and gird on sackcloth, and lament before Abner." King David followed the bier. [4] They buried Abner in Hebron, and the king wept aloud at Abner's grave and all the people wept.

---

a most beautiful woman and forced to marry Paltiel by her father, who was the king. Paltiel and Michal lived in the same house but Paltiel put a sword between himself and Michal to keep him from temptation. In thus recognizing his duty and restraining his passions and governing his *yetzer ha-ra*, Paltiel merited the addition of God's name to his own.

&ᴣ [4] KING DAVID FOLLOWED THE BIER: According to the law, a king must not follow the bier. In this case, however, David did so to appease the people. So it is written: "And all the people of Israel understood on that day that the king was not involved in the slaying of Abner."

קִרְעוּ בִגְדֵיכֶם וְחִגְרוּ שַׂקִּים וְסִפְדוּ לִפְנֵי אַבְנֵר . וְהַמֶּלֶךְ דָּוִד הֹלֵךְ אַחֲרֵי הַמִּטָּה.

David also chanted this lament for Abner:

> Must Abner die as a base fool dies?
> Your hands were not bound,
> Your feet were not put in fetters
> As one falls before bandits did you
>   fall.

Then all the people wept afresh for Abner. And afterward all the people came to persuade David to eat some food before the day ended. But David swore, saying: "God do so to me, and more also, if I taste bread or anything else before the sun sets." So all the people and all Israel were convinced that day that the king had nothing to do with the murder of Abner.

Then the king said to his servant: "You know that a prince and a great man has fallen this day. I am weak and newly anointed king and the sons of Zeruiah are too hard for me."

KING OVER ALL ISRAEL

THEN ALL the tribes of Israel came to David at Hebron, and said: "We are of your bone and of your flesh. Even when Saul was king, it was you who led out and brought Israel back. Furthermore, the Lord said to you: 'You shall shepherd My people Israel, and you shall be prince over Israel.'" So David made a covenant with the elders of Israel in Hebron before the Lord, and they anointed David king over Israel.

David was thirty years old when he became king; and he reigned forty years. He reigned over Judah in Hebron seven years and six months, and in Jerusalem he reigned thirty-three years over all Israel and Judah.

DAVID CAPTURES JERUSALEM

THE KING and his men went to Jerusalem against the Jebusites, the inhabitants of the land. They said to him: "You will never enter here, even if we left only the blind and the lame." [5] Then David said [to his men]: "Whoever goes up to smite the Jebusites and gains the water shaft will be made chief." Joab, the son

---

    [5] THE BLIND AND THE LAME: When Abraham wanted to buy the Cave of Machpelah as a burial-place for Sarah, the people of Heth agreed to let Sarah be buried there for a large sum. However, he had to agree that his descendants would not take over the city of Jerusalem "except by the consent of the children of Jebus." The Jebusites then made copper images which they set up all over their

בֶּן שְׁלֹשִׁים שָׁנָה דָוִד בְּמָלְכוֹ; אַרְבָּעִים שָׁנָה מָלָךְ.

of Zeruiah, went up first, and he was made chief.

David captured the stronghold of Zion, [6] and he settled in the city and called it the City of David. [7] And

then he built an encircling wall from Millo and inward.

And Gad came to David and said: "Go, build an altar to the Lord in the threshing floor [8] of Araunah, the Jebu-

---

city and on each image they inscribed the covenant Abraham had made with their ancestors. And they broke the covenant.

So when the Jebusites now told David that he could not enter the city unless he took away the lame and blind, David understood what they meant. The blind and the lame referred to the copper images which have eyes and see not, feet and walk not, and, as it was said, "That are hated of David's soul."

᪣ [6] DAVID CAPTURED THE STRONGHOLD OF ZION: When Joshua divided the land Jerusalem was not included in the territory of any tribe because the city was still in the hands of the Jebusites. Now that it was to be the capital, to whom would it belong? David declared that it would belong to all of the tribes together and assured that by having all the tribes contribute fifty shekels of gold each so that they could all together buy the city from Ornan (Araunah).

᪣ [7] THE CITY OF DAVID: When David placed the center of worship of the Lord in Jerusalem, he sang: "Let me dwell in Thy tent forever" (Psalms 61:5). The Rabbis ask: "Did David want to live forever?" No, but in his joy, he wished his thanksgiving to endure forever. Then the Lord replied: "Because your joy is for Me and not for you, because you were the first to think of it and because you wished to build My House for My sake and not for your own, even though it shall be your son who will build it, yet will I attribute its building to you."

᪣ [8] THE THRESHING FLOOR: When David came to buy the threshing floor, Ornan, the Jebusite, offered him a yoke of oxen for a burnt-

אָמַר דָּוִד: יְהִי רָצוֹן שֶׁיְּהִי שִׁירוֹת וְתִשְׁבָּחוֹת שֶׁלִּי נֶאֱמָרוֹת לְעוֹלָם.

site." Araunah saw the king and his servants coming to him and bowed down with his face to the ground, saying: "Why does my lord, the king, come to his servant?" And David said: "To buy an altar to the Lord." And so Araunah said: "Let my lord, the king, then take all that seems to be good to him. Behold the oxen for the burnt-offering, and the threshing instruments and the yoke of the oxen for the wood." All this did Araunah give to the king. Then Araunah said to the king: "The Lord your God accept you." And the king said to Araunah: "No, but I will buy it from you at a price, nor will I offer burnt-offerings to the Lord which cost me nothing." So David bought the threshing floor and the oxen for fifty shekels of silver. David built an altar to the Lord there and offered burnt-offerings and peace-offerings.

David became greater and greater, for the Lord was with him.

Hiram, king of Tyre, sent messengers to David with cedar trees and carpenters and masons, and they built a house for David. Then David realized that the Lord had established him king over Israel, and that the Lord had made his kingdom exalted for the sake of His people Israel.

---

offering and the threshing implements to be used as the wood for the sacrificial fire and wheat for the meal-offering. But David refused Ornan's generous offer, saying: "No, but I will buy these things for the full price, for I will not take that which is yours to offer a burnt-offering to the Lord without cost to me." And David paid Ornan for the oxen and the wood and the wheat. So Ornan blessed David as he went up to prepare the sacrifice. Then the people said: "Despise not the blessing of a simple common man, nor even of a gentile, for Ornan's blessing was acceptable to God."

וַיֵּדַע דָּוִד כִּי הֱכִינוֹ יְיָ לְמֶלֶךְ עַל יִשְׂרָאֵל, וְכִי נִשֵּׂא מַמְלַכְתּוֹ בַּעֲבוּר עַמּוֹ יִשְׂרָאֵל.

17. II SAMUEL [5–12]

WAR WITH PHILISTINES

WHEN THE Philistines heard that David was anointed king over all Israel, they went up in search of David. When David heard it, he went down to his stronghold, and the Philistines spread themselves in the valley of Rephaim. Then David inquired of the Lord: "Shall I go up against the Philistines? Wilt Thou deliver them into my hand?" And the Lord said to David: "Go up, for I will certainly deliver the Philistines into your hand."

David came to Baal-perazim and defeated them there. The Philistines left there their idols, and David and his men burned them with fire.

DAVID'S COMPASSION

WHEN THE armies of the Philistines were in the valley of Rephaim, David at that time was in the stronghold at the cave of Adullam. A garrison of Philistines occupied Beth-lehem. Then David said longingly: "Oh, that some one would give me a drink of water from the well of Beth-lehem, that is by the gate." Three of his stalwarts broke through the Philistine lines, and drew water from the well at Beth-lehem and brought it

וַיֹּאמֶר יְיָ אֶל דָּוִד: עֲלֵה, כִּי נָתוֹן אֶתֵּן אֶת הַפְּלִשְׁתִּים בְּיָדֶךָ.

to David. But David refused to drink it and he said: "The Lord forbid that I should. Am I to drink the blood of these men? For at the risk of their lives they have brought the water." And he poured it out for the Lord.

DAVID'S WARS

DAVID DEFEATED the Philistines and subdued them. He took Metheg-ammah from the hands of the Philistines. He defeated Moab, and the Moabites became subject to him, and paid him tribute. He also defeated the king of Zoba when he attempted to establish his dominion over the River. When the Aramean of Damascus came to help Hadadezer, king of Zoba, David defeated him and put a garrison in Aram of Damascus. The Arameans became subject to David, and paid tribute to him. David put a garrison in Edom, and the Edomites paid tribute to him. He dedicated to the Lord all the silver and gold that he had captured from Aram, Moab, the Philistines and Amalek.

The Lord gave victory to David wherever he went. David was king over all Israel, and he administered justice, righteousness for all his people. [1]

THE ARK IS BROUGHT TO JERUSALEM

DAVID BUILT for himself houses in Jerusalem, and he prepared a place for the Ark of God. Then David gathered all the chosen men of Israel and David arose and went with all the people to bring up the Ark of God, the Lord of hosts. They brought the Ark to the City of David. And David danced before the Lord with all his might, and he was girded with a linen ephod. So David and all the house of Israel brought up the Ark of the Lord with shouting and with the sound of the *Shofar*.

And it was when the Ark of the Lord

ᵉ§ [1] HE ADMINISTERED JUSTICE, RIGHTEOUSNESS FOR ALL HIS PEOPLE: The original Hebrew says, "He did what is just and charitable," and our Rabbis inquired, "How can those two terms be reconciled? If it is just, according to strict law, it is not charitable; if it is charitable, then it cannot be just, because it is not decided according to strict law."

The Sages comment that this verse means that David employed arbitration, which contains both justice and charity, as his method of judgment, telling the people who came to him that they must compromise their differences.

וְדָוִד מְכַרְכֵּר בְּכָל עֹז לִפְנֵי יְיָ, וְדָוִד חָגוּר אֵפוֹד בָּד.

came into the city, that Michal, the daughter of Saul, looked out of the window, and she saw King David whirling and dancing before the Lord, and she despised him in her heart. They brought the Ark of the Lord, and set it in its place within the tent that David pitched for it. Then David offered sacrifices to the Lord. And he blessed the people in the name of the Lord, and distributed to all the people, both to men and women, to every one a loaf of bread, a portion of meat and a sweet cake. So the people departed each to his home.

David went home to bless his household. Michal came to meet David, and she said to him: "How dignified was the king of Israel today as he stripped himself before the eyes of the handmaids of his servant! You bared yourself [2] as a common fellow shamelessly uncovers himself."

David said to Michal: "It is before the Lord who chose me rather than your father, or any of his house, to appoint me prince over Israel, that I danced. As to the maidservants, I shall be held in honor by them."

DAVID'S KINDNESS

AND DAVID said: "Is there anyone left [3] of the house of Saul to whom I may show kindness for the sake of Jonathan?" Now there was a servant in the house of Saul whose name was Ziba, and they called him to David. And David said: "Is there still someone left of the house

---

⤶ [2] YOU BARED YOURSELF: Michal railed at David when she saw him dancing before the multitude bared. She berated him for having behaved like a common lout and told him that her father and brothers had conducted themselves with more modesty and regal dignity. Then David replied: "Your family was always concerned with their own dignity and honor. I am more concerned with the honor and praise of the Lord than with what men may say about me."

⤶ [3] IS THERE ANYONE LEFT? The commentators ask: "Did not David know how many children Saul and Jonathan had? Did he not also know that only three of Saul's sons were killed on Mount Gilboa?" The Rabbis explain that David knew the children of Saul were living but he did not know where they were. Because in those days kings customarily killed the descendants of the old dynasty, Saul's children had gone into hiding. But David inquired after them and

לִפְנֵי יְיָ אֲשֶׁר בָּחַר בִּי מֵאָבִיךְ וּמִכָּל בֵּיתוֹ לְצַוּוֹת אוֹתִי נָגִיד עַל עַם יְיָ, עַל יִשְׂרָאֵל, וְשִׂחַקְתִּי לִפְנֵי יְיָ.

of Saul, that I may show the kindness of God to him?" Ziba answered: "Jonathan left a son and he is lame in his feet. When he was five years old, the news came of Saul's and Jonathan's deaths. His nurse took him up and fled. But as she hurried he fell and became lame. His name is Mephibosheth."

David said to Ziba: "Where is he?" And Ziba said to the king: "He is in Lo-debar."

Then King David sent for him, and Mephibosheth came to David and prostrated himself. And David said: "Fear not, for I will surely show you kindness for the sake of Jonathan, your father." Then he called Ziba, Saul's servant, and said to him: "I give to your master's son the entire estate of Saul. And you and your sons and your servants shall till the land for him, but Mephibosheth shall sit at my table."

Then Ziba said to the king: "As my lord, the king, commanded his servant, so shall your servant do." Mephibosheth remained in Jerusalem, and ate regularly at the king's table.

DAVID'S SIN WITH BATH-SHEBA

NOW AT THE return of the spring, at the time when kings go forth to battle, David sent Joab with the whole army of Israel, and they besieged Rabbah. David remained in Jerusalem. [4] One day at sunset David walked upon the roof of the king's house, and he saw a woman bathing. The woman was very beauti-

---

declared: "They should be told that no harm will befall them," so that all would know he intended no harm to any member of Saul's household.

&ৣ [4] DAVID REMAINED IN JERUSALEM: When the country was at last at peace and Jerusalem established David spent his days governing and meting out justice. At night, exhausted from the labors of his day, he would fall asleep worn out. But at midnight his harp, which hung over his bed, would resound with the night breezes and fill his room with music. Then David would arise, go to the roof of the palace with his harp, and there survey the beautiful night skies of Jerusalem. Words of praise would spring to his lips and melodies from his lyre and all through the night he would chant the praises of the Lord.

כִּנּוֹר הָיָה תָּלוּי לְמַעְלָה מִמִּטָּתוֹ שֶׁל דָּוִד. כֵּיוָן שֶׁהִגִּיעַ חֲצוֹת לַיְלָה – הָיְתָה מְנַשֶּׁבֶת רוּחַ צְפוֹנִית וְהָיָה מְנַגֵּן מֵאֵלָיו.

ful. David sent and inquired about the woman. He was told: "Is she not Bath-sheba, the wife of Uriah, the Hittite?" David sent messengers, and took her to the king's house. Then he wrote a letter to Joab: "Put Uriah in the forefront on the hottest fighting, then draw back from him, that he may be struck down and die."

When Joab assigned the watch of the siege, he put Uriah [5] at a place where he knew the valiant troops were. When the men of the city went out and fought with Joab, some of the men fell, and Uriah died also.

Then Joab sent and told David all concerning the war, and he said to the messenger: "If King David will become angry and ask: 'Why did you go so near the wall?' then you shall say: 'Also Uriah, the Hittite, is dead.' " The messenger came and told David all that Joab charged him to say.

Thereupon David said: "Tell Joab, let not this thing depress you, for in one manner or another, the sword devours. Strengthen your attack upon the city and overthrow it."

Now when the wife of Uriah heard that her husband was dead, she lamented for her husband. When the mourning period was over, David sent and brought her to his house, and she became his wife, [6] and she bore him a son. But

---

&S; [5] HE PUT URIAH: Why did Joab do David's bidding and deliberately send a valiant fellow-officer to his death? And why wasn't Joab punished for such treachery to Uriah?

Some Rabbis maintained that Uriah merited his death for disobeying his king. David had told him to "go down to your house and wash your feet," but instead Uriah had stayed at the king's palace. When David on the morrow asks why he did not go, Uriah speaks of "my lord Joab and the servants of my lord." In naming Joab lord before David and the soldiers servants of Joab, he was committing treason. Joab did not know what had happened in Jerusalem, but when Uriah brought him the note from David he was led to understand that Uriah had rebelled against the king and was thus being sentenced to death to avoid public notice.

&S; [6] AND SHE BECAME HIS WIFE: The Rabbis explain that David was not forbidden to Bath-sheba. Like all soldiers of the court Uriah had

הָבוּ אֶת אוּרִיָּה אֶל מוּל פְּנֵי הַמִּלְחָמָה הַחֲזָקָה, וְשַׁבְתֶּם מֵאַחֲרָיו וְנִכָּה וָמֵת.

the thing that David had done displeased the Lord.

THE PROPHET'S REBUKE

THE LORD sent Nathan to David, and he came to him and said: "There were two men in a city, one rich, the other poor. The rich man owned very many flocks and herds, but the poor man had nothing but a single ewe lamb. He fed it and it grew up with his children. It would eat from his food and drink from his cup, nestle in his bosom, and it was like a daughter to him.

"Then a traveler came [7] to visit the rich man, but he spared his own sheep and cattle. He took the poor man's lamb, and prepared it for the man who came to him."

---

given Bath-sheba a divorce when he went off to battle lest she become an *agunah*. An *agunah* was a woman whose husband had deserted her, or had gone off on a journey or to battle, and had never returned. With no witnesses to confirm his death, his widow must then remain alone awaiting his return. If the man never returns, the woman must remain a widow and not remarry to her dying day. Thus, because Bath-sheba was given a divorce by Uriah, she was free to go to David even before Uriah's death.

[7] THEN A TRAVELER CAME: The Talmud pointed out that Nathan was doing far more than showing David that he had sinned with Bath-sheba. Nathan was reminding the king that sin grows until it fills the whole heart and mind.

Rava observed that first the evil inclination is called a "passerby"; then it is called a "guest"; and finally it is called an "occupant of the house." Why is the *yetzer ha-ra* referred to in this way? Because the soul which is holy, dwells in the body, which is the house of the soul. When the person admits the evil inclination, at first it is like a wayfarer who can shortly be sent on his way. But as the *yetzer ha-ra* remains it is like a household guest who acquires certain privileges. And soon the guest takes over and becomes the man, driving out the original soul which dwelt there and so becoming master of the house.

לְעָשִׁיר הָיָה צֹאן וּבָקָר הַרְבֵּה מְאֹד, וְלָרָשׁ אֵין כֹּל כִּי אִם כִּבְשָׂה אַחַת קְטַנָּה.

David's anger blazed furiously, and he said to Nathan: "As the Lord lives, the man who has done it deserves to die, because he had no pity. He shall restore the lamb fourfold."

Then Nathan said to David: "You are the man! Thus said the Lord: 'I anointed you king over Israel, and I delivered you out of the hand of Saul; I gave you your master's house, and gave you the house of Israel and Judah.' Why did you despise the word of the Lord by doing that which is evil in His eyes? You have slain Uriah, and you have taken his wife. Now, thus said the Lord: 'The sword shall never depart from your house.'"

David said to Nathan: "I have sinned [8] against the Lord."

Nathan said to David: "You shall not die. Nevertheless, because you have openly spurned the Lord by this deed, I will let your sin be known to all. You did it secretly, but I will do it before all the eyes of Israel. I will raise up evil against you out of your own household. The child that will be born to you shall die!" And Nathan departed.

THE CHILD DIES

THE CHILD that the wife of Uriah bore to David became very sick. David prayed to the Lord in behalf of the child, he fasted, and lay on the earth in sackcloth before the Lord. The elders of his house came and stood over him to raise him from the earth, but he would not get up nor eat with them. On the seventh day the child died. The servants of David feared to tell him for they said: "While the child was alive we spoke to him and he did not listen to us, how can we tell him that the child is dead? He may do himself some harm."

When David saw that his servants were whispering together, he understood. He said to his servants: "Is the child dead?" They said: "Dead." Thereupon David arose from the earth and

---

⋘ [8] I HAVE SINNED: When Nathan left, David realized how great was his sin and he begged God's forgiveness. He prayed and pleaded, but the Lord would not listen to him. Finally David cried out: "O Lord, if only You will forgive me, Israel may learn from my example. They will see that if a man turns to You with all his heart in full atonement, You will pardon him, for even David, that grave sinner, was forgiven." And then God heeded his words and gave ear to his plea.

וַיֹּאמֶר נָתָן אֶל דָּוִד׃ אַתָּה הָאִישׁ!

bathed, anointed himself, changed his garments, went to the house of the Lord and worshiped. Then he went to his own house and told the servants to set bread before him, and he ate.

The servants said to him: "What is the meaning of the thing that you have done? You have fasted and wept for the child while it was alive, but when the child died you arose, bathed, changed your garments, and have eaten food?"

David answered: "While the child was still alive I fasted and wept, for I said: 'Who knows, the Lord might have mercy and the child may live.' But now that he is dead, why should I fast? Can I bring him back again? I shall go to him, but he will not return to me."

David comforted Bath-sheba, his wife, and she bore him a son, and he called his name Solomon. The Lord loved him, and He sent a message through Nathan, the prophet, and he called his name Jedidiah, "the beloved of the Lord."

וַיְנַחֵם דָּוִד אֵת בַּת־שֶׁבַע אִשְׁתּוֹ ... וַתֵּלֶד בֵּן וַיִּקְרָא אֶת שְׁמוֹ שְׁלֹמֹה.

18. II SAMUEL [14–17]

ABSALOM SEEKS SUPPORT

ABSALOM, WHOSE mother was Maacah, was born to David in Hebron. In all Israel there was no man so much praised for his beauty as Absalom. From the sole of his foot to the crown of his head there was no blemish in him. At the end of every year he would cut his hair, as it was heavy on him; it weighed two hundred shekels by the king's weight. Absalom had chariots and horses, and fifty men to run before him. He would rise early and stand at the gate of the city. When any man had a suit to come before the king for judgment, Absalom would call him and ask him: "Of what city are you?"

The man answered: "Your servant is from one of the tribes of Israel." Absalom said to him: "Your cause is good and right, but the king has not appointed any man to hear you. Oh, that I were made judge [1] in the land, that

[1] THAT I WERE MADE JUDGE: David had proved himself to be a particularly good judge, why therefore does Absalom make such a point of being a good judge?

וּכְאַבְשָׁלוֹם לֹא הָיָה אִישׁ יָפֶה בְּכָל יִשְׂרָאֵל לְהַלֵּל מְאֹד.

any man who had a suit or cause might come to me. I would see that he received justice." Also, when a man came near to prostrate himself, he would put out his hand and take hold of him and kiss him. In this manner Absalom stole the hearts of the men of Israel.

BEGINNING OF THE REVOLT

IT WAS SOME time later that Absalom said to the king: "Let me go to Hebron [2] and pay my vow, that I have vowed to the Lord." The king said to him: "Go in peace." So he arose and went. He sent secret messengers throughout all the tribes of Israel, saying: "As soon as you hear the sound of the trumpet, you shall say: 'Absalom reigns in Hebron.'" With Absalom went two hundred men from Jerusalem who went in all innocence for they were invited as guests,

---

David was so busy with so many things, government, military preparations, the Tabernacle, his own studies and writing that he could not hear even a few cases each day. So he arranged court days each month and all the litigants were heard then, but they all had to wait for those days. Absalom promised instant justice, which appealed to the common people for, as the saying has it, "Justice delayed is not justice."

[2] LET ME GO TO HEBRON: Absalom deceived both David and the elders of Israel. Absalom came to David, saying: "Father, I want to go to Hebron to bring fat sheep from there to sacrifice to God. Please give me a letter empowering me to select two elders to accompany me." David asked if he wanted any man in particular and Absalom replied, "No, just empower me to select any two."

With that document Absalom went from city to city and in each showed the two most prominent men in the town the letter, saying: "My father empowered me to select any two men and I chose you because I have particular affection for you." In that fashion Absalom succeeded in gathering around him the heads of two hundred councils who knew nothing of his conspiracy with Ahithophel. When the elders discovered the plan for the rebellion, they gave only half-hearted assent to it. And they prayed: "O Lord, hear our prayer.

כְּשָׁמְעֲכֶם אֶת קוֹל הַשּׁוֹפָר וַאֲמַרְתֶּם: מָלַךְ אַבְשָׁלוֹם בְּחֶבְרוֹן.

and were not aware of any plot. Before Absalom offered the sacrifice, he sent for Ahithophel, [3] David's counselor. Ahithophel came and the conspiracy became strong as the people who joined Absalom increased.

Then a messenger came to David and said: "The hearts of the men of Israel are with Absalom." David said to the men who were with him: "Arise and let us flee. Make speed lest Absalom overtake us quickly and bring calamity upon us, and smite the city with the edge of the sword."

The king left the city on foot, and he stopped at the last house of the city. All the countryside wept in a loud voice as the people passed by. Then the king came and stood in the river bed of Kidron, and all the people passed before him, toward the way of the wilderness. And, behold, among the people were the priests Zadok and Abiathar and all the Levites bearing the Ark of the Covenant of God. They set down the Ark until all the people had passed out of the city. Then the king said to Zadok: "Carry back the Ark of God into the city. If I find favor in the eyes of the Lord, He will bring me back, and He will let me see the Ark and its abode. But if He will say: 'I have no delight

May we fall into the hands of David, for he will be merciful. Only let not King David fall into our hands, because Absalom and Ahithophel will show him no mercy."

⇛ [3] AHITHOPHEL, THE GILONITE: Ahithophel was the grandfather of Bath-sheba. He was a great scholar, the most prominent courtier of David's retinue, and David's most intimate friend. Whenever David had a question of law he consulted Ahithophel and whatever Ahithophel's decision the assembly of elders abided by it.

But Ahithophel lacked true piety. He thought that his wisdom and learning made him best suited to be king of Israel. He enticed Absalom to rebel against his father and to violate David's wives. Ahithophel hoped to have Absalom defeat David's followers and then to kill his father. Ahithophel then planned to bring Absalom to judgment before the council of elders, holding Absalom to account and condemning him to death for his crimes. Then he, Ahithophel, the great sage, would be anointed king of Israel.

וַיָּבֹא הַמַּגִּיד אֶל דָּוִד לֵאמֹר: הָיָה לֵב אִישׁ יִשְׂרָאֵל אַחֲרֵי אַבְשָׁלוֹם.

in you,' let Him do to me whatever He wills." Zadok and Abiathar carried the Ark of God back to Jerusalem, and they remained there.

HUSHAI SENT TO OPPOSE AHITHOPHEL

THEN DAVID was told that Ahithophel was among the conspirators with Absalom. David said: "O Lord, I pray Thee, turn the counsel of Ahithophel into foolishness." When David came to the top of the mountain, [4] Hushai, the Archite, came to meet him, his garment rent and earth upon his head. David said to him: "If you go with me, you will be a burden. But if you return to the city, and say to Absalom: 'I will be your servant, O king, as I have been your father's servant,' then you will help me defeat the counsel of Ahithophel. There will also be with you Zadok and Abiathar, the priests. They have with them their two sons, Ahimaaz, Zadok's son, and Jonathan, Abiathar's son. By them you shall send me everything which you shall hear."

Hushai, David's friend, returned to the city. David and all the people with him came to Bahurim weary and stopped there to rest. Absalom and all the people of Israel came to Jerusalem, and Ahithophel was with him.

SHIMEI CURSES DAVID

WHEN DAVID came to Bahurim, behold, there came a man of the family of the house of Saul, whose name was Shimei,

---

ᏺ [4] TO THE TOP OF THE MOUNTAIN: When David looked around him and saw that his courtiers and officers kept their places around him according to their rank, as if they were all still in the palace of Jerusalem, and that all his friends had remained loyal to him and still considered him king, he forgot his grief and self-pity. He saw it as a sign that the Lord had not deserted him and he burst into a song of joy. It was a new psalm which began: "A song of David when he fled from Absalom, his son:

"Lord, how many are my adversaries
Many are they that rise against me.
Many that are, that say of my soul:
'There is no salvation for him in God.'
But Thou, O Lord, art my shield above me,
My glory, and the lifter up of my head" (Psalms 3:1-4).

וְאַתָּה יְיָ מָגֵן בַּעֲדִי, כְּבוֹדִי וּמֵרִים רֹאשִׁי.

the son of Gera; he came out, and kept on cursing as he came. And he cast stones at David, and at all the servants of King David; and all the people and all the mighty men were on his right hand and on his left. And thus said Shimei when he cursed: "Begone, be-gone, you man of blood, and base fel-low; the Lord has returned on you all the blood of the house of Saul, in whose stead you have ruled; and the Lord has delivered the kingdom into the hand of Absalom, your son; and, behold, you are undone by your own mischief, be-cause you are a man of blood."

Then Abishai, the son of Zeruiah, said to the king: "Why should this dead dog curse my lord, the king? Let me go, I pray you, and take off his head." And the king said: "What have I to do with you, you sons of Zeruiah? So let him curse, because the Lord has said to him: Curse David; [5] who then shall say: Why have you done so?"

David said to Abishai and all his servants: "My son, who came out of my body, seeks my life; how much more this Benjamite now? Let him alone, and let him curse; for the Lord has bid him curse. It may be that the Lord will re-quite me [6] good for his cursing of me this day." So David and his men went

---

&ß [5] CURSE DAVID: How is it that David says the Lord told Shimei to curse him? The Sages said that David had told Abishai: God has given Shimei room to curse me, for look at my condition. Were I still monarch in Jerusalem, would he dare to open his mouth? But like many men, God gives them *pithon peh* (permission to speak) and they speak far more than God intended and so earn God's en-mity and man's.

And David added: "Let God see that despite Shimei's false charges and cursing I seek no revenge; and so it may be to my credit in these dire straits."

&ß [6] THE LORD WILL REQUITE ME: Why did God allow David to sin? David was His own anointed, the man who welded God's own peo-ple together. Rabbi Joshua ben Levi said that it was part of God's plan, just as He allowed the Hebrews fresh from Sinai to sin with the golden calf. Each sin was an opening to repentance. Rabbi Simeon ben Yoḥai said: David was not suited for his sin; the Israel-ites were not suited for their sin. Why then did they occur?

וַיֹּאמֶר הַמֶּלֶךְ: מַה לִּי וְלָכֶם בְּנֵי צְרֻוּיָה? כֹּה יְקַלֵּל כִּי יְיָ אָמַר לוֹ: קַלֵּל אֶת דָּוִד, וּמִי יֹאמַר: מַדּוּעַ עָשִׂיתָה כֵּן?

their way; and Shimei went along on the hillside and cursed as he went, and threw stones at him, and cast dust.

HUSHAI COMES TO ABSALOM

WHEN HUSHAI, David's friend, came to Absalom, he called out: "Long live the king! Long live the king!"

Absalom said to him: "Is this your loyalty to your friend? Why did you not go with your friend?"

Hushai answered: "I am for the man whom the Lord and Israel have chosen; his will I be. Again, whom should I serve? Should it not be his son? As I served your father, so will I serve you."

AHITHOPHEL'S PLAN

THE COUNSEL of Ahithophel which he gave in those days was as if one inquired the word of God. So was all the advice of Ahithophel considered by David and by Absalom. Now Absalom said to Ahithophel: "Give us counsel, what shall we do?"

Ahithophel said: "Let me now choose twelve thousand men, and I will pursue David tonight. I will come upon him while he is weary and discouraged. And him and all the people with him I will throw in a panic. I will strike down the king alone, and I will bring back all the people to you, and the people will be at peace." The plan pleased Absalom and all the elders of Israel. But Absalom said: "Call now Hushai, the Archite: let us also hear what he has to say."

When Hushai came Absalom said to him: "This is what Ahithophel said. Shall we listen to him? If not, speak out yourself."

And Hushai said: "The counsel that Ahithophel has given this time is not good. You know your father and his men; they are mighty warriors. They are embittered as a bear in the field robbed of her cubs. Your father is a man of war. He will not lodge with the people. He has hidden himself in some pit, or in some other place. When some of the attacking men will fall, whoever hears the report will say: 'There has been a slaughter among the people who follow Absalom.' Then the most coura-

---

So that in the future if the community or an individual should sin, he could see that the Hebrews right after Sinai, and David, after he had established his glory, had sinned likewise. So, whether a sin is private or public—David's was private, Israel's was public— or an individual or communal sin, repentance sincerely offered will be accepted and the sin forgiven.

אַתָּה יָדַעְתָּ אֶת אָבִיךָ וְאֶת אֲנָשָׁיו כִּי גִבּוֹרִים הֵמָּה, וּמָרֵי נֶפֶשׁ הֵמָּה כְּדֹב שַׁכּוּל בַּשָּׂדֶה.

geous man, whose heart is like the heart of a lion, will utterly melt.

"Therefore, I counsel that all Israel, from Dan to Beer-sheba, shall be gathered, as many as the sands by the sea, and you yourself lead them in battle. So you will come upon him, and we will fall upon him [and the men who are with him] as dew falls on the ground; and of him and all the men who are with him not one shall be left. If he withdraws into a city, then all Israel will bring ropes to that city, and will drag it into the river until not even a single pebble can be found there."

Then Absalom and all Israel said: "The counsel of Hushai, the Archite, is better than the counsel of Ahithophel." The Lord had ordained to defeat the good counsel of Ahithophel, so that He might bring evil upon Absalom.

HUSHAI WARNS DAVID

THEN HUSHAI told the priests Zadok and Abiathar: "Ahithophel gave such and such advice to Absalom. Therefore send quickly and tell David not to camp tonight at the fords of the wilderness, but to cross the Jordan lest he be destroyed and all those with him."

Jonathan and Ahimaaz, the sons of Zodak and Abiathar, stayed outside the city, and a maidservant was sent to them with the message, and they went to tell King David. But a lad saw them and told Absalom. Both of them went quickly and came to the house of a man in Bahurim who had a well in his court, and they hid down there. The woman spread a cloth over the mouth of the well, and spread groats upon it. When Absalom's men came to the woman's house, they said: "Where are Ahimaaz and Jonathan?"

She said: "They have crossed the brook." So when they looked for them and could not find them, they returned to Jerusalem.

After they were gone, Ahimaaz and Jonathan came up out of the well, and went and told King David: "Pass quickly over the water, for thus has Ahithophel counseled against you." David arose, and all the people who were with him, and they crossed the Jordan.

When Ahithophel saw that his counsel was not followed, he saddled his donkey and went home to his city. He gave instructions to his household, and then he hanged himself. He was buried in the burial-place of his father.

וּבָאנוּ אֵלָיו בְּאַחַד הַמְּקוֹמוֹת אֲשֶׁר נִמְצָא שָׁם וְנַחְנוּ עָלָיו כַּאֲשֶׁר יִפֹּל הַטַּל עַל הָאֲדָמָה.

19. II SAMUEL [17-24]

ABSALOM DEFEATED

DAVID CAME to Mahanaim, and Absalom crossed the Jordan, he and all the men of Israel with him. Absalom had set Amasa in command of all of the army in place of Joab. So Absalom and Israel encamped in the land of Gilead.

David mustered the people who were with him, and appointed captains of thousands and captains of hundreds. Then he divided the people: one third he put under the command of Joab; another third under the command of Abishai, Joab's nephew; and another third under the command of Ittai, the Gittite. The king said to the people: "I also will go with you."

But the people said: "You shall not go with us, because if we run away, or if even half of us die, no one will care. But you are worth ten thousand of us. The important thing is for you to be ready to help us from the city."

The king said to them: "Whatever seems good in your eyes I will do."

So the king stood at the side of the gate, and all the people went out by hundreds and by thousands. The king commanded Joab and Abishai and Ittai, saying: "Deal gently for my sake with

לֹא תֵצֵא, כִּי אִם נֹס נָנוּס לֹא יָשִׂימוּ אֵלֵינוּ לֵב, וְאִם יָמֻתוּ חֶצְיֵנוּ לֹא יָשִׂימוּ אֵלֵינוּ לֵב, כִּי עַתָּה כָמֹנוּ עֲשָׂרָה אֲלָפִים.

the lad Absalom." All the people heard when the king gave charge to all the captains concerning Absalom.

The people took to the field against Israel, and the battle was in the forest. And the forest that day devoured more people than the sword. The people of Israel were defeated by the followers of David. Absalom chanced to meet the servants of David. Absalom was riding on his mule, and the mule went under the thick branches of a great oak. His head was caught fast in the branches; the mule under him passed on, and he was left hanging between heaven and earth. A man saw it and told Joab: "I saw Absalom hanging under an oak."

Joab said: "You saw him; why did you not kill him? I would have given you ten [shekels of] silver and a belt."

The man answered: "Even if I felt in my hand a thousand, I would not lay a hand on the king's son. We all heard the king charge you and Abishai and Ittai: 'Deal gently with the lad Absalom.'"

Joab said: "I have no time to waste with you." He took three darts and thrust them into the body of Absalom. The ten young men who bore Joab's armor surrounded Absalom and killed him. They took the body of Absalom and cast it into a great pit in the forest. Then Joab blew the *Shofar*, and the people stopped pursuing Israel. All Israel fled away, every one to his home.

THE NEWS OF ABSALOM'S DEATH

NOW AHIMAAZ said: "Let me run now and bring the news to the king, that the Lord avenged him of his enemies." Joab said: "You are not to carry tidings today; you shall not do so, for the king's son is dead." Then Joab said to the Cushite: "Go and tell the king what you have seen." The Cushite bowed to Joab and ran.

Then Ahimaaz said again: "Come what may, do let me run after the Cushite." Joab said: "Why is it that you desire to run, my son? You will not be rewarded for the news you bring." But Ahimaaz said: "Come what may, let me run." So Joab said: "Run." Ahimaaz ran by the way of the plain [of the Jordan], and he overtook the Cushite.

David was sitting between the two gates, and the watchman had gone up on the roof of the gate. When he looked he saw a man running alone. The watchman called and told the king, and the king said: "If he is alone, there are tidings in his mouth." Then the watchman saw another man running. He called: "I see another man running alone." The king said: "He is also bringing good tidings."

Then the watchman said: "I think the running of the first is like the running of Ahimaaz."

כִּי בְאָזְנֵינוּ צִוָּה הַמֶּלֶךְ אוֹתְךָ וְאֶת אֲבִישַׁי וְאֶת אִתַּי לֵאמֹר, שִׁמְרוּ־מִי בַנַּעַר, בְּאַבְשָׁלוֹם.

The king said: "He is a good man, he comes with good news." Ahimaaz came near the king and said: "All is well." Then he bowed and said: "Blessed be the Lord, who has delivered up the men who raised up their hand against the king."

The king said: "Is it well with the lad Absalom?" Ahimaaz said: "When Joab sent me, I saw a great tumult and I did not know what it was."

Then the Cushite came, and said: "Tidings for my lord, the king, for the Lord has avenged you this day from all those who are against you."

The king said to the Cushite: "Is it well with the lad Absalom?" The Cushite answered: "Let all the enemies of the lord, the king and all who rise against you for evil, be as the young man is."

DAVID'S GRIEF

THE KING was much moved and as he went up to the chamber over the gate, he wept and cried: "O my son Absalom, my son, my son Absalom. Would I had died for you O Absalom, my son, my son." [1]

The victory of that day turned into mourning for all the people, since they heard that the king was grieving for his son. The people slipped into the city stealthily, like people ashamed when they flee in battle.

The king cried in a loud voice, "O my son Absalom, Absalom, my son, my son." Joab came into the house of the king and said: "You have shamed this day all your followers who have saved your life and the lives of your sons, your daughters, and the lives of your wives, for you love your enemies and hate those who love you. You have declared today that all the princes and your followers are nothing to you. For now I know that if Absalom were alive and all of us dead today, you would be well pleased. Now arise and go out, and speak to the people. I swear by the Lord,

[1] ABSALOM, ABSALOM: David was not only calling his son Absalom's name. *Av shalom* means Father of Peace and David was also calling on God, praying: If I have found favor in Your sight, O Father of Peace, have mercy on my son Absalom's soul.

Why is "my son" repeated eight times? Seven times to raise Absalom from the seven divisions of Gehenna; and, as for the last, some say to unite Absalom's severed head to his body and others say to bring him into the World to Come.

בְּנִי אַבְשָׁלוֹם, בְּנִי בְנִי אַבְשָׁלוֹם, מִי יִתֵּן מוּתִי אֲנִי תַחְתֶּיךָ, אַבְשָׁלוֹם, בְּנִי בְנִי.

if you do not go out and speak, not a man will be left with you tonight."

The king arose and sat at the gate. When all the people were told: "The king is sitting at the gate," all of them came to greet the king.

DAVID RETURNS

SO THE KING returned and Judah came to Gilgal to meet the king and to bring him over the Jordan. Shimei, the son of Gera, [2] came down to meet King David with a thousand men of Benjamin. Shimei fell down before the king, when he would go over the Jordan. And he said: "Let not my lord hold me guilty, neither should you remember that which I did evilly the day that the king went out of Jerusalem. For your servant knows that he has sinned; therefore, I have come this day the first of the house of Joseph to meet my lord, the king."

But Abishai, the son of Zeruiah, answered and said: "Shall not Shimei be put to death for this because he cursed the Lord's anointed?"

David said: "Shall there any man be put to death this day in Israel?" And the king said to Shimei: "You shall not die." And the king swore it.

Mephibosheth, the son of Saul, came down to meet the king. And the king

---

⤙ [2] SHIMEI, THE SON OF GERA: After Absalom's death, the people were concerned to see if King David would forgive those who had followed after the rebel. But none dared approach David until Shimei ben Gera came and knelt before the king. All were astonished because it was Shimei who had cursed David and stoned him as he fled. Then Shimei said: "My lord, even Joseph's brothers, his own flesh and blood, were forgiven after they wronged him. Joseph treated them with kindness and generosity and forgave them. Therefore, O king, forgive my sins against you. I deserve no forgiveness, I know, but the people will say: 'None deserved punishment more than Shimei, for his crimes were the worst, yet King David forgave him.' So let this be a sign to all Israel that you will forgive your people for their sins."

And David replied: "So be it. I have forgiven as you asked."

And because David forgave him, Mordecai was born out of the seed of Shimei and called by his name.

וּלְכָל הָעָם הִגִּידוּ לֵאמֹר: הִנֵּה הַמֶּלֶךְ יוֹשֵׁב בַּשַּׁעַר. וַיָּבוֹא כָל הָעָם לִפְנֵי הַמֶּלֶךְ.

said to him: "Why did you not go with me, Mephibosheth?" He answered: "My lord, my servant deceived me. For your servant said: I will saddle a donkey that I may ride on it and go with the king for I am lame. And he has slandered me to my lord, the king; but my lord, the king is as an angel of God. Do therefore what is good in your eyes." And he said: "For all my father's house were deserving of death at the hand of my lord, the king; yet you set your servant among those who ate at your own table. What right therefore have I yet? Or why should I cry any more to the king?"

And the king said: "Why do you speak of these matters any more? I say: You and Ziba divide the field." [3]

Mephibosheth said: "Let him take all, for since my lord, the king, is come in peace into his own house."

ABISHAI SAVES DAVID

THE PHILISTINES had war with Israel again; and David went down and fought against the Philistines; and David waxed faint. [4] Ishbi-benob, who was of the sons of the giant, thought to have slain David. But Abishai, the son of Zeruiah, saved him and killed the Philistine. Then the men of David said: "You shall

---

⤐ [3] DIVIDE THE FIELD: Rather than take the time and energy to discover the truth, David impatiently told Mephibosheth and Ziba to divide the land themselves. This was neither judgment nor just. So the Talmud states that when David said, "You and Ziba divide the field," a Heavenly Voice called out: "Rehoboam and Jeroboam shall thus divide your kingdom!"

⤐ [4] AND DAVID WAXED FAINT: All through the hot day David and his warriors fought the Philistine armies and then stopped to rest. The only water they found was brackish and foul-tasting and David, in a moment of recollection, said, "Would that I could drink from the well near the gate of Beth-lehem!"

Three young soldiers heard his words. Carrying only their weapons and a skin bag, they went through the Philistine lines which stood between them and Beth-lehem, eluding sentries where they could, fighting their way when they had to, until finally they reached Beth-lehem. There, having filled the skin with water from the well,

וַיֹּאמֶר לוֹ הַמֶּלֶךְ: לָמָּה תְּדַבֵּר עוֹד דְּבָרֶיךָ? אָמַרְתִּי, אַתָּה וְצִיבָא תַּחְלְקוּ אֶת הַשָּׂדֶה!

not go out with us to battle any more lest you quench the lamp of Israel."

A TEMPLE TO THE LORD

AFTER THE LORD had given rest to the king from all his enemies and he had settled in his palace, the king said to Nathan, the prophet: "See now, I dwell in a house of cedar, but the Ark of the Covenant of the Lord still dwells under curtains."

The same night the word of the Lord came to Nathan saying: "Go and tell My servant David: 'You shall not build a house unto My name, because you have made great wars and you have shed much blood. Your son Solomon, he shall build My house [5] and My courts and I will establish his throne forever. His

---

they returned as they had come, fighting their way back to David's camp. Bloody and proud, they presented the waterskin to their king. "Let the king drink from the well of Beth-lehem," they said, "and restore his strength."

But David, appalled by their wounds, cried out, "No! I will not drink water bought at the price of your blood."

[5] HE SHALL BUILD MY HOUSE: When David was settled in Jerusalem he built a palace for himself and his family. Then he began to plan to build the Temple to the Lord. But the Lord spoke to Nathan, saying: "Go quickly to David because he is a hasty man and tell him, 'You shall not build My house.'"

David was saddened and asked the Prophet why. Nathan explained: "Solomon, your son, will think first of the Lord and build the Lord's house before he builds his own." Then he told David that he was a man of war and therefore not fit to build the Lord's Temple.

David was saddened and wept. But then he said, "If I am not fit to build the house, at least I am fit to prepare for it." And so he gathered together on Mount Moriah beams and stone, iron and brass (I Chronicles 22).

Then the Lord sent the prophet Nathan to David once again to tell him: "Solomon will build the Temple and within its walls the

דָּם לָרֹב שָׁפַכְתָּ וּמִלְחָמוֹת גְּדוֹלוֹת עָשִׂיתָ – לֹא תִבְנֶה בַיִת לִשְׁמִי, כִּי דָּמִים רַבִּים שָׁפָכְתָּ.

name is Solomon and I will give peace and quietness to Israel in his days. I will not take away My mercy from him as I took it away from him who was before you. But I will settle him in My house and in My kingdom forever, and his throne shall be established forever.' "

So did Nathan speak to David. Then David went in and sat before the Lord, and he said: "Who am I, O Lord God, and what is my house, that Thou hast brought me so far? For Thy word's sake and according to Thine own heart, hast Thou wrought all this greatness. Thou art great, O Lord God; for there is none like Thee, neither is there any God besides Thee."

DAVID ADDRESSES ISRAEL

DAVID ASSEMBLED in Jerusalem all the princes of Israel, the chiefs of the tribes, the captains of thousands and the captains of hundreds, and all the valiant men. David rose to his feet and said: "Hear me, my kinsmen and my people. It was in my heart to build a house of rest for the Ark of the Covenant of the Lord. I had prepared to build it, but God said to me: 'You shall not build a house to My name, because you are a man of war and you have shed blood.' And He then said to me: 'Solomon, your son, he shall build My house and My courts.'

"And you, Solomon, my son, know the God of your father and serve Him with a whole heart and willing mind. Take heed now, for the Lord has chosen you to build a house for the Sanctuary. Be strong and do it!"

Then David said to all the congregation: "Now bless the Lord." And all the congregation blessed the Lord, the

---

Children of Israel will chant: 'A song at the dedication of the House of David,' for it was you who first desired to build it."

[5] HE SHALL BUILD MY HOUSE: Some commentators explained that God had said to David: "As you merited My love through the Psalms, which you wrote with all the fervor of your heart, so will they be established forever. Israel will daily speak them in their prayers. So will your name endure. If you build My Temple, you will do it with equal love and dedication and it will be established forever. If in the future Israel sins, the Temple will stand and Israel will have to be destroyed for its iniquity. But let your son

וְאַתָּה, שְׁלֹמֹה בְנִי, דַּע אֶת אֱלֹהֵי אָבִיךָ וְעָבְדֵהוּ בְּלֵב שָׁלֵם וּבְנֶפֶשׁ חֲפֵצָה.

God of their fathers, and bowed down
their heads before the Lord and before
the king.

DAVID'S LAST WORDS

These are the last words of
David, [6]
The saying of David, the son of
Jesse,
The saying of the man raised on
high,
The anointed of the God of
Jacob,
The sweet singer of Israel:
"The spirit of the Lord has spoken
by me,
And His word is upon my tongue.

"The God of Israel said,
The Rock of Israel [7] spoke to
me:
He who rules over man
righteously,
He who rules in the fear of God,
He is like the light of morning
When the sun rises,
A morning without clouds;
When from the sunshine after the
rain,
The tender grass springs from the
earth.

"Is not my house founded by God?
He has made with me an
everlasting covenant,
Fully and clearly set forth.

Solomon build the Temple. He is a fine man but his heart is not
as your heart. Then if Israel sins, the Temple can be destroyed as
punishment, but Israel will live!"

&§ [6] THE LAST WORDS OF DAVID: Why do some of David's religious
poems occur here and others in the Book of Psalms? The Rabbis
explained that there are two spirits that flow from God, the Spirit
of Prophecy and the Holy Spirit (the Shechinah). David had both
spirits, the only man to be so blessed. The Spirit of Prophecy produced the poems that are in the historical books; the gift of the
Holy Spirit produced the Psalms and the Shechinah descended only
when one was happy or enthusiastic.

&§ [7] THE ROCK OF ISRAEL: Why does David speak these two lines,
the second of which adds nothing to the first? Because David was

כִּי לֹא כֵן בֵּיתִי עִם אֵל, כִּי בְרִית עוֹלָם שָׂם לִי, עֲרוּכָה בַכֹּל וּשְׁמוּרָה.

Will then all my desires and
longings not be fulfilled?
But the ungodly rulers are as
thorns to be thrust away,
all of them,
That cannot be taken with the
hand.
If a man touches them,

He must be armed with iron and
spearshaft;
And they shall have to be burned
with fire at their place."

Then David blessed the Lord before
the congregation and built an altar to
the Lord and offered burnt-offerings.

---

stressing that he was not speaking as David the king, but as David
the man, not of his own will or for his own glory, but with words
put into his mouth by the Lord. The source was important; the
message essential, not the speaker. By thus speaking he demonstrated his own humility for he might easily have taken pride in
being chosen by God to be the Lord's mouthpiece.

God said that a ruler over man shall be righteous, even if he rules
through the fear of God. The Rock of Israel said: "I rule man; who
rules Me? The righteous rule Me, for I make a decree and the
righteous may annul it with supplication."

וַיְבָרֶךְ דָּוִיד אֶת יְיָ לְעֵינֵי כָּל הַקָּהָל.

20. I KINGS [1–5]

STRIFE BETWEEN BROTHERS

KING DAVID was old and well advanced in years. Now Adonijah, who was born after Absalom, and who was very handsome, cherished the idea that he would be king. He provided chariots and horsemen for himself, and fifty retainers to run before him. His father had never restrained him, by saying: "Why have you done so?"

Joab, the son of Zeruiah, and Abiathar, the priest, gave him their support. But Zadok, the priest, and Benaiah, the commander of David's bodyguard, the prophet Nathan and David's bodyguard were not with Adonijah.

Then Adonijah made a solemn feast and he invited all his brothers, the king's sons, and all the royal officials of Judah, but he did not invite Nathan, the prophet, nor Benaiah, nor the bodyguard, nor Solomon, his brother. Then Nathan said to Bath-sheba, the mother of Solomon: "Have you not heard that Adonijah, the son of Haggith, has proclaimed himself king and that David, our lord, does not know it? Now let me advise you, so that you may save your own life and the life of your son Solomon. Go to David and say to him: 'Have you not, my lord, O king, sworn to your maidservant saying, "Solomon your son shall be king after me"? Why

וַאֲדֹנִיָה בֶן חַגִּית מִתְנַשֵּׂא לֵאמֹר: אֲנִי אֶמְלֹךְ... וְגַם הוּא טוֹב תֹּאַר מְאֹד וְאוֹתוֹ יָלְדָה אַחֲרֵי אַבְשָׁלוֹם.

then has Adonijah been made king?' And while you are speaking with the king, I will come and will confirm your words."

Bath-sheba went into the king's chamber and she bowed and prostrated herself before the king. The king said to her: "What is your wish?" And she said to him: "My lord, you yourself swore to your maidservant by the Lord your God: 'Solomon, your son, shall be king after me and he shall sit upon my throne.' Now Adonijah has proclaimed himself king without the knowledge of my lord. The eyes of all Israel are upon you, that you shall tell them who shall sit on the throne of my lord after him; otherwise when my lord, the king, shall sleep with his fathers, I and my son, Solomon, will be considered rebels."

While she talked they told the king: "Nathan, the prophet, is here." [Bath-sheba left the chamber] and Nathan entered and bowed before the king, and he said: "My lord, O king, have you said: 'Adonijah shall be king after me, and he shall sit on my throne'? For he has gone down this day and made a solemn feast. He invited all the king's sons and Abiathar, the priest, and Joab, the commander of the army, and they are eating and drinking and have said: 'Long live King Adonijah!' But I, Zadok, the priest, Benaiah and your son Solomon were not invited. Now, if this all

has been brought about with the knowledge of the king, then why has this thing not been told to your servant?"

Then David answered and said: "Call Bath-sheba to me." She came and stood before him, and the king swore this oath: "As the Lord lives, who saved my life in all adversity, and as I have sworn to you by the Lord, God of Israel, saying: 'Solomon, your son, shall be king after me,' so will I do this day." Bath-sheba bowed and prostrated herself before the king and said: "May my lord, the king, live forever." Then David said: "Call Zadok, the priest, Nathan, the prophet, and Benaiah, the commander of my bodyguard." They came and stood before the king. The king said to them: "Take with you the warriors commanded by Benaiah and let my son Solomon ride upon my own mule. Bring him to the spring Gihon and there let Zadok, the priest, and Nathan, the prophet, anoint him king over Israel. Afterward, blow the *Shofar* and say: 'Long live King Solomon.' He shall go and sit upon my throne, and he shall be king after me, over Israel and Judah."

SOLOMON IS ANOINTED

THEN ZADOK, the priest, Nathan, the prophet, together with Benaiah and David's bodyguard went out and put Solomon on David's mule and brought

וּבָא וְיָשַׁב עַל כִּסְאִי, וְהוּא יִמְלֹךְ תַּחְתָּי וְאוֹתוֹ צִוִּיתִי לִהְיוֹת נָגִיד עַל יִשְׂרָאֵל וְעַל יְהוּדָה.

him to the spring of Gihon. Zadok, the priest, took a horn of oil from the tent and anointed Solomon. Afterward they blew the ram's horn and all the people said: "Long live King Solomon!" Then all the people went up after him playing upon flutes and rejoicing with a great tumult.

Adonijah and all the guests with him heard it as they finished feasting. And they were all of them terrified. They arose and every man went his way, but Adonijah was in such fear of Solomon that he went and caught hold of the horns of the altar. It was told to Solomon: "Adonijah is in fear of King Solomon, so he has caught hold of the horns of the altar and has said: 'I will not go out of the Sanctuary unless King Solomon swears to me that he will not kill me.'" Then Solomon said: "If he be a worthy man, not a hair of his shall be touched. But if he be found guilty of treason then he will die." So Solomon sent and brought him down from the altar. And Adonijah came and prostrated himself before King Solomon and Solomon said: "Go to your home."

SOLOMON ANOINTED A SECOND TIME

DAVID ASSEMBLED in Jerusalem all the princes of Israel, the captains of the companies that serve the king, the captains of thousands, the captains of hundreds, and all the officers and mighty men of valor. And he said to all the congregation: "Solomon, my son, whom God alone has chosen is young and tender; and the work to build is great, for it is not a palace for man but for the Lord God. I have prepared with all my might for the house of my God the gold, the silver, the copper, the brass, the iron, the wood and all the precious stones. Now, who will make a voluntary offering today unto the Lord?" Then the heads of the families and the princes of the tribes of Israel, the captains and the overseers of the king's work willingly offered gold, silver, brass and iron. Those who had precious stones offered them to the treasure of the house of the Lord. Then the people rejoiced, for they offered willingly to the Lord.

Thereupon David blessed the Lord before all the congregation: "Blessed be Thou O Lord, the God of Israel, our Father, forever and ever. Thine, O Lord, is the greatness and the power and the glory and the victory and the majesty, for all that are in heaven and earth are Thine. Thine is the kingdom, O Lord, and Thou art exalted as head above all.

"Solomon, my son, know the God of your fathers, and serve Him with a whole heart and willing mind: for the Lord searches all hearts and understands all thoughts. If you seek Him you will be able to find Him: Take heed now,

כִּי כָל לְבָבוֹת דּוֹרֵשׁ יְיָ, וְכָל יֵצֶר מַחֲשָׁבוֹת מֵבִין. אִם תִּדְרְשֶׁנּוּ יִמָּצֵא לָךְ.

for the Lord has chosen you to build a house for the Sanctuary. Be strong and do it!"

Then David said to all the congregation: "Bless the Lord your God."

And all the congregation blessed the Lord, the God of their fathers, and bowed their heads. They sacrificed unto the Lord and they did eat and drink with great rejoicing. Afterward they made Solomon, the son of David, king, and again anointed him to the Lord to be ruler, and Zadok to be high priest.

David slept with his fathers [1] and

---

[1] DAVID SLEPT WITH HIS FATHERS: As the angel of death took David's soul his body fell to the grass in the royal courtyard. Guards quickly called for the king's physician, for Solomon, for the priests and the elders. When the physician had pronounced the king dead, Solomon ordered the soldiers to carry his father's body into the palace, but the elders intervened. "It is Sabbath," they said, "and it is not permitted to move a dead body on the Sabbath."

"Then what shall be done for my father's body?" the new king asked of the elders.

"The body should be covered and let the guards remain near until the Sabbath is done."

Just then a clamor of barking was heard. "What is that?" Solomon asked his guards.

After investigating, one of the guards returned and explained that the dogs in the king's kennel had not been fed at the appointed time and were barking because they were hungry.

"Feed them that they may be quiet," Solomon ordered.

"Your majesty," the guard explained, "the man in charge left because his mother is sick and he did not cut up the meat for the dogs. Is it permitted to cut the meat on the Sabbath?"

Solomon inquired of the elders and they replied: "To feed a dumb animal, you may cut up the meat."

Solomon then reflected, "To remove my father's body to his room is not allowed, but to cut up meat for dogs to eat is allowed. Now I see how true it is that 'a live dog is greater than a dead lion!' (Ecclesiastes 9:4)."

כִּי יְיָ בָּחַר בְּךָ לִבְנוֹת בַּיִת לַמִּקְדָּשׁ; חֲזַק וַעֲשֵׂה!

he was buried in the city of David. He reigned over Israel forty years, seven years he reigned in Hebron, and thirty-three years in Jerusalem. Solomon sat upon the throne of David, his father, and his kingdom was established firmly.

SOLOMON'S VISION

THE KING went to Gibeon to sacrifice there; a thousand burnt-offerings [2] did Solomon offer upon that altar. In Gibeon the Lord appeared to Solomon in a dream that night, and said: "Ask, what shall I give you?"

Solomon said: "Thou hast shown Thy servant David, my father, great kindness. Now O Lord, my God, Thou hast made me king instead of my father, and I am still but a little child; I know not how to go out or come in. Give Thy servant, therefore, an understanding heart to judge Thy people, that I may discern between good and evil. For who is able to judge [3] this Thy great people?"

The Lord was pleased that Solomon asked this thing, and God said to him: "Because you have not asked for yourself a long life neither have you asked riches for yourself, nor have you asked the life of your enemies, but you have asked understanding to discern justice, so I have given you a wise and understanding heart. Also I have given you riches and wealth and honor, which you have not asked."

Solomon awoke, and it was a dream.

• [2] A THOUSAND BURNT-OFFERINGS: When Solomon offered a thousand sacrifices to the Lord in Gibeon, the people were saddened. They said, "Who can equal King Solomon to find favor in the eyes of the Lord? No man can afford so many sacrifices." Then God spoke to the people, saying: "Beloved is he to Me who is merciful to his fellow man more than all the sacrifices that King Solomon offered. 'For I desire mercy not sacrifices, the knowledge of God rather than burnt-offerings' (Hosea 6:6)."

• [3] FOR WHO IS ABLE TO JUDGE: Our Sages explain that Solomon asked for an understanding heart because he said: "A pagan prince may judge in any way he wishes, to hang, to strangle, to have a man beaten or to set him free. He is responsible to no one, for his word is the law. But a Jewish prince may judge only by Your law

וְנָתַתָּ לְעַבְדְּךָ לֵב שֹׁמֵעַ לִשְׁפֹּט אֶת עַמְּךָ, לְהָבִין בֵּין טוֹב לְרָע, כִּי מִי יוּכַל לִשְׁפֹּט אֶת עַמְּךָ הַכָּבֵד הַזֶּה?

He stood before the Ark of the Covenant of the Lord, and offered peace-offerings and made a feast for his followers.

THE JUDGMENT OF SOLOMON

TWO WOMEN, innkeepers, came to the king and stood before him. One woman said: "O my lord, I and this woman dwell in the same house. I gave birth to a child while she was in the house. Then on the third day after I was delivered, this woman also gave birth. We were alone in the house, there was no stranger with us. This woman's child died in the night, because she lay on it. She arose in the middle of the night, and took my son from beside me, while your maidservant slept, and laid him in her bosom, and laid her dead child beside me. When I arose in the morning to nurse my son I saw he was dead. But when I looked at him closely, I saw that it was not the son whom I did bear."

The other woman said: "No, but the dead is your son and the living is my son." So they disputed before the king.

Then the king said: "One says: 'The one who is alive is my son, and the one who is dead is your son.' The other claims: 'No, but your son is the dead, and my son is the living.' So, get me a sword."

They brought a sword to Solomon. The king said: "Cut the living child in two, [4] and give half to one and half to the other."

---

and Your teachings and if he fails to judge aright, he is then responsible to You."

So God saw that Solomon had asked wisdom not to seek empire or for his own vanity, but truly to judge the people and so He granted Solomon's desire.

⋙ [4] CUT THE LIVING CHILD IN TWO: When Solomon heard each woman claim the living child as her son, he said: "Cut the living child in two and give half to one and half to the other, so no one will be wronged."

When the king's counselors heard that, they lamented, "Woe to the land whose king is but a youth. Solomon is only twelve years old so he talks like a child. Is it not enough that one child is dead? Now he will kill the other."

גִּזְרוּ אֶת הַיֶּלֶד הַחַי לִשְׁנָיִם, וּתְנוּ אֶת הַחֲצִי לְאַחַת וְאֶת הַחֲצִי לְאֶחָת.

At that, the woman to whom the living child belonged spoke to Solomon, for her heart yearned for her son: "O my lord, give her the living child, and by no means put it to death."

But the other woman said: "It shall be neither mine nor yours; split it!"

Then the king said: "Give the first woman the living boy, and by no means kill him. She is his mother."

When all Israel heard of the decision the king had rendered, they stood in awe of the king; for they saw the wisdom of God was in him to do justice.

SOLOMON'S KINGDOM

KING SOLOMON ruled over all Israel, and over all the kingdoms, from the Euphrates to the land of the Philistines and to the border of Egypt. These kingdoms paid tribute and served Solomon all his life.

Solomon appointed twelve governors over all Israel, who provided food for the king and his household; each governor had to make provision for one month in the year. King Solomon gathered together chariots and horsemen. He had a thousand and four hundred chariots, and twelve thousand horsemen. He placed them in chariot cities, and some were with the king in Jerusalem. All the drinking vessels of King Solomon were of gold, and all the utensils of the house of the forest of Lebanon were of rare gold. And silver in Jerusalem was as common as stones, cedars were as plentiful as the sycamore trees in the lowland. He had peace on all sides about him. Judah and Israel dwelt safely, each man under his vine and under his fig-tree, from Dan to Beer-sheba. Judah and Israel were as the sand [5] which is by the sea for multitude, eating and drinking and making merry.

No sooner had Solomon ordered the deed when the true mother cried out: "O my lord, by no means put the child to death. Give the child to her."

Immediately the assembly understood that Solomon's clever ruse had revealed the true mother and they acclaimed him in unison: "Happy is the land whose king is mature in judgment and not the pawn of his counselors!"

&ε [5] AS THE SAND: Were there really that many Israelites? Obviously there were not. But the Rabbis say that a man cannot be counted

יְהוּדָה וְיִשְׂרָאֵל רַבִּים כַּחוֹל אֲשֶׁר עַל הַיָּם לָרֹב, אוֹכְלִים וְשׁוֹתִים וּשְׂמֵחִים.

THE WISDOM OF SOLOMON

GOD GAVE Solomon great wisdom and
understanding and largeness of heart.
[6] Solomon's wisdom surpassed the wisdom of all the wise people of the East
and all the wisdom of Egypt, and his
fame spread to all neighboring nations.

He composed three thousand parables
and a thousand and five songs. He spoke
concerning trees, from the cedar of Lebanon to the hyssop that springs from
the wall. He spoke concerning beasts,
of fowl and of creeping things, and of
fishes. Men came from all the kings of
the earth who had heard of the wisdom
of Solomon.

---

as one counts clay counters or coins. A person is counted according
to his worth so that when the Hebrews sinned in the wilderness,
Moses was considered more than all Israel. But when the people
repented, each Israelite was again considered the equal of Moses.
Now, under Solomon, because the people lived according to God's
commandments, each was worth an infinite amount so that Scripture
can compare them to the sands of the sea. The Jews are like sand in
lime; without the sand the lime has no substance.

[6] LARGENESS OF HEART: Solomon was said to have the wisdom of
all Israel: the young and the old, the learned and the unlearned.
Each of these has its own peculiar wisdom: the young have daring,
the old experience, the scholars learning, and the unlearned the
shrewd common sense of those close to nature. Solomon had all
their wisdoms combined.

וַתֵּרֶב חָכְמַת שְׁלֹמֹה מֵחָכְמַת כָּל בְּנֵי קֶדֶם וּמִכֹּל חָכְמַת מִצְרָיִם.

21. I KINGS [5–8]

THE RESOLVE TO BUILD
THE TEMPLE

WHEN HIRAM, king of Tyre, heard that Solomon was anointed king after the death of his father, he sent his officers [to congratulate him], for Hiram had ever been friendly to David. Then Solomon sent a message to Hiram, saying: "You know that David, my father, could not build a temple in honor of the Lord, his God, because of the wars which surround him. But now the Lord, my God, has given me tranquillity on every side. There is no adversary nor evil occurrence. I am resolved, therefore, to build a house to honor the Lord, my God.

"Now the house which I am to build is to be great, for our God is greater than all gods. Who is able to build Him a house, for the heavens cannot contain Him? Who am I to build Him a house? I build a house only to hallow it to Him, a place to burn before Him incense of sweet spices and for the burnt-offerings every morning and evening, on the Sabbath, on the new moon, and the festivals.

"Now send me men skilled to work in gold and silver, in bronze and iron, in purple, crimson and violet stuffs, and who know how to engrave. Also command men to cut the cedar-trees of Lebanon, and my servants shall be with your servants, I will pay the hire of

וְעַתָּה הֵנִיחַ יְיָ אֱלֹהַי לִי מִסָּבִיב, אֵין שָׂטָן וְאֵין פֶּגַע רָע. וְהִנְנִי אוֹמֵר לִבְנוֹת בַּיִת לְשֵׁם יְיָ אֱלֹהָי.

your servants according to all you say, for you know that there is no one among us, who has the skill to hew timber like the Zidonians."

Hiram sent to Solomon, saying: "I will do as you desire concerning the timber of cedar and cypress. My servants shall bring them down from Lebanon to the sea, and I will make the logs into rafts to go by the sea to the place you shall direct. There I will have them broken up. And you shall receive my servants, and you shall provide food for my household.

"Now, I am sending a skillful man filled with wisdom and understanding. He is the son of a woman of the daughters of Dan, and his father is of the tribe of Naphtali, who resides in Tyre. He is skillful to work in gold, in silver, in brass, in iron, in stone, in timber, in purple, in blue, in fine linen and in crimson. He also can perform all manner of engraving and do whatever may be set before him."

King Solomon raised a levy of thirty thousand forced laborers out of all Israel. He sent them to Lebanon, ten thousand a month in relays. And [from the aliens in the country] Solomon took seventy thousand porters, and eighty thousand hewers in the mountains. There were also three thousand and three hundred officers who had charge of the people who did the work. The king commanded and they quarried heavy [1] stones to lay the foundation of the Temple.

THE BUILDING OF THE TEMPLE

IN THE four hundred and eightieth year after the Israelites left Egypt, in the fourth year of Solomon's reign over Israel, in the second month of the year, Solomon began to build the Temple. The house which King Solomon built for the Lord was sixty cubits long, its breadth twenty cubits, and its height thirty cubits. The porch in front of the Temple was twenty cubits, corresponding to the breadth of the Temple and ten cubits wide. The windows of the Temple [2] were broad within and narrow without. The house was built of stones made ready in the quarry; neither

---

[1] HEAVY STONES: The Hebrew for "heavy stones" may also mean "costly stones." The Rabbis said that not only did Solomon order the parts of the Temple which were visible to be properly ornamented but also those parts which were buried in the ground and were unseen, because it was all for the glory of God who sees all.

בַּשָּׁנָה הָרְבִיעִית בְּחֹדֶשׁ זִו, הוּא הַחֹדֶשׁ הַשֵּׁנִי לְמֶלֶךְ שְׁלֹמֹה עַל יִשְׂרָאֵל, וַיִּבֶן הַבַּיִת לַיְיָ.

hammer, nor ax, nor any iron tool [3] was heard in the house while it was being built.

Hiram who was brought from Tyre and who was a skillful master in metal, [made the vessels of the Temple] and all the metal work. He fashioned two columns of bronze. He made two capitals, a capital of lily-work on top of each column. And the pomegranates were two hundred, in rows about each capital. He set up the columns at the porch of the

---

ᑫᔕ [2] THE WINDOWS OF THE TEMPLE: Why did Solomon have the Temple windows built broadly within and narrowly without? The usual way allowed for more light to enter and would have illuminated the Temple more brightly.

Our Sages tell us that Solomon wanted to emphasize that the Lord needs no light, but radiates His own light to the world. As Scripture has it (Daniel 2:22): "The light dwells within Him." The pagans believed that their gods needed light to see what to do. Pagan gods also needed nourishment so that their worshipers prepared bread and sacrificed animals to them to sustain them. The Temple had similar paraphernalia, a *menorah*, an altar, a table with showbread, but these were used in a different way. In order to demonstrate that the *menorah* was not to give light so that the Lord should see how to eat, it was placed on the south side of the Temple, the table with showbread on the north side, and the altar between the two of them.

Why then did the Lord command the making of these things if He had no need of them? "The Holy One, Blessed Be He, did so to make Israel able to acquire merit. Therefore, He multiplied the Torah and the precepts for them."

ᑫᔕ [3] ANY IRON TOOL: Because Solomon wished the Temple to be a symbol of peace and dedicated to peace, he did not want implements of war made of iron used in it or in its construction. From the spirits Solomon heard of a strange worm of wonderful powers called the *shamir*. The *shamir* cut or split any material, stone or metal, into any shape, and without exertion. But where to find the *shamir*?

רָצָה הַקָּדוֹשׁ בָּרוּךְ הוּא לְזַכּוֹת אֶת יִשְׂרָאֵל, לְפִיכָךְ הִרְבָּה לָהֶם תּוֹרָה וּמִצְווֹת.

Temple. The column which he set up at the right hand he called Jachin, and that on the left side he called Boaz.

So Solomon built the house, and finished it. And he built the walls of the house within with boards of cedar; from the floor of the house up to the joists of the ceiling, he covered them on the inside with wood; and he covered the floor of the house with cypress boards. And in the Sanctuary he made two cherubim of olive wood and doors of olive wood. [4] And he built the inner court with three rows of hewn stone, and a row of cedar beams.

He made ten lavers of bronze, and he made ten bases of bronze. Solomon had made all the vessels of the house of the Lord: the golden altar, the golden table upon which was the showbread; and he

---

Only Ashmodai, king of the evil spirits, might know. By a ruse Solomon's men captured Ashmodai and chained in bonds that bore the seal of the name of the Lord they brought him before the king. Solomon promised Ashmodai that he would release him if Ashmodai told where the *shamir* might be found and Ashmodai obliged.

Solomon then sent an expedition to the mountains of darkness. There his men placed a huge pane of glass over the nest of a roc, trapping its young. The mother roc, when she could not break the glass with her beak, flew off and returned with the *shamir*. As she split the glass Solomon's men leaped screaming from their hiding places and the roc, frightened, dropped the *shamir*. Solomon's men seized the *shamir* and brought it back to Jerusalem.

There Solomon had it used to split all the rock and metal for the Temple and then returned the *shamir* to the roc's nest. The roc swiftly carried it back to its secret hiding place.

៚ [4] OF OLIVE WOOD: The Ralbag notes that the wood was taken from old olive trees which no longer bore fruit. We are told that acacia was prescribed for the Tabernacle in order to teach man that when he wants to build a house, he must remember that God Himself used wood for His own house from a tree that does not bear fruit. How much more so then should an ordinary man refrain from using fruit-bearing trees for timber.

וַיָּקֶם אֶת הָעַמּוּד הַיְמָנִי וַיִּקְרָא אֶת שְׁמוֹ יָכִין, וַיָּקֶם אֶת הָעַמּוּד הַשְּׂמָאלִי וַיִּקְרָא אֶת שְׁמוֹ בֹּעַז.

made a *menorah*, five branches on the right side and five on the left, before the Sanctuary. They were both made of pure gold.

When all the work of the House of the Lord was finished, Solomon brought in all the sacred objects of his father David, the silver, the gold, and all the vessels, and placed them in the treasuries of the House of the Lord.

BRINGING THE ARK TO THE TEMPLE

THEN SOLOMON assembled in Jerusalem all the elders of Israel, and all the heads of the tribes, and the princes of the families of Israel, to bring the Ark of the Covenant from the City of David which is Zion. All the men of Israel assembled before King Solomon at the festival of Tabernacles, which is in the seventh month of the year. The priests and the Levites took up the Ark of the Covenant, the Tent of Meeting, and all the holy vessels that were in the Tent. Then the priests placed the Ark of the Covenant of the Lord in the Sanctuary of the Temple, in the most holy place, under the wings of the cherubim. There was nought in the Ark except the two tablets of stone which Moses put there in Horeb, when the Lord made a Covenant with the Children of Israel, when they came out of Egypt.

The Levites who were the singers stood at the end of the altar robed in fine linen, holding cymbals, flutes and lyres. Beside them stood a hundred and twenty priests with trumpets. The trumpeters and the singers joined in a loud song of praise and thanksgiving to the Lord. They played and sang:

> For He is good,
> His mercy endures forever.

When the priests came out of the holy place, a cloud filled the House of the Lord, and the priests could not stand to minister because of the cloud, for the glory of the Lord filled the House of the Lord. Then said Solomon:

> I have built Thee a house of habitation,
> For Thee to dwell in forever.

SOLOMON'S PRAYER

THE KING turned his face and blessed the congregation of Israel, and said: "Blessed be the Lord, the God of Israel, who said to my father David: 'Since the day that I brought My people Israel from out of Egypt, I chose no city out of all the tribes of Israel to build a house, that My name might be there; but I chose David [5] to be over My people Israel,' and the Lord also said to him: 'It was in your heart to build a house to Me; you did well, that you

בָּנֹה בָנִיתִי בֵּית זְבוּל לָךְ, מָכוֹן לְשִׁבְתְּךָ עוֹלָמִים.

thought of it. Nevertheless, you yourself shall not build the house, but your
son, he shall build it.' Now the Lord
has made good His word, for I have
risen in the place of my father, and I
have built the house for the Lord. And
I have provided a place for the Ark, in
which is the Covenant of the Lord,
which He made with our fathers, when
He brought them out of Egypt."

Then Solomon stood before the altar
of the Lord, in the presence of the
whole assembly of Israel. He spread his
hands toward the heavens, and said:

"O Lord, the God of Israel, there is
no God like Thee in heaven above, nor
upon the earth beneath, who keeps a
covenant and mercy with Thy servants,
who walk before Thee with all their
hearts. But can God really dwell on the
earth? Behold, heaven and the heaven
of heavens cannot contain Thee, [6]
how much less this house which I have
built? Yet, turn to the prayer of Thy
servant and to his supplication, that
Thine eyes may be open toward this
house night and day, that Thou mayest
listen to the supplication of Thy servant
and Thy people Israel, when they shall
pray toward this place.

"If a man sins against his neighbor,
and an oath is to be exacted of him, he
shall come and swear before Thy altar
in this house. Hear Thou in heaven,

❧ [5] BUT I CHOSE DAVID: What connection is there between "I chose
no city . . . but I chose David"? The Lord considers who shall lead
the people and only then does He build the city and bring the people
into it. The Rabbis said that the duty to choose the king comes even
before the duty to build the Temple. The verse therefore means:
"I chose no city until I had seen that David was a fitting shepherd
of Israel."

❧ [6] HEAVEN CANNOT CONTAIN THEE: God does not need a place to
stand much less a place in which to dwell. God's glory can be revealed to man's senses in a cloud or a fire, or in a still small voice.
But it cannot be said that God is in a place, for He is not a body
with dimension that space can surround. For this reason the Rabbis
called God "Place" (Makom) as in "Blessed be the Place [God]
who gave the Torah to Israel." So, too, the Psalmist (90:1) could
say: "Lord, Thou hast been our dwelling place."

הִנֵּה הַשָּׁמַיִם וּשְׁמֵי הַשָּׁמַיִם לֹא יְכַלְכְּלוּךָ, אַף כִּי הַבַּיִת הַזֶּה אֲשֶׁר בָּנִיתִי.

and judge Thy servants, punishing the wicked and justifying the righteous.

"When Thy people Israel are defeated before an enemy, because they sinned against Thee, if they turn to Thee and confess, and make supplication in this house, then hear Thou in heaven, and forgive the sin of Thy people.

"If there be famine in the land, if there be pestilence, locust or caterpillar, if their enemy besiege them at any of their gates; whatever plague or sickness there be; all prayer or supplication offered by any man of all Thy people Israel, who will stretch out his hand toward this house in prayer—hear Thou in heaven and forgive his acts. Render to each according to his ways, for Thou alone knowest the hearts of all men.

"Also, concerning the stranger, [7] who is not of Thy people, but comes from a far country, for Thy name's sake. If he shall come and pray to this house, then listen to him, and do all that the stranger requests of Thee, so that all the people of the earth may know Thy name and fear Thee, as does Thy people Israel.

"If Thy people go out to battle, and they pray to the Lord toward the city [8] which Thou hast chosen, and toward the house which I have built for Thy name, then hear Thou in heaven their prayer and their supplication, and maintain their cause."

A JOYFUL FEAST

WHEN SOLOMON finished praying, he arose from before the altar of the Lord and stood and blessed all the congregation of Israel with a loud voice, saying:

≈§ [7] CONCERNING THE STRANGER: God is asked by Solomon to answer each Israelite "according to his ways." In other words, God is to judge each Israelite, then answer him if he merits an answer. But the stranger is not to be judged the same way. Solomon asks God to do all "that the stranger requests of Thee," whether the stranger merits it or not. Why does Solomon ask more for the non-Jew than he asks for the Jew? Solomon does so in order that the stranger, the non-Jew, should thereby be able more easily to appreciate the holiness of God and of His Temple.

≈§ [8] THEY PRAY TO THE LORD TOWARD THE CITY: In Diaspora the worshipers should turn in prayer toward the Land of Israel, to the

לְמַעַן יֵדְעוּן כָּל עַמֵּי הָאָרֶץ אֶת שְׁמֶךָ לְיִרְאָה אוֹתְךָ כְּעַמְּךָ יִשְׂרָאֵל.

"Blessed be the Lord, who has given rest to His people Israel as He promised. May the Lord our God be with us, as He was with our fathers; may He not leave us nor forsake us. Let your heart be completely with the Lord our God, to walk in His statutes and to keep His commandments, as at this day."

Then the king and all Israel with him offered sacrifices before the Lord. They made a feast for seven days, after celebrating for eight days the festival of Tabernacles. Then he sent the people away. They blessed the king, and went home joyful and glad of heart for all the goodness that the Lord had shown to David, His servant, and to Israel, His people.

---

east. In the Land of Israel, they should turn their faces toward Jerusalem, the Holy City. In Jerusalem, toward the Temple. In the Temple toward the Holy of Holies. So does all Israel direct its heart toward one place and toward God alone.

יְהִי יְיָ אֱלֹהֵינוּ עִמָּנוּ, כַּאֲשֶׁר הָיָה עִם אֲבוֹתֵינוּ, אַל יַעַזְבֵנוּ וְאַל יִטְּשֵׁנוּ.

22. I KINGS [7-14]

BUILDING KING SOLOMON'S PALACE

SOLOMON WAS thirteen years [1] in building his own palace until he finished the entire house. He also built the Forest of Lebanon House. Its length was one hundred cubits, its breadth was fifty cubits and its height thirty cubits. Now

King Solomon made two hundred shields of beaten gold, twenty pounds of gold went into each shield. He also made three hundred small shields of beaten gold, about six pounds of gold in each of them. Then the king put them in the Forest of Lebanon House.

He also made a great throne of ivory,

---

[1] THIRTEEN YEARS: Why did Solomon take thirteen years to build his palace and only seven to build the Temple? The Temple was larger and should have taken twice as long, not half as long. Because, our Sages explain, Solomon was inspired and eager to finish the Temple for it was a holy project. His own palace did not excite this same sense of enthusiastic dedication. The Sanctuary was more

וְאֶת־בֵּיתוֹ בָּנָה שְׁלֹמֹה שְׁלֹשׁ עֶשְׂרֵה שָׁנָה וַיְכַל אֶת־כָּל־בֵּיתוֹ.

and overlaid it with fine gold. The throne had six steps. Behind the top of the throne was a round canopy. There were arms on both sides of the throne. Two lions stood beside the arms, and twelve lions stood on each side of six steps. There was not the like in any kingdom.

His own residence was behind the hall of the throne, built of like work. He also made a house for Pharaoh's daughter, [2] whom Solomon married.

KING SOLOMON AND THE QUEEN OF SHEBA

WHEN THE Queen of Sheba heard of the fame of Solomon, she came to test him with riddles. She came to Jerusalem with a very large retinue, with camels bearing spices, and very much gold and precious stones. When she came to Solomon she spoke to him about all that was in her mind. Solomon answered all her questions, there was not a thing which he could not explain to her. The Queen of Sheba saw the wisdom of Solomon, the palace that he had built, the food of his table, the seating of his courtiers, and the magnificent retinue which accompanied him when he went up to the House of the Lord. And she said to the king: "The report which I heard in my own land of your acts and your wisdom was true. I did not believe it until I came and saw it with my own eyes. And now I see not half was told me; you surpass in wisdom and prosperity all that I had heard. Happy are your people, happy are your servants who

---

magnificent than the king's palace. And Solomon was assiduous in building the Sanctuary but remiss in completing his own house. In this Solomon was more meritorious than David who built his own palace first.

[2] THE DAUGHTER OF PHARAOH: When Shimei ben Gera, Solomon's teacher, died, Solomon approached Pharaoh and arranged to marry Pharaoh's daughter. Solomon brought her to Jerusalem and took her into his palace.

On that very day the angel Gabriel plunged earthward and placed a reed in the sea. The sea was in turmoil, mud clung to the reed, then earth formed, and soon it was a large land. That land became the center of the imperial city of Rome.

וְהִנֵּה לֹא הֻגַּד לִי הַחֵצִי, הוֹסַפְתָּ חָכְמָה וָטוֹב אֶל הַשְּׁמוּעָה אֲשֶׁר שָׁמָעְתִּי.

stand continually before you and hear your wisdom. Blessed be the Lord your God, who set you on the throne of Israel; because the Lord loved Israel for ever, [3] therefore He made you king to do justice and righteousness." Then she returned and went to her land, she and her servants.

KING SOLOMON'S SINS

BESIDES THE daughter of Pharaoh, King Solomon loved many foreign women, Moabites, Ammonites, Edomites, Zidonians, and Hittites, of the nations concerning which the Lord said to the Children of Israel: "You shall not go among them, neither shall they come among you; for surely they will turn away your heart after their gods." [4] He had seven hundred wives of princely birth, and three hundred concubines. When Solomon grew old his wives turned his heart away after their gods and Solomon did that which is evil in the eyes of the Lord. He built a high place for the

---

⇜ [3] THE LORD LOVED ISRAEL FOR EVER: But how does God show His love? In the wilderness God performed miracles for the people. Later He sent His judges and prophets, bringing truth and justice to Israel. But after the miracles and the prophecies, the Lord expresses His love in the wisdom He instills in His righteous ones, from ancient times until this very day.

⇜ [4] THEY WILL TURN AWAY YOUR HEART AFTER THEIR GODS: Rabbi Sh'muel in the name of Rabbi Jonathan said: "Though King Solomon did not himself actually sin in idolatry, he did not stop his wives from serving their pagan idols. Scripture therefore assigns him the burden of having committed the idolatry himself. When Solomon married the daughter of Pharaoh, she brought a thousand varied musical instruments to him. "Each of these," she pointed out, "is used to worship a different idol." She played for him and Solomon made no objection.

When Solomon's other wives saw that, they all built their own high places and sacrificed there to their own idols. Since Solomon could have prevented that, Scripture also assigns the responsibility for it to him, and the verse says: "Then did Solomon build a high

וַיְהִי לְעֵת זִקְנַת שְׁלֹמֹה, נָשָׁיו הִטּוּ אֶת לְבָבוֹ אַחֲרֵי אֱלֹהִים אֲחֵרִים.

Chemosh, the destestable idol of Moab, in the mountain that is before Jeru-salem, and for Molech, the destestable idol of Ammon. So he did for all his foreign wives, he built high places, burn-ing incense and sacrificing to their gods.

The Lord became angry with Solomon, because his heart was turned away from the Lord, the God of Israel, who had appeared to him twice, and He said to Solomon: "Since you have not kept My covenant and My statutes which I have commanded you, I will rend the king-dom from you and give it to your serv-ant. However, I will not do it in your lifetime for the sake of David, your father. I will rend it out of the hand of your son. Still I will not tear away the whole kingdom, but I will leave one tribe to your son for David, My serv-ant's sake, and for the sake of Jerusalem which I have chosen."

JEROBOAM'S REVOLT

JEROBOAM, THE son of Nebat, was a man of much valor, and he lifted up his hand against the king, because Solomon built Millo, and repaired the breach [5] of the City of David, his father. Solomon

---

place for the Chemosh, the detestable idol of Moab . . . and for Molech the detestable idol of the children of Ammon" (I Kings II:7).

Rabbi Jonathan commented: "He who has the power to protest against the wrongs committed in a household and does not do so is held responsible for the wrongs committed by each member of the household. He who has the power to protest the wrongs done in his city and does not protest is held responsible for the wrongs committed in the city. He who has power to protest the wrongs committed by the whole world and does not protest, he is held responsible for the wrongs of the whole world."

[5] REPAIRED THE BREACH: Rabbi Johanan said: Why did Jeroboam deserve to be king? Because he admonished the king in the name of heaven. And why was he punished? Because he did so publicly.

Jeroboam said to Solomon: "Your father tore the breaches in the wall so that the people of Israel might readily come up on their pilgrimages to Jerusalem, but you have repaired the breaches to provide a pleasure pavilion for your Egyptian wife."

יַעַן אֲשֶׁר הָיְתָה זֹאת עִמָּךְ, וְלֹא שָׁמַרְתָּ בְּרִיתִי וְחֻקֹּתַי אֲשֶׁר צִוִּיתִי עָלֶיךָ, קָרֹעַ אֶקְרַע אֶת הַמַּמְלָכָה מֵעָלֶיךָ וּנְתַתִּיהָ לְעַבְדֶּךָ.

saw that the young man was industrious, so he put him in charge of all the forced labor of the tribe of Joseph. Once, when Jeroboam went out of Jerusalem, the prophet Ahijah of Shiloh met him on the road. Now Ahijah had put on a new garment, and the two were alone in the field. Then Ahijah took hold of his new garment and tore it in twelve pieces, and he said to Jeroboam: "Take for yourself ten pieces, for thus said the Lord, the God of Israel: 'I will tear the kingdom from the hand of Solomon, and will give ten tribes to you; but he shall have one tribe, for David, My servant's sake, and for the sake of Jerusalem, the city which I have chosen out of all the tribes of Israel, because they have forsaken Me.'" [6]

Solomon sought to kill Jeroboam, but he fled to Egypt, and he was there until Solomon died.

Solomon reigned over all Israel forty years. Then Solomon slept with his fathers, and was buried in the City of David.

THE DISRUPTION OF THE KINGDOM

REHOBOAM WENT to Shechem, for all Israel had come to Shechem to make him king. When Jeroboam heard of the death of Solomon, he still dwelt in Egypt. Then the people sent for him, and he and all the congregation of Israel came and spoke to Rehoboam, saying: "Your father made our yoke heavy. Now lighten the heavy yoke of your father, and we will serve you."

Then he said to them: "Depart for three days and then return to me." The people departed.

King Rehoboam took counsel with the old men who had stood before Solomon, his father: "How do you advise that we reply to these people?" They said to him: "If you comply with their demands this day and talk kindly to them, they will be your servants forever."

Then he took counsel with the young men, who had grown up with him and who were his companions: "What do

---

[6] FORSAKEN ME: The reader might think that the "they" refers to the tribes, but the Rabbis said: "No, they refer to Solomon's wives." Israel remained loyal to God but the wives had been converted to Judaism at Solomon's insistence not because they themselves were committed to the worship of the true God, but to please the king. They therefore relapsed quickly into their idolatry and forsook the Lord.

אָבִיךָ הִקְשָׁה אֶת עֻלֵּנוּ, וְאַתָּה עַתָּה הָקֵל מֵעֲבוֹדַת אָבִיךָ הַקָּשָׁה וּמֵעֻלּוֹ הַכָּבֵד...
וְנַעַבְדֶךָ.

you advise that we reply to the people who have spoken to me?"

The young men spoke to him, saying: "Thus shall you say to them: 'My little finger is thicker than my father's loins. My father burdened you with a heavy yoke, and I will add to your yoke. My father chastised you with whips, but I will chastise you with scorpions.' "

When Jeroboam and all the people came to Rehoboam on the third day, the king answered them harshly, saying: "My father made your yoke heavy, but I will add to your yoke. My father chastised you with whips, and I will chastise you with scorpions."

When the people heard it, they called out: "What portion do we have in David? To your tents, O Israel!" So Israel departed.

Then King Rehoboam sent Adoram, who was head of the forced labor, to quell the revolt, but all Israel stoned him to death. King Rehoboam leaped into his chariot and fled to Jerusalem.

Thus Israel rebelled against the house of David. The whole assembly made Jeroboam king over Israel: only the tribe of Judah followed the house of David.

SHEMAIAH AVERTS A CIVIL WAR

REHOBOAM CAME to Jerusalem and assembled a hundred and eighty thousand warriors from the tribe of Judah and from the tribe of Benjamin to fight against the house of Israel, to bring the kingdom back. But the word of God came to Shemaiah, the man of God, saying: Speak to Rehoboam and to all the house of Judah and Benjamin, and the rest of the people, saying: "Thus said the Lord: 'You shall not go and fight your brothers, the Children of Israel. Return every man to his house for this is the way I, the Lord, have planned it.' "

So they listened to the word of the Lord, and turned and went away according to His command.

THE GOLDEN CALVES

JEROBOAM FORTIFIED Shechem in the highland of Ephraim, and dwelt there. He also fortified Penuel. Then he said in his heart: "If the people go up to offer sacrifices in the House of the Lord in Jerusalem, their heart will turn back to Rehoboam, and they will kill me, and the kingdom will return to the house of David." So Jeroboam made two golden calves. He set up one in Beth-el, and the other in Dan, and said to the people: "You have gone up long enough to Jerusalem. Here are your gods, O Israel, who brought you up out of the land of Egypt."

He also made sanctuaries in high places, and appointed priests, people

אָבִי יִסַּר אֶתְכֶם בַּשּׁוֹטִים, וַאֲנִי אֲיַסֵּר אֶתְכֶם בָּעַקְרַבִּים.

who were not from the sons of Levi. He ordained the feast on the fifteenth day in the eighth month, a month which he had devised of his own heart.

The Lord spoke to Ahijah, saying: "Go say to Jeroboam: 'Thus said the Lord, the God of Israel: I exalted you from the midst of the people, and made you a prince over My people, Israel. I tore the kingdom away from the house of David, and gave it to you, but you have done evil and made for yourself other gods and molten images to provoke Me. Therefore I will utterly sweep away the house of Jeroboam as a man sweeps away waste. The Lord will raise up a king over Israel, who shall cut off the house of Jeroboam.'" [7]

꛳ [7] TWO GOLDEN CALVES: The Lord tried to persuade Jeroboam to repent because He remembered Jeroboam's piety, scholarship and devotion to the common people. So the Lord spoke to Jeroboam, saying: "Repent, My son, and I, and David, and you will walk in the Garden of Eden." Then Jeroboam asked: "Who will lead?" The Lord said: "The son of Jesse." So Jeroboam rejoined: "If that is so, I refuse." Thus was Jeroboam designated the greatest sinner of all generations: "He sinned and caused many to sin, and therefore the sins of many are ascribed to him."

וְהֵקִים יְיָ לוֹ מֶלֶךְ עַל יִשְׂרָאֵל, אֲשֶׁר יַכְרִית אֶת בֵּית יָרָבְעָם.

23♦ I KINGS [14-19]

CHRONOLOGY OF THE KINGS

JEROBOAM REIGNED for twenty-two years. His son Nadab became king and reigned over Israel for two years. He did evil in the sight of the Lord. Then Baasa conspired against Nadab, and smote all the house of Jeroboam, and became king over Israel. Baasa reigned for twenty-four years, and his son Elah became king. He ruled for two years.

His servant Zimri, a captain of the chariots, conspired against him, and killed him and all the household of Baasa. Omri, the chief of the army, besieged Zimri in Tirzah, and Zimri died in the battle. He reigned for seven days and Omri became king.

Rehoboam was succeeded by his son Abijam. Asa succeeded his father Abijam. Jehoshaphat reigned after the death of his father Asa.

THE REIGN OF OMRI

IN THE thirty-first year of the reign of Asa, king of Judah, Omri began to reign over Israel. He reigned in Tirzah six years. Then he bought the mountain of Samaria from Shemer for two talents of silver. He built a city on the mountain, and called it Samaria, after the name of

וַיִּבֶן אֶת הָהָר, וַיִּקְרָא אֶת שֵׁם הָעִיר אֲשֶׁר בָּנָה ... שֹׁמְרוֹן.

Shemer, the owner of the hill. Omri walked in the ways of Jeroboam, and made Israel sin. He reigned for twelve years and died. He was buried in Samaria, and his son Ahab reigned in his stead.

THE REIGN OF AHAB

AHAB, THE SON of Omri, reigned over Israel in Samaria twenty-two years. The least of his transgressions was that he walked in the ways of Jeroboam for he took to wife Jezebel, daughter of Ethbaal, king of the Zidonians, and served Baal and worshiped him. He built in Samaria a temple to Baal, and erected an altar there. Ahab did more to provoke the Lord, the God of Israel, than all the kings of Israel who were before him.

In his days Hiel rebuilt Jericho. He laid its foundations upon his first born son Abiram, and set up its gates upon his youngest son Segub.

ELIJAH AND THE DROUGHT

THEN ELIJAH of Tishbi said to Ahab: "As the Lord the God of Israel lives whom I serve, there shall be neither dew nor rain these years except according to my command."

Then the word of the Lord came to him saying: "Depart from here and turn eastward and hide yourself by the riverbed of Cherith, east of the Jordan. You shall drink from the river and I have commanded the ravens [1] to feed you there." So he went and did according to the word of the Lord and dwelt at the river-bed of Cherith, and the ravens brought him bread [2] and meat in the morning and bread and meat in the evening and he drank the water from the river.

❧ [1] I HAVE COMMANDED THE RAVENS: Some of our Sages translate the Hebrew *orvim* not as ravens but as merchants. Others explain that the Lord told Elijah to hide in the city of Oreb where the inhabitants would feed him.

❧ [2] RAVENS BROUGHT HIM BREAD: God created the ravens on condition that in time to come they would feed Elijah. So it is with all the miracles in Scripture; when the Lord created the world, He did so arranging the appointed time and place when these miracles would occur.

חַי יְיָ אֱלֹהֵי יִשְׂרָאֵל אֲשֶׁר עָמַדְתִּי לְפָנָיו, אִם יִהְיֶה הַשָּׁנִים הָאֵלֶּה טַל וּמָטָר כִּי אִם לְפִי דְבָרִי.

After a time the river-bed dried up [3] because there was no rain. Then the word of the Lord came to him, saying: "Arise, go to Zarephath, which belongs to Zidon, and stay there. I have ordered a widow there to provide for you."

꙳ [3] THE RIVER-BED DRIED UP: Rabbi Yosé said: "Elijah was very hot-tempered and dealt too severely with Ahab. The Lord promised Elijah that there would be no rain except on Elijah's command." Our Sages, in their picturesque language, said that the Lord had given Elijah the key to rain. But the Lord thought Elijah would have pity on the suffering people and not withhold the rain too long. For that reason He commanded the ravens to feed the prophet so that Elijah would see that even the ravens, the cruelest of birds, can perform acts of kindness and so learn to be more compassionate himself. But Elijah did not relent.

Then the Lord made the river-bed dry up to let Elijah suffer too, so that perhaps he would release the Lord from His promise and permit rain to flow. But Elijah was adamant.

So the Lord sent Elijah to the pious widow of Zarephath. She was known as an upright and God-fearing woman and when the child died, she said to Elijah: "Formerly God had been gracious to me, because in comparison to the inhabitants of the city, I was righteous. But now He has abandoned me because my virtues are nothing in the presence of a great and pious man such as you are, Elijah."

Then Elijah prayed to the Lord and said: "Almighty God, revive the child so that people will not say that as a guest I repaid the widow's hospitality with evil. Take pity on the poor woman."

Then the Lord said to Elijah: "You are concerned with the widow's grief, but you have no compassion for My children who suffer. I will pay no heed to your petition until you release Me from My promise to withhold the rain."

So Elijah returned the key of rain to the Lord and the Lord gave the prophet the power to revive the child, and then told him: "Go, show yourself to Ahab and I will send rain on the land."

קוּם לֵךְ צָרְפַתָה אֲשֶׁר לְצִידוֹן וְיָשַׁבְתָּ שָׁם, הִנֵּה צִוִּיתִי שָׁם אִשָּׁה אַלְמָנָה לְכַלְכְּלֶךָ.

He arose and went to Zarephath, and as he came to the gates of the city there was a widow gathering sticks. He called out to her: "Bring me, I beg you, a little water in a vessel that I may drink." As she was going to bring it, he called out to her: "Bring me, I beg you, a bit of bread with it." She replied: "As the Lord your God lives, I have nothing but a handful of meal in the jar and a little oil in a cruse. I am just gathering a few sticks that I may go and prepare it for myself, and my son, that we may eat before we die." Then Elijah said to her: "Fear not, go and do as you have said. But first make me from it a little cake and bring it to me, afterward make one for yourself and your son. Because this is what the Lord, the God of Israel, said: 'The jar of meal shall not be exhausted nor shall the cruse of oil give out until the day that the Lord sends rain upon the land.'"

So she went and did according to the word of Elijah, and she and he and her household did eat day after day. The jar of the meal was not exhausted, neither did the flask of oil fail, as the word of the Lord which He spoke to Elijah.

In the third year of the drought, the word of the Lord came to Elijah, saying: "Go, show yourself to Ahab, [4] and I will send rain upon the land." So Elijah went to Ahab. Now, when Ahab saw Elijah, he said to him: "Is it you, you troubler of Israel?"

And he said: "It is not I who has scourged Israel, but you and your father's house, for you follow the Baalim. Now, therefore, send and gather to me all Israel, to Mount Carmel, together with the four hundred and fifty prophets of the Baal, and the four hundred prophets of the Asherah who eat at Jezebel's table."

ELIJAH AND THE PRIESTS OF BAAL

AHAB SENT to all Israel, and gathered the prophets together at Mount Carmel. Then Elijah approached the people, and

---

ᴥ§ [4] GO, SHOW YOURSELF TO AHAB: When the Lord spoke thus to Elijah, the prophet said: "Almighty God, why should You send rain to relieve the famine when Ahab has not repented?" Then the Lord answered: "I sent rain upon the land when Adam was one man though he might afterward sin and when he did become a sinner. Therefore shall I still give rain, though the people sin, because whatever man is he is man and My creature."

לֹא עָכַרְתִּי אֶת יִשְׂרָאֵל, כִּי אִם אַתָּה וּבֵית אָבִיךָ, בַּעֲזָבְכֶם אֶת מִצְוֹת יְיָ וַתֵּלֶךְ אַחֲרֵי הַבְּעָלִים.

said: "How long will you falter between two opinions? If the Lord is God, follow Him, but if Baal, follow him." The people answered him not a word.

Then Elijah said to the people: "I, I alone am left as a prophet of the Lord, but the prophets of Baal are four hundred and fifty men. Let them give us two young bullocks, and let them choose one bullock for themselves, and cut it in pieces, and lay it on the wood, and put no fire under it. I will prepare the other bullock and place it on the wood, and put no fire under it. Then you call to your god, and I will call [5] to the Lord, and the God who answers by fire, He is God." Thereupon all the people answered: "It is well-spoken."

Then Elijah said to the prophets of Baal: [6] "You choose a bullock and

---

[5] I WILL CALL: Why did Elijah enter such a contest with a detested foe? It meant he had to set up an altar away from Jerusalem, far from any recognized shrine. It meant he had to use a "high place" which was particularly forbidden. It meant that he, who was neither priest nor Levite, would have to assume their duties, which was also forbidden. In trying to bring the people of Israel back to the Lord, Elijah would thereby be shattering the law in the presence of a multitude easily led astray.

In normal times no altar could be built or sacrifices offered outside of the Temple in Jerusalem. But, our Rabbis say, the Lord said: "Let no one think that Elijah transgressed by sacrificing on Mount Carmel while the Temple was in being. Though it was prohibited by the Torah, it was I who commanded him."

[6] THE PROPHETS OF BAAL: Why did the prophets of Baal accept the contest so willingly? They had seen what Elijah could do in withholding the rain. Were they not afraid?

Not at all. They brought an altar with a hollow base from a nearby shrine and inside it concealed Hiel the Beth-elite with a pot of burning charcoal. When the priests called loudly on "the name of Baal," Hiel was to insert the charcoal through a hole in the altar, but, we are told, a snake emerged from under the altar and

עַד מָתַי אַתֶּם פּוֹסְחִים עַל שְׁתֵּי הַסְּעִיפִים? אִם יְיָ הָאֱלֹהִים – לְכוּ אַחֲרָיו, וְאִם הַבַּעַל – לְכוּ אַחֲרָיו.

prepare it first, for you are many. Put no fire under it and call to your god." So they took the bullock which he gave them and they prepared it, and called to Baal from morning till noon, saying: "O Baal, answer us!" But there was no voice, nor answer. Then they danced a halting dance around the altar which they had made.

When it was noon, Elijah mocked them: "Call with a loud voice for he is god! He may be meditating, or he is on a journey, or perchance he is asleep and must be awakened." They cried aloud and slashed themselves, as their custom was, with swords and lances till the blood gushed. They worked themselves into a frenzy; the midday passed; it was time for the evening sacrifice, but there was no voice, nor any answer.

Then Elijah said to the people: "Draw near." [7] The people came near to him. Elijah took twelve stones, the number of the tribes of the sons of Israel, and with the stones he rebuilt the altar of the Lord that was thrown down. He made a trench around the altar. He arranged the wood on the altar, cut the bullock, and laid it upon the wood, and he said: "Fill four jars with water, and pour it on the burnt-offering and on the wood." Then he said: "Do it again." And they did. He said: "Do it a third time." And they did, so the water ran around the altar.

When it was time for the evening offering, Elijah came near and said: "O Lord, God of Abraham, of Isaac, and of Israel, let it be known today that Thou art God, and I am Thy servant, and I did all this at Thy command. Answer me, O Lord, answer me, so that this

---

bit Hiel so that he died. The priests then danced and sang and shouted, thinking that Hiel had fallen asleep and that they would so awaken him, but Hiel was beyond waking.

෴ [7] DRAW NEAR: Why did Elijah ask the people to draw near before he repaired the altar? The Rabbis said he did so in order to have all Israel participate in repairing the altar as a united people. When Elijah had made the repairs with the hearts of the people united behind him, then the *Shechinah*, God's presence, was drawn, for when the people are united in peace, then the spirit of God descends on them.

יְיָ אֱלֹהֵי אַבְרָהָם, יִצְחָק וְיִשְׂרָאֵל, הַיּוֹם יִוָּדַע כִּי אַתָּה אֱלֹהִים בְּיִשְׂרָאֵל וַאֲנִי עַבְדֶּךָ.

people may know that Thou Lord art God."

Then the fire of the Lord fell, and consumed the burnt-offering, the wood, the stones, the dust, and licked up the water that was in the trench. When all the people saw it, they prostrated themselves, and called out: "The Lord, He is God. The Lord, He is God."

Elijah said to the people: "Seize the prophets of Baal: let not a man of them escape." So they seized them, and Elijah brought them down to the river-bed of Kishon, and there they were killed.

Elijah said to Ahab: "Go up, eat and drink, for there is the rushing sound of a heavy rain." So Ahab went up to eat and drink and Elijah went up to the top of Carmel and crouched down upon the earth and hid his face between his knees. He said to his servant: "Go up now and look toward the sea." He went up and looked and said: "There is nothing." Elijah said: "Go again seven times." The seventh time the servant said: "There arises a cloud out of the sea as small as the palm of a man's hand." Elijah said: "Go and say to Ahab: 'Harness your chariots and go down, that the rain may not hinder you.'"

In a short time the heavens grew black with clouds; there was wind and a great downpour. Ahab rode and arrived at Jezreel. The hand of the Lord was upon Elijah, so that he girded up

his loins and ran before Ahab to the entrance of Jezreel.

THE VISION OF MOUNT HOREB

AHAB TOLD Jezebel what Elijah had done, and how he had killed the prophets of Baal. Then Jezebel sent a messenger to Elijah, saying: "May the gods do so [to me] and more also if by this time tomorrow I do not make your life the same as the life of any one of them."

When Elijah saw this he fled for his life, and came to Beer-sheba, and left his servant there. He himself went a day's journey into the wilderness, and sat down under a broom tree, and prayed that he might die, saying: "It is enough. O Lord, take my life, for I am not better than my fathers." He lay down and slept under the broom tree.

Behold, an angel touched him and said: "Arise and eat." He looked and there was at his head a cake baked on hot stones and a flask of water. He ate and drank, and lay down again. The angel of the Lord returned a second time, and touched him and said: "Arise and eat because the journey is long." He arose, and he ate and drank and, with the strength of that food, he went for forty days and forty nights to Horeb, the Mount of God. He came there to a cave and lodged there.

הִנֵּה עָב קְטַנָּה כְּכַף אִישׁ עוֹלָה מִיָּם. וַיֹּאמֶר: עֲלֵה אֱמֹר אֶל אַחְאָב, אֱסֹר וָרֵד
וְלֹא יַעֲצָרְכָה הַגָּשֶׁם.

The word of the Lord came to him and when Elijah heard it he wrapped his face in his mantle and he went out and stood at the entrance of the cave. There came a voice to him: "What are you doing here, Elijah?" [8] And he said: "I have been zealous for the Lord because the Children of Israel have forsaken Thy covenant, Thine altars they have thrown down, they have slain Thy prophets with the sword and I, only I, am left and they seek to take away my life."

Then the Lord said: "Go outside, and stand upon the mountain before Me." A great and strong wind that rent mountains and broke rocks in pieces came before the Lord, but the Lord was not

---

[8] WHAT ARE YOU DOING HERE, ELIJAH? When Elijah hid in the cave at Mount Horeb and stood in the cleft of the rock he heard a still small voice saying, "God is compassionate, mild and considerate. He draws the people to Himself with bonds of love and soft speech. What are you doing here, Elijah?"

Elijah wrapped his face in his mantle and replied: "I have been zealous for the Lord. The Children of Israel have forsaken Your covenant. They have stopped circumcizing children. They have thrown down Your altars and they seek to take my life."

Then the Lord retorted: "You should have learned from Moses to be forbearing and compassionate. When the Children of Israel sinned with the golden calf, Moses prayed for their forgiveness. But you are angry and zealous. You say that the people of Israel do not keep the command of circumcision. Therefore do I decree that from now to eternity, My children shall put a chair for you at every circumcision feast and you shall come to sit in that chair and witness the B'rit for thousands of years."

But still Elijah did not desist, and then the Lord said: "You disparage the people of Israel. Go to Damascus and see where the people worship 365 idols, one for each day of the year, yet still do I make My rain to fall and dew to descend there. But you want Me to destroy My people. You are no longer fit to be My prophet and to dwell in the world. My people who are only human cannot contend with you. Go, anoint Elisha as your successor."

קַנֹּא קִנֵּאתִי לַיָי אֱלֹהֵי צְבָאוֹת כִּי עָזְבוּ בְרִיתְךָ בְּנֵי יִשְׂרָאֵל.

in the wind. After the wind followed an earthquake, but the Lord was not in the earthquake. After the earthquake a fire, but the Lord was not in the fire. After the fire a still small voice.

Then the Lord said to him: "Go back, take the desert road to Damascus, and when you arrive there anoint Hazael to be king over Aram, Jehu, the son of Nimshi, you shall anoint to be king over Israel, and Elisha, the son of Shaphat, you shall anoint to be prophet in your place. I will punish Israel, but I will spare all the knees that have not bowed to Baal, and every mouth that has not kissed him."

וְאַחַר הָרַעַשׁ אֵשׁ, לֹא בָאֵשׁ יְיָ. וְאַחַר הָאֵשׁ קוֹל דְּמָמָה דַקָּה.

24. I KINGS [19-22]

HE DEPARTED from there, and he found Elisha as he was plowing behind twelve yoke of oxen. Elijah came to him, and threw his mantle upon him. He left the oxen, and ran after Elijah, and said: "Let me kiss my father and mother, and then I will follow you."

Elijah said to him: "Go and return, for what have I done [1] to you?"

So Elisha returned and took a pair of oxen and slew them, and took their

---

[1] WHAT HAVE I DONE: The Rabbis disagreed about what Elijah meant. Some said Elijah was angry that Elisha should think of anything but his new calling. Others said that Elijah was pleased that Elisha should still remember, even at that climactic moment in his life, to observe the Lord's commandment to honor his father and his mother. The Rabbis interpreted Elijah's words to mean: "Go back

וַיַּעֲזֹב אֶת הַבָּקָר וַיָּרָץ אַחֲרֵי אֵלִיָּהוּ וַיֹּאמַר: אֶשְּׁקָה־נָּא לְאָבִי וּלְאִמִּי וְאֵלְכָה אַחֲרֶיךָ.

yoke to boil the flesh, and gave it to the people to eat. Then he arose, and went after Elijah and became his attendant.

THE VINEYARD OF NABOTH

NABOTH, THE JEZREELITE, had a vineyard adjoining the palace of Ahab. Ahab spoke to Naboth, saying: "Give me your vineyard, that I may have a garden of herbs, because it is near my house. I will give you for it a better vineyard, or if you prefer, I will give you its value in money."

Naboth said: "The Lord forbid that I should give you the inheritance of my fathers."

When Ahab heard it, he went into his house sullen and dejected, and lay down on his bed, turned his face to the wall, and refused to take food.

Jezebel, his wife, came to him, and said: "Why are you so dejected, that you refuse food?"

He said: "Because I said to Naboth, the Jezreelite: 'Give me your vineyard for money, or if you prefer, I will gladly give you another vineyard for it,' and he said: 'I will not give you my vineyard.'"

Jezebel said to him: "Is this the way you govern the kingdom of Israel? Arise, eat and set your mind at ease. I will give you the vineyard of Naboth."

JEZEBEL'S SCHEME

SHE WROTE letters in Ahab's name, sealed with his seal, and sent the letters to the elders and nobles who lived in Naboth's city. She wrote in the letters: "Proclaim a fast, and set Naboth at the head of the people, and set two men, base fellows, against him and let them bear witness, saying: 'You have cursed God and the king.' Then take him out, and stone him to death."

The elders and nobles of Naboth's city did as Jezebel had written in the letters. They proclaimed a fast, and set Naboth at the head of the people. Two base fellows came and sat before him, and bore witness against Naboth in the presence of the people, saying: "Naboth cursed God and the king."

So they took him outside the city, and stoned him to death. Then they sent to Jezebel, saying: "Naboth is stoned and is dead." Jezebel said to Ahab: "Arise, and take possession of the vineyard of Naboth, who refused to give it to you for money, for Naboth is not alive but dead."

---

to your parents, but remember what I have done to you by dedicating your life to God, and return."

אַתָּה עַתָּה תַּעֲשֶׂה מְלוּכָה עַל יִשְׂרָאֵל? קוּם אֱכָל לֶחֶם וְיִיטַב לִבֶּךָ. אֲנִי אֶתֵּן לְךָ אֶת כֶּרֶם נָבוֹת.

When Ahab heard that Naboth was dead, he went to the vineyard to take possession of it.

ELIJAH PRONOUNCES
GOD'S JUDGMENT

THEN THE word of the Lord came to Elijah, saying: "Arise, and go down to meet Ahab, king of Israel, who is now in the vineyard of Naboth, where he has gone down to possess it. You shall say to him: 'Have you slain and also taken possession?' Thus said the Lord: In the place where the dogs licked the blood of Naboth, shall dogs lick your blood."

And Ahab said to Elijah: "Have you found me, O my enemy?" And he answered: "I found you, because you have sold yourself to do that which is evil in the eyes of the Lord. Therefore, I will bring evil upon you. I will make your house like the house of Jeroboam for making Israel sin. And the dogs shall eat Jezebel in the valley of Jezreel."

When Ahab heard these words, he tore his garments and put on a sackcloth and fasted. He slept in sackcloth and walked barefoot. The word of the Lord came to Elijah, saying: "Have you seen that Ahab has humbled himself before Me? Because of that, I will not bring the evil in his days but in his son's days."

THE DEATH OF AHAB

THE KING of Israel, and Jehoshaphat, king of Judah, went up to Ramoth-gilead: The king of Israel said to Jehoshaphat: "I will disguise myself and go into battle, but you put on your own robes." So the king of Israel disguised himself before he went into battle. Now an archer drew his bow at random, and shot the king of Israel between the breast plate and the lower part of the armor.

But the battle grew fiercer that day, so the king held himself upright in his chariot facing the Arameans until evening. The blood from the wound ran out into the bottom of the chariot. He said to the driver of his chariot: "Wheel about and take me out of the battle, for I am badly wounded." In the evening he died. [2] About sunset the cry passed throughout the army: "Every man to his city, every man to his land [for the king is dead]!"

So the king died and was brought to Samaria, and they buried him there. When they washed the chariot by the

---

ᴥ᷄ [2] IN THE EVENING HE DIED: Ahab repented after his crime against Naboth. He fasted and prayed morning and night; and the Lord

וְדִבַּרְתָּ אֵלָיו לֵאמֹר: כֹּה אָמַר יְיָ, הֲרָצַחְתָּ וְגַם יָרָשְׁתָּ?

pool of Samaria, the dogs licked his blood, according to the word of the Lord which He spoke.

The rest of the acts of Ahab, and all that he did, and the ivory palace which he built, and all the cities which he built, all is written in the Book of Chronicles of the king of Israel. Ahab slept with his fathers, and his son Ahaziah reigned in his stead.

---

forgave him. When he was mortally wounded in battle, his blood ran out onto the floor of his chariot. Then Ahab exerted all his strength and courage to remain standing in order not to frighten and panic his soldiers.

וַיִּשְׁכַּב אַחְאָב עִם אֲבוֹתָיו, וַיִּמְלֹךְ אֲחַזְיָהוּ בְנוֹ תַּחְתָּיו.

25. II KINGS [2–7]

ELIJAH ASCENDS TO HEAVEN

IT WAS before the Lord took up Elijah by whirlwind into heaven. Elijah and Elisha went on their way from Gilgal. Elijah said to Elisha: "I pray you, remain here, for the Lord has sent me to Beth-el." Elisha answered: "As the Lord lives, and as your soul lives, I will not leave you." So they went down to Beth-el.

Then the sons of the prophets [1] who were in Beth-el came out to Elisha, and said: "Do you know that the Lord will take your master away from you today?" He said: "Yes, I know, only hold your peace."

Elijah said again to Elisha: "Remain here, I pray you, for the Lord has sent

---

[1] THE SONS OF THE PROPHETS: Why were the followers of the prophets called "the sons of the prophets"? Our Sages answer that the disciples are called sons and the teachers called fathers, because a teacher gives spiritual life to his disciples as a father gives physical life to his sons.

וַיֹּאמֶר אֱלִישָׁע: חַי יְיָ וְחֵי נַפְשְׁךָ אִם אֶעֶזְבֶךָ.

me to Jericho." And he said: "As the Lord lives and as your soul lives, I will not leave you." So they entered Jericho. Elijah said again to Elisha: "Remain here, I beg you, for the Lord has sent me to the Jordan." Elisha said: "As the Lord lives, I will not leave you." So the two of them went on.

Now fifty men of the followers of the prophets went and stood opposite them at a distance, while they too stood by the Jordan. Elijah took his mantle, rolled it up, and struck the waters of the Jordan and they divided on either side, and they crossed on dry ground. And it was when they crossed over, Elijah said to Elisha: "Ask what I shall do for you, before I am taken from you."

Elisha said: "Let there be a double portion of your spirit [2] upon me." He answered: "You have asked a hard thing. If you see me as I am being taken away [3] from you, it shall be so with you, but if not, it shall not be so."

---

[2] DOUBLE PORTION OF YOUR SPIRIT: Rabbi Yosé said: "Every man is jealous of his friends, except his sons and his disciples." A man is generally jealous of his reputation and achievement and often envious of friends or even relatives who advance higher and more swiftly than he does. But a teacher does not envy his student when the student outdoes the teacher. Nor does a father feel envy when his son accomplishes more than he has. Both teacher and father rejoice in their pupils' and sons' achievements.

When the servant came to David to congratulate him on Solomon's assumption of the throne, he said to the king: "Let God make Solomon's name better than your name and his throne greater than your throne" (I Kings 1:47). And David did not resent it but blessed the Lord. And when Elisha asked of Elijah, "Let a double portion of your spirit be on me," Elijah was not angry; he wished only for Elisha's desire to be fulfilled.

[3] IF YOU SEE ME TAKEN AWAY: No man can endow another with the gift of prophecy. Elijah said to Elisha, if you have the merit, if God has granted you the inner sight to see me taken from you, then you may become what you ask. But if you do not see me taken from you, then God has not granted you the gift of prophecy and then I cannot grant you your wish.

בְּכָל אָדָם מִתְקַנֵּא, חוּץ מִבְּנוֹ וְתַלְמִידוֹ.

As they walked and talked, [4] a chariot of fire and horses of fire came between them, and Elijah went up by a whirlwind into heaven.

Elisha saw it and cried out: "My father, my father! The chariots of Israel and its horsemen." And he saw him no more. Then he took hold of his clothes and rent them into two pieces. He took up the mantle of Elijah that had fallen from him, and returned.

The followers of the prophets who were at Jericho saw him and said: "The spirit of Elijah is upon Elisha." They came to meet him and bowed before him to the earth and said: "There are with your servants fifty stalwart men, let them go, we beg you, in search of your master."

He said: "Do not send."

But they pressed him [5] until he could not resist their request any longer, so he said: "Send." They sent the fifty men, and they searched for three days and did not find him. They returned to him while he stayed in Jericho.

THE FLASK OF OIL

THE WIFE of one of the followers of the prophets cried out [6] to Elisha: "Your servant, my husband, is dead, and you

⋘ [4] AND TALKED: What did they talk about? Elisha knew that Elijah was about to leave this world, and so he kept on asking questions concerning the Torah, and Elijah answered him. God had sent His angels with the chariot to remove Elijah but the angels would not interrupt the prophets' discussion of Torah. Finally, the angels removed the cloud that hid the chariot so that both Elijah and Elisha could see it—and the chariot's brightness filled the sky. The two prophets ceased their talk of Torah and, thunderstruck, gazed up at the heavens. Then the chariot swooped low and Elijah disappeared.

⋘ [5] THEY PRESSED HIM: Why did Elisha allow the young men to roam the wilderness for three days when he knew they would find nothing? When Elisha returned, the sons of the prophets crowded around him. They heard the story of the chariot and feared that Elijah might have fallen from it, or been put down in some remote and inaccessible place. That is why they asked if they might go out to seek him. At first Elisha refused, for he knew that Elijah had been transported, but when he realized that the young men sought

וֶאֱלִישָׁע רוֹאֶה וְהוּא מְצַעֵק: אָבִי אָבִי, רֶכֶב יִשְׂרָאֵל וּפָרָשָׁיו.

know that your servant feared the Lord. Now the creditor has come to take away my two children as bondsmen."

Elisha said to her: "What have you in the house?" She said: "Only a small flask of oil." [7] He said to her: "Go borrow of your neighbor's empty vessels; borrow as many as you can, then shut yourself and your sons in the house, and pour the oil in the vessels."

She went from him, and she shut herself and her sons in the house. They brought the vessels to her and she poured. As soon as the vessels were full, she said to her son: "Bring me another." He said to her: "There is not another empty vessel." Then the oil stopped.

She came and told the man of God. He said to her: "Go, sell the oil, and pay your debt and you and your sons can live on what is left." [8]

THE SHUNAMMITE'S SON

ONE DAY Elisha went to Shunem, and

---

the older prophet out of love and zeal, and that they might suspect him of coveting his teacher's place, he permitted them to go.

◦§ [6] THE WIDOW WHO CRIED OUT: According to tradition the widow who cried out to Elisha about the great wrong done her was the wife of Obadiah, the man who had saved a hundred prophets from the wrath of Jezebel (I Kings 18:13). Obadiah hid the prophets in caves, fed them, and soon his money was gone because food and drink were very expensive. Then he had to borrow money from Jehoram, heir to the throne, at usurer's rates, and was soon so deeply in debt that he could not repay his debts before he died. Jehoram then wanted to take Obadiah's two children as slaves in forfeit for their father's debt.

◦§ [7] A SMALL FLASK OF OIL: Why did Elisha ask the widow whether she had anything in the house? And only after she told him that she had a flask of oil did Elisha say the blessing of the Lord would enter the oil, that the oil would then increase and fill all her vessels? Our Sages explain that no blessing from above can descend on a void. What is below and human must be prepared to receive and use the miracle from above.

לְכִי מִכְרִי אֶת הַשֶּׁמֶן וְשַׁלְּמִי אֶת נִשְׁיֵךְ, וְאַתְּ וּבָנַיִךְ תִּחְיִי בַּנּוֹתָר.

there was a great lady who persuaded him to partake of food. So it was afterward that as often as he passed there, he would turn to her to eat food. She said to her husband: "I see that this man, who often passes by us, is a holy man of God. Let us build a little chamber for him on the roof, and let us put there a bed, a table, a chair and a lamp, so that whenever he comes to us he can turn there."

One day he came there and went into the chamber and rested. He said to Gehazi, his servant: "Call this Shunammite woman." He called her, and she stood before him. He said to Gehazi: "Say to her: 'You have troubled yourself so much for our comfort, what is to be done for you? Is it to speak for you to the king, or to the commander of the army?'" She said: "I dwell among my own people." [9]

He said to Gehazi: "What then is to be done for her?" Gehazi said: "She has no son, and her husband is old." Elisha said: "Call her back." He called her, and she stood in the doorway. Elisha said: "At this time next year you shall embrace a son." She said: "No, my lord, man of God, do not deceive your servant." But the next year the woman gave birth to a son, at the time that Elisha had said.

When the child was grown, he went

◦§ [8] ON WHAT IS LEFT: When the woman went to sell her oil she found that the price had risen greatly and she had enough money to live on. But the widow asked could she hold the oil even longer because the price was rising. No, the prophet said, go and sell the oil now. You will have enough to pay your husband's debts and afterward to live for the rest of your life. The miracle was performed to help you and your sons but not to make you rich by speculation.

◦§ [9] I DWELL AMONG MY OWN PEOPLE: When Elisha asked the Shunammite woman what he could do for her, whether he might speak to the king, or the commander of the army for her, she replied: "I dwell among my people." Rabbi Baḥya ibn Pakuda said that the Shunammite meant to say, "If I am wronged in any way, I have my own people who will protect me and look after my interests; and, if necessary, who will appeal to the proper authorities." Therefore, it is written (Deuteronomy 10:19): "You shall love the stranger."

נַעֲשֶׂה־נָּא עֲלִיַּת קִיר קְטַנָּה וְנָשִׂים לוֹ שָׁם מִטָּה וְשֻׁלְחָן וְכִסֵּא וּמְנוֹרָה.

out one day to his father among the reapers. He said to his father: "My head, my head." The father said to his servant: "Carry him to his mother." When he was brought to his mother, the boy sat in her lap till noon and he died. She ascended and laid him on the bed of the man of God, closed the door, and went out.

Then she called her husband, and said: "Send me one of the servants and one of the donkeys, that I may hasten to the man of God, and return." He said to her: "Why do you go to him today? It is neither new moon nor Sabbath. [Is all well?]" She said: "It shall be well."

Then she saddled the donkey, and said to her servant: "Drive fast, do not slacken my pace unless I tell you." She went and came to the man of God at Mount Carmel.

When the man of God saw her at a distance, he said to Gehazi: "Look, there is the Shunammite woman. Run to meet her, and ask: 'Is all well with you? With your husband? With the child?'" She answered: "All is well," but when she came to the man of God at the mountain of Carmel, she grasped his feet. When Gehazi tried to push her away, Elisha said: "Let her alone, for her soul is bitter within her and the Lord has hidden it from me and has not told me."

Then she cried: "Did I ask a son of my lord? Did not I say: 'Do not deceive me'?"

Elisha said to Gehazi: "Make haste, take my staff in your hand and go! If you meet any man do not salute him. If any man salutes you answer him not, [10] and lay my staff on the face of the child." But the mother of the child said: "As the Lord lives, I will not leave you." So he arose, and followed her.

Now Gehazi had gone before them

---

 [10] ANSWER HIM NOT: Gehazi was proud of serving Elisha and downcast only in that he was permitted to do so little for his master. When he was sent with the staff, he set out hurriedly. Now he thought he was to perform a miracle on his own, but when people recognized him and Elisha's staff, and asked him where he was going, Gehazi scoffed and laughed and told them that he was off to perform a miracle. The people followed him and crowded into the room where the boy lay. They watched as Gehazi placed the staff on the boy's body—but nothing happened. His skepticism made him unworthy of being an agent through whom miracles are per-

הַרְפֵּה לָהּ כִּי נַפְשָׁהּ מָרָה לָהּ וַיָי הֶעְלִים מִמֶּנִּי וְלֹא הִגִּיד לִי.

and laid the staff on the face of the child. There was neither a sound nor hearing. He returned to meet them, and told him: "The child has not awakened."

Elisha came to the house. The boy was lying dead on his bed. He went in the chamber, closed the door upon the two of them, and prayed to the Lord. Then he lay upon the child, put his mouth to his mouth, his eyes upon his eyes and his hands upon his hands, and stretched himself upon him; the flesh of the child became warm. Then he rose and paced back and forth in the house. Then he went up and stretched himself upon the child, and the boy sneezed seven times, and he opened his eyes.

He called Gehazi and said: "Call the Shunammite." When she came to him, he said: "Take up your son." [11] She fell to his feet, and bowed herself to the ground, took up her son, and went out.

ELISHA CURES LEPROSY

NAAMAN, [12] COMMANDER of the king of Aram's army, was highly esteemed by his master because through him the Lord had given victory to Aram. He was

formed. Gehazi failed because he doubted Elisha's power to revive the child. Then Elisha came, emptied the room of the intruders, and prayed for the boy.

&⁊ [11] TAKE UP YOUR SON: Our Sages ask: "Why did neither Elijah nor Elisha revive their own parents after they died?" The Rabbis explained that when one performed a miracle he endangered his own life because the miracle worker wearies God by making Him change the laws of nature. So the miracle worker was in danger of dying before his time but not when the miracle is performed for one who merited it. The woman of Zarephath had endangered her life to feed Elijah. The Shunammite had served and fed Elisha unselfishly and without thought of reward. Both were worthy and merited the prophets' miracles.

&⁊ [12] NAAMAN: In the eyes of the king of Aram, Naaman was a great and important man because it was Naaman, the archer, who in the battle of Gilead drew the bow and killed Ahab, king of Israel.

וַיַּעַל וַיִּגְהַר עָלָיו, וַיְזוֹרֵר הַנַּעַר עַד שֶׁבַע פְּעָמִים וַיִּפְקַח הַנַּעַר אֶת עֵינָיו.

a valiant man, but a leper. The Arameans had gone out on a marauding expedition and carried off a little girl from the Land of Israel. She became a servant to the wife of Naaman. She said to her mistress: "Would that my master saw the prophet who is now in Samaria, then he would cure him of his leprosy." When Naaman heard it he went and told it to the king of Aram. The king said: "Go now and I will send with you a letter to the king of Israel."

Naaman departed and took with him ten talents of silver, six thousand pieces of gold and ten festal robes. He brought the letter to the king of Israel and the letter said: "Now, when this letter reaches you, be informed that I have sent Naaman, my servant, to you, that you may cure him of his leprosy."

When the king of Israel read the letter he rent his garments and cried out: "Am I a god to kill and make alive, that this man sends me a letter to cure a man of leprosy? Clearly he seeks an occasion to make war against me."

When Elisha, the man of God, heard that the king of Israel had rent his clothes he sent to the king, saying: "Why have you rent your clothes? Let him come to me and he shall know that there is a prophet in Israel." So Naaman came with his horses and chariots and stood at the door of Elisha's house.

Elisha sent a messenger to him, saying: "Go and wash in the Jordan seven times and your flesh will be well and clean."

Naaman was enraged and left. He said: "I thought he would come out to me, stand and call on the Name of the Lord his God, wave his hand over the leprous place and so cure the leprosy. Are not the rivers of Damascus better than all the waters of Israel? Could I not wash in them and be clean?" So he turned and went away in a rage.

Then his servants went up to him and said: "Master, if the prophet had demanded of you some great thing, would you not have done it? Why not then when he says to you: 'Wash and be clean.'" Then Naaman went down and dipped himself seven times in the Jordan as the man of God told him to do and his flesh became once more like the flesh of a little child.

He returned to the man of God, with all his company, and stood before him and said: "Now I know that there is no God in all the earth, but in Israel. Therefore, I beg you, accept a present from your servant." Elisha said: "As the Lord lives, I will take nothing." Naaman urged him but he refused. Then Naaman said: "If not, at least let there be given to your servant two mules' loads of earth. [13] For henceforth your servant will offer neither burnt-offering,

לָמָּה קָרַעְתָּ בְּגָדֶיךָ? יָבוֹא נָא אֵלַי וְיֵדַע כִּי יֵשׁ נָבִיא בְּיִשְׂרָאֵל.

nor any sacrifice to any other gods but to the Lord. Only in this matter may the Lord pardon your servant: When my master, the king, goes into the house of Rimmon to worship there, he will be leaning on my arm, and I also will have to bow in the house of Rimmon when he bows. Then may the Lord pardon your servant in this matter." And Elisha said: "Go in peace."

FAMINE IN THE BESIEGED SAMARIA

AND IT came to pass that Ben-hadad, king of Aram, assembled all his army, and besieged Samaria. The famine was so severe in the city that a donkey's head was sold for eighty shekels of silver. As the king of Israel was passing by upon the wall a woman cried out: "Help, my lord, O king!" He said: "If the Lord did not help you, how can I help from the threshing floor or the wine press? But what is your trouble?"

The woman said: "This woman said to me: 'Give your son that we may eat him today, and we will eat my son tomorrow.' So we cooked my son and ate him. On the next day I said to her:

'Give your son that we may eat him,' but she has hidden her son." When the king heard the words of the woman, he rent his clothes and the people saw that he wore sackcloth next to his skin.

Now Elisha was sitting in his house, with the elders sitting beside him. While he was talking with them, the king of Israel came down to him, and said: "See, this evil is from the Lord. Why should I hope for the Lord any longer?"

Elisha said: "Hear you the word of the Lord. Thus said the Lord: 'Tomorrow about this time shall a measure of fine flour be sold for a shekel, and two measures of barley for a shekel, at the gate of Samaria.'" Then the captain, upon whose hand the king leaned, answered the man of God: "Even if the Lord would make windows in the heavens, could this thing be?" .

Elisha said: "You yourself shall see it with your own eyes, but you shall not eat of it."

THE PLENTY AFTER THE FAMINE

NOW THERE were four lepers at the entrance of the gate, and they said one

---

ɜ૭ [13] TWO LOADS OF EARTH: When the Children of Israel live according to the laws of their Father in heaven, then no one would dare to take even a load of earth from their land without permission.

וַיֹּאמֶר: הִנֵּה יְיָ עוֹשֶׂה אֲרֻבּוֹת בַּשָּׁמַיִם, הֲיִהְיֶה הַדָּבָר הַזֶּה? וַיֹּאמֶר: הִנְּכָה רוֹאֶה בְּעֵינֶיךָ וּמִשָּׁם לֹא תֹאכֵל.

to another: "If we enter the city, the famine is in the city, and we shall die there, and if we remain here, we die also. Therefore let us desert to the camp of the Arameans. If they let us alive, we shall live; if they kill us, we shall but die."

So at twilight they set out to go to the camp of the Arameans. When they came to the edge of the camp, there was no man there; for the Lord had caused the army of the Arameans to hear a noise of chariots, of horses, and of a great army. So they said one to another: "The king of Israel has hired the kings of the Hittites and the kings of Egypt to come against us." So they arose and fled in the twilight, and abandoned their tents, their horses, their donkeys, everything was left as it was, and they fled for their lives.

When the lepers came to the outermost part of the camp they entered into a tent, ate, drank and carried away silver, gold, and raiment, and went and hid it. They returned and entered another tent, and carried away what was there, and went and hid it.

Then they said to one another: "We are not doing right. This is a day of good news, but we are keeping still. Let us go and inform the house of the king." They came and called to the gatekeepers of the city, and said: "We came to the camp of the Arameans, but there was no one there; no sound of man, but the horses tied, the donkey tied and the tents were as they have been."

The gatekeepers called out, and informed the house of the king within. The king arose in the night, and said to his officers: "Let me tell you what the Arameans have done. They know that we are hungry. Therefore they have gone from the camp and hid themselves in the field, thinking: 'When they come out of the city we shall take them alive, and so get into the city.'"

One of the officers answered: "Send some men with the five of the horses that are left. If they die, they will be like all the multitude of Israel that perish here. Let us send and see."

They took two chariots with horses, and the king sent them after the army of the Arameans, and said: "Go and see."

They followed them to the Jordan and all the way was full of garments and vessels, which the Arameans had thrown away in their haste. The messengers returned, and told the king.

The people went out and plundered the camp of the Arameans. So a measure of fine flour was sold for a shekel and two measures of barley for a shekel, according to the word of the Lord! The king appointed the captain upon whose hand he leaned to guard the gate, but

וַיְהִי סְאָה סֹלֶת בְּשֶׁקֶל וְסָאתַיִם שְׂעוֹרִים בְּשֶׁקֶל, כִּדְבַר יְיָ.

in the rush the people trampled him to death. It happened as the man of God had spoken: "Tomorrow about this time shall a measure of fine flour be sold for a shekel and two measures of barley for a shekel at the gate of Samaria." When the captain said: "Even if the Lord Him- self would make windows in the heavens, could this be?" And the man of God said: "You yourself shall see it with your own eyes, but you shall not eat it." So it happened to him, for the people tram- pled upon him in the gate so that he died.

וַיְהִי לוֹ כֵּן, וַיִּרְמְסוּ אֹתוֹ הָעָם בַּשַּׁעַר וַיָּמֹת.

26. II KINGS [8–15]

ELISHA AND THE KING OF ARAM

ELISHA CAME to Damascus [1] and Benhadad, the king of Aram, was sick. When he was told: "The man of God has come here," the king said to Hazael: "Take a gift in your hand and go to meet the man of God and through him inquire of the Lord whether I shall recover from this illness."

---

[1] ELISHA CAME TO DAMASCUS: Our Sages say that Gehazi came to Damascus to demand payment from Naaman for the suffering that had befallen him. Elisha had transferred Naaman's leprosy to Gehazi. Elisha came to Damascus to persuade Gehazi to repent, but Gehazi said that the Lord does not accept the repentance of those who sin and cause many others to sin. Elisha disagreed with him, but Gehazi persisted.

What were the other sins of Gehazi? Our Sages tell us that he made a magnet which lifted Jeroboam's idols and suspended them

קַח בְּיָדְךָ מִנְחָה וְלֵךְ לִקְרַאת אִישׁ הָאֱלֹהִים, וְדָרַשְׁתָּ אֶת יְיָ מֵאוֹתוֹ לֵאמֹר: הַאֶחְיֶה מֵחֳלִי זֶה?

So Hazael took a gift and went to meet him. When he came to Elisha he stood before him and said: "Your son Ben-hadad, the king of Aram, has sent me to ask you whether he will recover from his illness." Elisha said to him: "Go and say to him: 'You shall surely recover,' but the Lord has told me that he will certainly die." Hazael stared at Elisha a long time, then the man of God wept. [2] Hazael said: "Why does my lord weep?" And Elisha answered: "Because I know the cruelties which you will inflict on the Children of Israel; their fortresses you will set on fire, their young men you will put to the sword, their little children you will dash to pieces and you will rip their unborn children from their women's wombs." Hazael said: "Your servant is but a dog,

how can he achieve this great thing?" Elisha said: "The Lord has shown me that you are to be king of Aram."

When Hazael returned to his master, Ben-hadad said to him: "What did Elisha say to you?" Hazael answered: "He said to me that you would surely recover." But on the next day Hazael took the bathcloth, dipped it in water and spread it over the king's face, so that he died. And Hazael became king in his stead.

CONSPIRACY AGAINST AHAB'S HOUSE

ELISHA, THE PROPHET, called one of the sons of the prophets [3] and said: "Gird up your loins, and take this flask of oil in your hand, and go to Ramoth-gilead. When you come there look for Jehu,

---

between heaven and earth so that the people were persuaded that the idols had supernatural powers.

⤐ [2] THE MAN OF GOD WEPT: Elisha wept when he saw that Hazael would become king. He foresaw the cruelties Hazael would commit and the horrors shocked him. But Hazael did not recoil from the atrocities or from the thought that he would commit them. He considered them great deeds, the heroic bouts of war.

⤐ [3] ONE OF THE SONS OF THE PROPHETS: The young man was said to be the prophet Jonah, the son of Amittai, Elisha's disciple. As Elisha had served Elijah, so had Jonah served Elisha until he was ready for prophecy himself.

לֵךְ אֱמָר לוֹ: חָיֹה תִחְיֶה, וְהִרְאַנִי יְיָ כִּי מוֹת יָמוּת.

the son of Nimshi, and bring him to an inner chamber. Then take the flask of oil, pour it on his head, and say: 'Thus said the Lord: I have anointed you king over Israel.' Then open the door and flee, and do not tarry."

The young man went to Ramoth-gilead, and when he came there, the officers of the army were sitting together. He said: "I have a word for you, O captain." Jehu said: "For which one of us?" And he said: "For you, commander."

Jehu arose and went in the house. [The young man] poured the oil on his head, and said: "Thus said the Lord, the God of Israel: 'I have anointed you king over the people of the Lord, over Israel. You shall smite the house of Ahab, your master, to avenge the blood of My servants, the prophets.'" Then he opened the door and fled.

Jehu came out to the officers of his master, and one said to him: "Is all well? Why did this madman come to you?" He answered: "You know how a man like that talks." They said: "Tell us what he said."

He answered: "He said: 'Thus said the Lord: I have anointed you king of Israel.'"

Then every man of them quickly took his garment and put it under Jehu on the top of the stairs, blew the horn and cried: "Jehu has become king!"

Jehu said: "If this is your will, then see that none escapes out of the city to tell it in Jezreel." He rode his chariot to Jezreel, where Joram, king of Israel, was recuperating from his wounds in the war with Hazael, king of Aram. Ahaziah, king of Judah, the son of Athaliah, the daughter of Ahab and Jezebel, was also there, because he had come down to see Joram.

Now the watchman who stood on the tower in Jezreel caught sight of the dust cloud raised by Jehu's company as it came. He called out: "I see a company!"

King Joram said: "Take a horseman, and send him to meet them and let him say: 'Is it in peace?'" So the rider on the horse went and met them, and said: "Thus said the king: 'Is it in peace?'"

Jehu said: "What have you to do with peace? Turn behind me and follow." The watchman reported: "The messenger came to them, but he does not return. However, the driving is like the driving of Jehu, for he drives like a madman." King Joram said: "Harness my chariot." As soon as they harnessed the chariot, Joram, king of Israel, and Ahaziah, king of Judah, set out each in his chariot, and they drove to meet Jehu. They reached him in the field of Naboth, the Jezreelite. And it came to pass, when Joram saw Jehu, that he said: "Is it peace, Jehu?" And he answered: "How can there be peace so long as the harlotries of your mother Jezebel and her

כֹּה אָמַר יְיָ אֱלֹהֵי יִשְׂרָאֵל: מְשַׁחְתִּיךָ לְמֶלֶךְ אֶל עַם יְיָ, אֶל יִשְׂרָאֵל.

witchcrafts are so great?" And Joram turned and fled, and said to Ahaziah: "There is treachery, O Ahaziah." And Jehu drew his bow with all his strength, and smote Joram between his arms, and the arrow went out of his heart, and he sank down in his chariot. Then [Jehu] said to Bidkar, his captain: "Remember how when you and I were riding side by side after Ahab, his father, the Lord pronounced this prophecy against him: 'Surely I saw yesterday the blood of Naboth and the blood of his sons, [4] and I will punish you in the same field.' Now, go, cast him into the same plot of ground."

Ahaziah, king of Judah, fled by the way of the garden house. Jehu said: "Follow him, and kill him also in the chariot." [And they smote him.] He fled to Megiddo, and died there.

THE EXECUTION OF JEZEBEL

JEHU CAME to Jezreel. As soon as Jezebel learned of it, she painted her eyelashes, adorned her head, and looked out of the window. When Jehu came in the gate, she said: "Is it all well with you, traitor, your master's murderer?" He raised his eyes to the window, and called out: "Who is on my side? Who?" Two or three officers looked out to him. He said to them: "Throw her down!" They threw her down and some of her blood spattered on the wall, and the horses trampled her down.

He went in and ate and drank, and then said: "Look after this cursed woman, and bury her, for she is a king's daughter." They went to bury her, but they found no more than the skull, the feet, and the palms of her hands. [5] They

---

⋑ [4] BLOOD OF HIS SONS: Why did Jehu speak of Naboth's sons dying with him? Scripture had not mentioned them before as having been stoned with their father. The Rabbis give two explanations: first, that although it was against Jewish law, when Naboth was stoned, his family was killed with him, as Jezebel had ordered, so that none might thereafter claim the vineyard; second, the blood refers to the blood of the sons of Naboth who would have been born had Naboth been spared so that, as in the case of Abel, their unborn blood had to be avenged.

⋑ [5] SKULL AND FEET: When Jehu heard that the dogs had not eaten some parts of Jezebel's body, he asked the elders of Samaria why.

וַיָּבֹא וַיֹּאכַל וַיֵּשְׁתְּ וַיֹּאמֶר: פִּקְדוּ־נָא אֶת הָאֲרוּרָה הַזֹּאת וְקִבְרוּהָ, כִּי בַת־מֶלֶךְ הִיא.

returned and told him. He said: "This is what the Lord spoke to Elijah, saying: 'In the field of Jezreel shall the dogs eat the flesh of Jezebel!'" [And they buried her.]

JEHOASH

JEHOASH WAS seven years old [6] when he became king, and he reigned forty years in Jerusalem. Jehoash did what was right in the eyes of the Lord [7] all the days of Jehoiada, the priest. But Jehoiada became old and he died. After the death of Jehoiada, the princes of Judah came to the king and prostrated themselves before him and persuaded him to forsake the ways of the Lord. The king listened to them. They forsook the way of the Lord, the God of

---

They told him that Jezebel had not been all evil. If a young couple passed on their way to be married, she would clap her hands and dance and sing before them. And if a body was brought out to be buried, she would wring her hands, bow her head and walk after the bier lamenting. Because her hands and feet and head displayed sorrow toward her fellow human beings or rejoiced with them, the dogs had mercy on those organs and did not devour them.

⋙ [6] JEHOASH WAS SEVEN YEARS OLD: Jehosheba had hidden Jehoash for six years. While Athaliah was actively seeking to kill the boy, the boy was hidden in the one place she would not look, the Holy of Holies in the Temple.

⋙ [7] RIGHT IN THE EYES OF THE LORD: One of our Sages declares that the people and the young king Jehoash did "what was right in the eyes of the Lord" only because they blindly followed the leadership of the High Priest Jehoiada. Theirs was only a mechanical conformity and repentance; they had not truly returned to the Lord. As soon as Jehoiada died, the people went back to their old sinful ways. They even deified the king. His followers came and said to Jehoash: "Surely you are a god. If you were not a god, how could you be hidden for six years in the innermost part of the Sanctuary and live?" Jehoash agreed with them and declared himself a god.

דְּבַר יְיָ הוּא אֲשֶׁר דִּבֶּר בְּיַד עַבְדּוֹ אֵלִיָּהוּ הַתִּשְׁבִּי לֵאמֹר: בְּחֵלֶק יִזְרְעֶאל יֹאכְלוּ הַכְּלָבִים אֶת בְּשַׂר אִיזָבֶל.

their fathers, and served the Asherim and the idols. Wrath fell upon Judah and Jerusalem for their guilt.

Then the spirit of God clothed Zechariah, the son of Jehoiada, the priest, and he stood above the people, and said: "Thus said God: 'Why do you transgress the commandments of the Lord?' Because you have forsaken the Lord, He has also forsaken you."

But they conspired against him, and stoned him with stones at the command of the king in the court of the house of the Lord. Before he died, he said: "May the Lord see and require an account."

A year later the army of Aram came up against Judah and Jerusalem. The army of the Arameans was a small company of men, but the Lord delivered the great army into their hand because they had forsaken the Lord, the God of their fathers. Then the servants of Jehoash conspired against him, for the blood of the sons of Jehoiada, and killed him on his bed. They buried him in the City of David, but not in the tombs of the king. Amaziah, his son, reigned in his stead.

When the kingdom was firmly established in the hands of Amaziah, he killed the servants who murdered his father. But the children of the murderers he did not put to death, according to which is written in the Torah in the book of Moses: "The fathers shall not be put to death for the children, neither shall the children be put to death for the fathers; only for his own sin shall anyone be put to death."

CONFUSION AND DISORDER

JEHOASH SLEPT with his fathers, and was buried in Samaria with the kings of Israel, and his son Jeroboam reigned in his place. He reigned in Samaria forty-one years. He restored the borders of Israel from the entrance of Hamath to the sea of Arabah, according to the word of the Lord, the God of Israel, which He spoke by the prophet Jonah, the son of Amittai, for the Lord saw the bitter affliction of Israel, so He saved them by the hand of Jeroboam.

Jeroboam slept with his fathers and Zechariah, his son, reigned in his place. Zechariah did evil in the eyes of the Lord. He reigned in Samaria six months. Shallum, the son of Jabesh, conspired against him and killed him, and reigned

---

Chronicles records (II 24:18), "And they forsook the house of the Lord, the God of their fathers . . .; and wrath came upon Judah and Jerusalem for their guilt."

לֹא יָמוּתוּ אָבוֹת עַל בָּנִים וּבָנִים לֹא יָמוּתוּ עַל אָבוֹת, כִּי אִישׁ בְּחֶטְאוֹ יָמוּתוּ.

in his place. Shallum reigned one month in Samaria. Then Menahem, the son of Gadi, came from Tirzah, and killed Shallum and reigned in his place. [8] He was king over Israel for ten years. He did evil in the sight of the Lord all his days.

Pul, the king of Assyria, invaded the land, and Menahem gave Pul a thousand talents of silver, that he might help him to establish the kingdom under his rule. And Menahem seized the money from the men of wealth, of each fifty shekels of silver, to give to the king of Assyria. The king of Assyria withdrew from the land.

Menahem slept with his fathers, and Pekahiah, his son, became king in his place. He also did evil in the eyes of the Lord, and Pekah, one of his captains, conspired against him, and smote him in Samaria and reigned in his place.

---

[8] REIGNED IN HIS PLACE: Our Rabbis state that there was no legitimate king after Zechariah, son of Jeroboam. For more than forty years one usurper after another reigned and all seized the throne by treachery and assassination. One of the Sages asked: "Did not Jehu, grandfather of Jeroboam, also ascend to the throne by treachery and assassination? He killed his master, King Joram, the son of Ahab." The other Sages answered: "Jehu's was a revolt against injustice and idolatry. Jehu was anointed by one of Elisha's disciples so that the revolt was blessed by the prophets. But Shallum and all who followed him killed for their own benefit and gain; therefore, none of them can be considered legitimate rulers."

וַיַּעַשׂ הָרַע בְּעֵינֵי יְיָ ... כָּל יָמָיו.

27. II KINGS [15–20]

WAR WITH JUDAH

IN THE DAYS of Pekah, king of Israel, came Tiglath-pileser, king of Assyria, and captured many cities in Israel, and carried them captive to Assyria. Ahaz reigned sixteen years in Jerusalem, he did not that which was right in the eyes of the Lord. But he walked in the ways of the kings of Israel, and also made molten images for the Baalim. He burnt his children in the valley of Ben-Hinnom in the abominations of the heathen. And the Lord delivered him into the hands of the king of Aram who carried away a great multitude as captives and brought them to Damascus. Pekah, king of Israel, also defeated him in a crushing disaster. He killed in Judah a hundred and twenty thousand fighting men, because they had forsaken the Lord, the God of their fathers. And the Israelites carried away captive two hundred thousand women, boys and girls. They also took an immense amount of spoil, and they brought the spoil to Samaria.

But a prophet of the Lord was there, Oded by name. And he went to meet the army that was coming to Samaria, and said to them: "Because of the wrath of the Lord, the God of your fathers, against Judah, He has delivered them into your hand. You have killed them with a fury that has reached up to

הִנֵּה בַּחֲמַת יְיָ אֱלֹהֵי אֲבוֹתֵיכֶם עַל יְהוּדָה נְתָנָם בְּיֶדְכֶם וַתַּהַרְגוּ בָם בְּזַעַף.

heaven. Now you intend to hold the people of Judah as slaves. Are you not yourself guilty of crimes against the Lord your God? Now hear me: Send back the captives of your brothers, for the fierce wrath of the Lord will be upon you." Then the chiefs of Ephraim stood up, and said to those who came from the war: "You shall not bring the captives here, for you will bring upon us guilt against the Lord."

So the armed men left the captives and their booty. The chiefs of Ephraim took the captives and clothed all those who were naked. They provided them with sandals, and gave them to eat and to drink, and carried all those who were feeble on donkeys; and they brought them to Jericho, to their kinsmen, and then returned to Samaria.

At that time the Edomites came and attacked Judah, and they carried them away captives. The Philistines also raided the cities of the lowland and captured Beth-shemesh.

AHAZ ASKS HELP FROM ASSYRIA

THEN AHAZ, king of Judah, sent messengers to Tiglath-pileser, king of As-

syria, saying: "I am your servant and your son. Come and save me from the hand of the king of Aram and from the hand of the king of Israel, who rise up against me." Ahaz took the silver and the gold that was found in the House of the Lord and in the treasures of the king's house, and sent it as tribute to the king of Assyria.

Then the king of Assyria listened to him, and went to Damascus, and captured it and carried away the inhabitants captive to Kir.

Hoshea, the son of Elah, conspired against Pekah king of Israel, and killed him, and reigned in his place. Hoshea reigned in Samaria nine years. He did evil in the eyes of the Lord, though not like the kings of Israel who were before him. [1] Against him came up Shalmaneser, king of Assyria, and Hoshea became his vassal, and paid him tribute.

THE FALL OF SAMARIA

THEN THE king of Assyria found conspiracy in Hoshea, for he sent messengers to the king of Egypt, and he did not bring up tribute to Assyria, as he had done year by year. The king of

---

≈§ [1] NOT LIKE THE KINGS BEFORE HIM: If, as the verse says, Hoshea "did evil in the eyes of the Lord, though not like the kings of Israel who were before him," why then were the ten tribes exiled

עַבְדְּךָ וּבִנְךָ אָנִי, עֲלֵה וְהוֹשִׁיעֵנִי מִכַּף מֶלֶךְ אֲרָם וּמִכַּף מֶלֶךְ יִשְׂרָאֵל הַקּוֹמִים
עָלָי.

Assyria shut him up in prison. Then the king of Assyria marched right through the land, and went up to Samaria and besieged it three years. In the ninth year of Hoshea's reign, the king of Assyria captured Samaria, and carried Israel captive to Assyria, and settled them in Halah, in Habor, and on the river of Gozan, and in the cities of the Medes.

WHY SAMARIA WAS DESTROYED

NOW THIS came about because the Israelites had sinned against the Lord their God who had brought them up from the land of Egypt. They had worshiped other gods and walked in the ways of the nations whom the Lord had dispossesed before them. They wrought wicked things to provoke the Lord of which He had said to them: "You shall not do these things." Yet the Lord warned Israel by all His prophets, saying: "Turn from your evil ways and keep My commandments and My statutes according to all the laws which I commanded your fathers and which I sent to you by My servants, the prophets."

However, they would not listen, [2] they were willful and stiff-necked, and

---

in his time? Our Sages explain that the Assyrians invaded the Northern Kingdom three times. The first time, in the reign of Pekah, they captured the golden calf at Dan and carried it off with some of the tribes to Babylon. The second time the Assyrians came was in the reign of Hoshea, when they carried off the other golden calf, which stood in Beth-el, together with four tribes.

After that Hoshea removed the guards on the frontiers between Judah and Israel who had kept the people from going up to Jerusalem to worship. But the people insisted on serving the Baalim and none went up to Jerusalem. Then the Lord spoke: "Before this, the people of Israel could blame the king and his guards for not worshiping Me. But now each is responsible for his own transgressions." Then the Assyrians invaded the Northern Kingdom for the third time, destroyed it and exiled the people.

⤷ [2] THEY WOULD NOT LISTEN: The Rabbis said that the relationship between God and Israel was like that of the king who at his wedding bound his wife to him with two fine jewels. When the wife lost one

בִּשְׁנַת הַתְּשִׁיעִית לְהוֹשֵׁעַ לָכַד מֶלֶךְ אַשּׁוּר אֶת שֹׁמְרוֹן וַיֶּגֶל אֶת יִשְׂרָאֵל אַשּׁוּרָה.

they rejected the Lord's statutes and
His covenant which He had made with
their fathers and the warning He had
given them. They went after things of
nought and became nought.

They forsook all the commandments
of the Lord and made molten images,
worshiped stars and served Baal. They
even made their sons and daughters to
pass through fire [to Molech]. They
practiced magic and witchcraft. They
gave themselves up to do evil in the
eyes of the Lord. Therefore the Lord
became exceedingly angry with Israel
and removed them out of His sight.
And there was none left but the tribe
of Judah only.

THE NEW SETTLERS IN SAMARIA

THE KING of Assyria brought people from
Babylon and from Cuthah and other
countries, and settled them in the cities
of Samaria, in place of the Israelites.
When they first dwelt there, they did
not fear the Lord. [3] Therefore the
Lord sent lions among them, which continued to kill them. They spoke to the
king of Assyria, saying: "The nations
which you have carried away and settled
in the cities of Samaria do not know
the custom of the God of the land,
therefore He has sent lions among them
and they kill them."

---

of them, the king said: "Be careful not to lose the other, or there
will be no sign left of our troth."

So, too, was it with Israel. When the Israelites sealed the covenant
at Sinai, the Lord gave them *na'aseh v'nishma—we will do* and *we
will hearken*. When Israel sinned with the golden calf, the Lord
said: "Now you have only *we will hearken*, for you have lost *we
will do*."

What is "do"? It is to do the *mitzvot*. What is "Hearken"? It is
to hearken to the Torah, to study the Law. When the Northern
Kingdom did not follow the *mitzvot*, God still considered them His
people, but when they refused to study Torah and did not allow
others to do so, they lost both parts of the covenant.

◁§ [3] THEY DID NOT FEAR THE LORD: After the king of Assyria exiled
the ten tribes, he sent some new peoples to settle in their place.
But the land was suddenly infested with wild beasts and lions killed

וַיִּמְאֲסוּ אֶת חֻקָּיו וְאֶת בְּרִיתוֹ אֲשֶׁר כָּרַת אֶת אֲבוֹתָם וְאֶת עֵדוֹתָיו אֲשֶׁר הֵעִיד
בָּם, וַיֵּלְכוּ אַחֲרֵי הַהֶבֶל וַיֶּהְבָּלוּ.

Then the king of Assyria gave command: "Send there one of the priests who was carried away from there, and let him dwell there, and teach the people the custom of the God of the land." One of the priests whom they carried away from Samaria came and dwelt in Beth-el, and taught them how they should serve the Lord. But each of the nations had also made gods of their own. So they worshiped the Lord, but they also worshiped their own gods, according to the custom of the nations which had been carried away.

So these people came to fear the Lord, and they served their carved images. Their children and children's children followed the custom of their fathers, so do they to this day.

HEZEKIAH, KING OF JUDAH

HEZEKIAH, THE SON of Ahaz, was twenty-five years old when he began to reign, and he reigned twenty-nine years in Jerusalem. He did that which was right in the eyes of the Lord, just as David, his father, had done. He trusted the Lord God of Israel; he cleaved to Him and departed not from following Him, but kept the commandments which the Lord commanded Moses.

So the Lord was with him, and he prospered in all his ventures. He re-

---

many of the new settlers. The king of Assyria called for the elders of the exiled Israelites and said to them: "All the years that you dwelt in your land the wild beasts did not afflict you. Now the lions are sorely grieving my people."

Hoping that the king would return the Israelites to their own land, the elders replied: "Our God will not permit a nation that does not live by the Torah to dwell in it." The elders thought that the king of Assyria would surely not force the settlers to convert but the king replied: "Send two of your number to teach my servants concerning your religion." So the elders sent Rabbi Dosetai and Rabbi Zechariah. They taught the new inhabitants the Torah and they wept, for the Rabbis saw that the new inhabitants would never become true converts to Judaism because they had not themselves wished to study the Torah but had had it thrust upon them. As the verse (17:33) tells us: "They appeared to fear the Lord, but in truth, they served their own idols."

בַּיְיָ אֱלֹהֵי יִשְׂרָאֵל בָּטָח ... וַיִּדְבַּק בַּיְיָ, לֹא סָר מֵאַחֲרָיו, וַיִּשְׁמֹר מִצְוֺתָיו אֲשֶׁר צִוָּה יְיָ אֶת מֹשֶׁה.

belled against the king of Assyria, and served him not. He defeated the Philistines as far as Gaza.

THE INVASION OF SENNACHERIB

NOW, IN THE fourteenth year of King Hezekiah, Sennacherib, king of Assyria, came up against [4] the fortified cities of Judah, and captured them. Then Hezekiah sent to the king of Assyria at Lachish, saying: "I have sinned. Withdraw from me and whatever you put on me, I will bear." The king of Assyria made Hezekiah pay three hundred talents of silver and thirty talents of gold.

Afterward the king of Assyria sent Tartan and Rab-saris and Rab-shakeh from Lachish to King Hezekiah with a great army to Jerusalem. They came and took up their position at the channel [5] of the upper pool, and they called

---

⋴§ [4] CAME UP AGAINST: How is it that Sennacherib made war on Judah during the reign of Hezekiah? Hezekiah had ordered all the people to study Torah and to walk in its ways. Every child, every woman and man soon became learned. When the Lord told Hezekiah, "I am sending Sennacherib against you," Hezekiah pleaded with the Lord that his people were righteous and did not deserve to be destroyed by the Assyrians.

Then God spoke, saying, "The monarch will come but he shall not prevail."

And still Hezekiah pleaded: "O Lord, neither the fright nor the victory!"

But the Lord replied: "Let the nations see that even the mightiest monarch cannot prevail against righteousness."

⋴§ [5] THEY TOOK UP THEIR POSITION AT THE CHANNEL: When Sennacherib and his army reached Jerusalem, the king of Assyria exclaimed: "Is this the famed city for whose sake I set my whole army on the march? It looks smaller and weaker than any of the cities I have subdued with my strong hand." His lieutenants said, "Let us take it immediately and make an end of it." But Sennacherib replied: "We have made the ten-day journey from Nob to Jerusalem in a single day. Our warriors are weary. Let us rest tonight." He

וּבְאַרְבַּע עֶשְׂרֵה שָׁנָה לַמֶּלֶךְ חִזְקִיָּהוּ עָלָה סַנְחֵרִיב מֶלֶךְ אַשּׁוּר עַל כָּל עָרֵי
יְהוּדָה הַבְּצֻרוֹת וַיִּתְפְּשֵׂם.

out for the king. There came out to them Eliakim who was the steward of the palace, Shebnah, the scribe, and Joah, the recorder.

Then Rab-shakeh said to them: "Say you now to Hezekiah: Thus says the great king, the king of Assyria: <u>What confidence is this in which you trust? Do you think that a mere word of the lips is council and strength for war?</u> Now in whom do you trust, that you have rebelled against me? You have put your trust in Egypt, in the staff of this broken reed, on which if a man lean, it will run into his hand and pierce it. But if you say to me, We trust in the Lord our God, is it not the Lord whose altars Hezekiah has taken away, and said to Judah, Worship at this altar in Jerusalem? So, make a wager with my master, the king of Assyria. I will give you two thousand horses, if you have the riders to set upon them. So you can then repulse the attack of the least of my master's servants."

Then Eliakim, Shebnah, and Joah said to Rab-shakeh: "Speak to us in Aramaic, for we understand it, but do not speak to us in Judean, with the people listening on the wall."

Rab-shakeh answered them: [6] "Did my master send me with this message to your master or to you? It was rather to the men who are sitting on the wall and die of hunger." Then he stood and cried with a loud voice in Judean, saying: "Hear the words of the great king, the king of Assyria: Thus says the king: Do not let Hezekiah deceive you, for he will not be able to deliver you. Have

---

waved his hand derisively toward the city, saying, "Tomorrow, each of you will take just one brick from the city wall and bring it to me and that will be the end of Jerusalem. There will not even be any need to besiege it."

That night the angel of the Lord came and slew Sennacherib's army, for the Lord had spoken: "I will protect the city and save it for My own sake and for My servant David."

⤹ [6] RAB-SHAKEH'S PREMONITION: While the army slept, Rab-shakeh stole to the top of the platform from which Sennacherib observed the city. He wanted to see what was going on in the city of his youth now doomed to be destroyed. He saw the Temple all lit and filled with the Jerusalemites. It was the first night of Passover and

מָה הַבִּטָּחוֹן הַזֶּה אֲשֶׁר בָּטָחְתָּ? אָמַרְתָּ אַךְ דְּבַר שְׂפָתַיִם עֵצָה וּגְבוּרָה לַמִּלְחָמָה.

any of the gods of the nations delivered his land from the hand of the king of Assyria? Was Samaria delivered out of my hand? Make peace with me, and surrender to me. Then can each man eat from his own vine and his own fig tree, and drink water from his own cistern, until I come and take you away to a land like your own, that you may live, and not die."

The people were silent, and answered not a word, for the king commanded: "Do not answer him."

ISAIAH'S PROPHETIC ASSURANCE

THEN KING HEZEKIAH rent his clothes, and covered himself with sackcloth, and sent Eliakim and Shebna, and the elders of the priests covered with sackcloth, to the prophet Isaiah, the son of Amoz. They said to him: "Thus said Hezekiah: 'This is a day of distress, rebuke, and disgrace. It may be that the Lord your God will hear all the words of Rab-shakeh whose master, the king of Assyria, has sent to insult the living God, and will rebuke the words which the Lord your God has heard.'"

Isaiah said to them: "Thus shall you say to your master: Thus said the Lord: Do not be afraid of the words of the lads of the king of Assyria who have blasphemed Me. He shall not enter the city, nor shoot an arrow there, neither shall he come before it with a shield, nor cast a mound against it. For I will defend and save the city for My own sake, and for the sake of My servant David. This is the word that the Lord has spoken against him:

---

the Levites were singing the *Hallel* Psalms. In the stillness of the night, he recognized the melody and the words:

> "When Israel came forth out of Egypt
> The House of Jacob from a people of a strange tongue,
> Jacob became His sanctuary
> Israel His dominion" (Psalms 114:1–2).

Suddenly he felt sure that Sennacherib would not be able to take the city, that somehow the army would be destroyed at the very gates of Jerusalem.

He went down to the king and said: "Master, abandon the siege of the city. I heard them reciting the *Hallel*, and reminded myself that many miracles happen to them on this night. Their God will not desert them now either. Put off taking the city."

וְגַנּוֹתִי אֶל הָעִיר הַזֹּאת לְהוֹשִׁיעָהּ לְמַעֲנִי וּלְמַעַן דָּוִד עַבְדִּי.

" 'The daughter of Zion,
She despises you, and laughs at
    you,
Whom have you insulted and
    blasphemed?
Against whom have you raised
    your voice?
Against the Holy One of Israel!
By your messengers you have
    insulted the Lord,
And said: With the multitude of
    my chariots
I have come up the heights of the
    mountains,
To the innermost parts of
    Lebanon,
I have cut down the tallest cedars,
    its choicest cypresses,
I have dug and drunk foreign
    waters,
And with the soles of my feet I
    dried up all the streams of Egypt.

Have you not heard, how I
    prepared it long ago,
And how I brought it to pass?
Because you have raged against
    Me,
And your arrogance has come up
    to My ears,
Therefore I will put My hook in
    your nose
And My bridle in your lips.
And I will turn you back the way
By which you came.' "

That night the angel of the Lord [7] went forth and smote in the camp of the Assyrians one hundred and eighty-five thousand men. Then Sennacherib, king of Assyria, returned to Nineveh. And when he was worshiping in the temple of Nisroch, his god, his sons smote him with the sword, and Esarhaddon, his son, reigned in his place.

Sennacherib only laughed and replied: "It was my wish that we should come to this city and take it. For this I have gathered a mighty army and tomorrow we shall take Jerusalem."

But Rab-shakeh's premonition came true.

∾§ [7] THE ANGEL OF THE LORD: According to tradition the Assyrians began their siege on the first night of Passover. Despite the beleaguering army, the Israelites celebrated the feast of their deliverance from bondage in Egypt. As they sang the *Hallel*, the song in praise of the Lord, the angels also sang the *Hallel* before the Celestial Throne. Amidst all this beauty the heavens were cleft, but the Israelites continued to chant God's praises unawares. The As-

וְשַׂמְתִּי חַחִי בְּאַפֶּךָ וּמִתְגִּי בִּשְׂפָתֶיךָ, וַהֲשִׁיבוֹתִיךָ בַּדֶּרֶךְ אֲשֶׁר בָּאתָ בָּהּ.

HEZEKIAH IS SAVED

IN THOSE DAYS Hezekiah was sick to death. Isaiah, the prophet, the son of Amoz, came and said to him: "Set your house in order; for you shall die, and not live." Hezekiah turned his face to the wall, and prayed to the Lord, [8] saying: "Remember now, O Lord, how I have walked before Thee in truth and with a whole heart, and have done that which is good in Thy sight." And Hezekiah wept bitterly.

Before Isaiah was gone out of the inner court of the city, the word of the Lord came to him, saying: "Return,

---

syrians looked up, and, overwhelmed by rapture, their souls departed from their bodies.

[8] PRAYED TO THE LORD: When Isaiah told Hezekiah that he would die, he added, "in this world and in the next." Hezekiah wept sorely and begged the prophet to tell him why. Isaiah said, "Because you have done evil in the sight of the Lord."

Hezekiah replied, "I have cleansed the idols from the land and taught the people Torah."

"But you disobeyed God's first injunction," Isaiah said. "You have never married and fathered children."

Hezekiah replied: "I saw a vision of my progeny and that they would all be evil. Better none than evil."

"No," Isaiah rebuked him, "why do you concern yourself with the mysteries of the Almighty? You must do your duty and the Lord will do whatever pleases Him."

"You are right," Hezekiah answered. "Give me your daughter to wife and with God's help we shall have children. And perhaps your merit and mine might cause the children to be virtuous."

"Too late," Isaiah said.

Then Hezekiah said, "Even if the sword is on your neck it is not too late to pray." So he prayed to God as Isaiah left and the Lord told Isaiah to return, for He had forgiven Hezekiah. And then the king married Isaiah's daughter.

אָנָּה יְיָ, זְכָר־נָא אֵת אֲשֶׁר הִתְהַלַּכְתִּי לְפָנֶיךָ בֶּאֱמֶת וּבְלֵבָב שָׁלֵם וְהַטּוֹב בְּעֵינֶיךָ עָשִׂיתִי.

and say to Hezekiah: 'Thus said the Lord, the God of David, your father: I have heard your prayer, I have seen your tears; behold, I will heal you; on the third day you shall go up to the House of the Lord. I will add fifteen years to your days; and I will deliver you and this city out of the hand of the king of Assyria; and I will defend this city for My own sake, and for My servant David's sake.'" And Isaiah said: "Take a cake of figs." And they took and placed it on the boil and Hezekiah recovered.

שָׁמַעְתִּי אֶת תְּפִלָּתֶךָ, רָאִיתִי אֶת דִּמְעָתֶךָ, הִנְנִי רֹפֵא לָךְ; בַּיּוֹם הַשְּׁלִישִׁי תַּעֲלֶה בֵּית יְיָ.

28. II KINGS [20–25]

KING MANASSEH

HEZEKIAH SLEPT with his fathers, [1] and Manasseh, his son, reigned in his place. He was twelve years old when he began to reign, and he reigned for fifty-five years in Jerusalem. He did evil [2] in the eyes of the Lord, after the abominations of the nations whom the Lord cast out before the Children of Israel. He built altars for Baal, and made an Asherah, and set the graven image of the Asherah in the House of the Lord. He made his son pass through the fire, and practiced soothsaying and witchcraft. He also shed very much innocent blood,

---

[1] SLEPT WITH HIS FATHERS: Despite Hezekiah's weaknesses he was a good man and a good king, beloved of his people. When he died, a great funeral cortège followed his coffin and over his grave the people built a house of study where Torah was studied every day. On the lintel over the entrance was carved this verse:

וְהֶעֱבִיר אֶת בְּנוֹ בָּאֵשׁ וְעוֹנֵן וְנִחֵשׁ וְעָשָׂה אוֹב וְיִדְּעֹנִים.

[3] until he filled Jerusalem from one end to another.

The Lord spoke by his servants, the prophets: "Because Manasseh has done these abominations, [4] I will bring such evil on Jerusalem and Judah that whosoever hears of it, both his ears shall ring. I will wipe Jerusalem as a man

---

If you would know who is buried here,
He who finds rest upon his bier,
What were his victories and what his fame,
The mass of his treasure, proud sound of his name,
Turn to the Torah that stands over his grave,
And seek what the Lord asks from king and from slave.
Here lies Hezekiah, of Judah the king,
Who to the Lord all devotion did bring.
Your gold and treasure before death do flee.
What is remembered? A good name and charity.

And they put above his grave a *Sefer Torah* and wrote over him: "Whoever lies in this casket fulfilled what is written here."

◄§ [2] MANASSEH DID EVIL: Manasseh was an idolator who served all the pagan gods. He also made a four-faced idol and placed it in the inner court of the Temple so that whatever direction one came in from one could immediately prostrate himself before it. Manasseh also had built another idol which was a colossus, so large that it required a thousand men to move it. Daily Manasseh forced men to drag it from one town to another and daily he had to replace the entire number of men because every evening the men died from their labors.

◄§ [3] MUCH INNOCENT BLOOD: Our Sages tell us that Manasseh sentenced his own grandfather, the prophet Isaiah, to death. When the prophet fled and hid in a hollow tree the king's men saw the edge of his garment exposed and reported it. Manasseh then ordered his men to saw the tree in two and they did so, thereby sawing the

הִנִּיחוּ סֵפֶר תּוֹרָה עַל מִטָּתוֹ וְאָמְרוּ: קִיֵּם זֶה מַה שֶּׁכָּתוּב בָּזֶה.

wipes a dish, wiping it and turning it
upside down."

Manasseh slept with his fathers, [5]
and was buried in the garden of his own

house, and Amon, his son, reigned in his
place. He reigned for two years and he
did evil in the sight of the Lord, as did
his father. His servants conspired against

---

prophet in half. Manasseh was the scourge of other prophets as well,
as the verse in Jeremiah (2:30) tells, "Your sword devoured your
prophets like a destroying lion."

 [4] MANASSEH'S SINS AND PRAYER: In the twenty-second year of
Manasseh's reign the Assyrians came and carried him off in fetters
to Babylonia. There they put him to torture and in his anguish he
called upon Baal and Molech and Ashtoreth, on all the pagan idols
he had worshiped, to help him, but there was no response. Then
he remembered the verses of the Torah his father Hezekiah had
taught him: "In distress you shall return to the Lord your God, and
you shall find Him if you will seek Him with all your heart and
with all your soul. For the Lord is merciful" (Deuteronomy 4:29-31).
And Manasseh repented and prayed to the Lord, saying, "You are
the Lord, Most High, tenderhearted, long-suffering and most merciful. You, God, Lord of the upright, have therefore not ordained
repentance for the upright. You have ordained repentance for a
sinner like me. I earnestly beseech You, forgive me Lord, forgive me."

When the angels heard his prayer, they shut the windows of
heaven so that his prayer should not be accepted. The angels said
to the Lord: "Manasseh put an idol in the inner court of the Temple;
he shed seas of innocent blood; he even killed his grandfather, the
prophet Isaiah; he is beyond redemption." And the Lord replied,
"Yes, his sins are many and his transgressions great. By applying the
law strictly his prayer should not be accepted; but then the people
would say that the Lord has shut the door in the face of the peni-
tent. I therefore accept his prayer and his repentance." And the
Lord made an opening under His throne of Glory to receive the
prayer of the repentant Manasseh.

אָכְלָה חַרְבְּכֶם נְבִיאֵיכֶם כְּאַרְיֵה מַשְׁחִית.

him, and killed him. The people of the land killed the conspirators, and his son Josiah became king in his place.

JOSIAH AND THE SCROLL

JOSIAH WAS eight years old when he began to reign, and he reigned thirty-one years in Jerusalem. He did right in the eyes of the Lord, and walked in the way of David.

In the eighteenth year of King Josiah,

the king sent Shaphan, the scribe, to the House of the Lord, saying: "Go to Hilkiah, the High Priest, and see that he shall take the money which the keepers of the doors have gathered from the people and deliver it into the hands of the workers who have supervision of the House of the Lord, that they may hire the carpenters, the builders, and the masons, to make repairs on the House."

Now when they brought out the money that had been taken to the House

---

  [5] SLEPT WITH HIS FATHERS: Rav Ashi appointed a time to lecture to his students about the three sinful kings: Jeroboam, Ahab and Manasseh. "Tomorrow," he said, "we shall discuss our colleague Manasseh." That very night Rav Ashi had a dream in which Manasseh appeared to him and said, "How dare you call me colleague! Do you think you are worthy to be my colleague or my father's? Answer this simple question: 'When we make the benediction of Hamotzi, from which part of the loaf of bread must we begin to cut?'"

Rav Ashi replied that he did not know.

Manasseh said, "If you do not know the answer to such a simple question, how dare you call me your colleague?"

Then Rav Ashi said, "Tell me your answer and I shall proclaim it in your name in my lecture tomorrow."

Manasseh said, "We begin to cut the bread from the part that is most browned."

So Rav Ashi asked, "If you were so wise in the laws of the Torah, why did you worship idols?"

Manasseh retorted, "Were you living in my generation you would have lifted the hem of your garment so that you might run faster after the idols to worship them."

אִלּוּ הָיִיתָ בְּאוֹתוֹ הַדּוֹר – הָיִיתָ תּוֹפֵס בְּשׁוּלֵי בִּגְדִי וְרָץ אַחֲרִי.

of the Lord, Hilkiah, the priest, found a scroll of the Torah of the Lord given to Moses.

Then Hilkiah said to Shaphan, the scribe: "I have found the scroll of the Torah [6] in the House of the Lord." Then Shaphan carried the scroll to the king, and said: "Hilkiah, the priest, has given me a scroll." Then Shaphan read it before the king.

And the king commanded Hilkiah, the priest, and Shaphan, the scribe: "Go inquire of the Lord for me and for all Judah concerning the words of this book that is found; for great is the anger of the Lord against us, because our fathers have not hearkened to the words of this scroll, to do all in it that is written concerning us."

So Hilkiah and Shaphan went to Huldah, [7] the prophetess, the wife of Shallum, the son of Tikvah. And she said to them: "Thus says the Lord: Tell the man that sent you to me: Behold, I will bring evil upon this place because they have forsaken Me, and have sacrificed to other gods. My wrath shall be kindled against this place, and it shall not be quenched. But to the king of Judah who sent you to inquire of the Lord, say to him: The Lord, God of Israel, says: Because your heart was tender and you did humble yourself before the Lord when you heard what I spoke against this place and its people, that they should become an astonishment and a curse, and have rent your clothes and wept before Me, I have also heard you. Therefore, I will gather you to your fathers in peace, neither shall your eyes see all the evil which I will bring upon this place." And they brought back word to the king.

---

      [6] I HAVE FOUND THE SCROLL OF THE TORAH: Where was the book of Law hidden and who hid it? When King Ahaz burned all the copies of the Torah, the priests hid one book between the lines of bricks in the Temple wall. When the High Priest Hilkiah, by the command of King Josiah, began to repair the breaches of the walls of the Temple, he found hidden there the Torah of Moses.

      [7] WENT TO HULDAH: Why did they go to Huldah? Jeremiah was also residing in Jerusalem, why did they not go to him?

     Some of our Sages believe that the officials went to Huldah because they thought a woman might be more tenderhearted, more ready to forgive the people.

כִּי גְדוֹלָה חֲמַת יְיָ אֲשֶׁר הִיא נִצְּתָה בָנוּ עַל אֲשֶׁר לֹא שָׁמְעוּ אֲבוֹתֵינוּ עַל דִּבְרֵי הַסֵּפֶר הַזֶּה לַעֲשׂוֹת כְּכָל הַכָּתוּב עָלֵינוּ.

A COVENANT BEFORE THE LORD

THEN THE KING gathered all the elders of Judah and Jerusalem. The king went up to the House of the Lord, together with all the men of Judah, and all the priests and prophets, and all the people small and great, and he read in their hearing all the words of the scroll of the covenant which was found in the House of the Lord.

Then the king stood on a platform, and made a covenant before the Lord, to follow the Lord and keep His commands, His decrees and His statutes, with all his heart, [8] and with all his soul, and to confirm the words of the covenant that were written in this scroll. And all the people accepted the covenant, and did according to the Covenant of the God of their fathers.

JOSIAH'S REFORMS

THEN THE KING commanded the priests to bring out of the Temple of the Lord all the vessels which were made for the Baal and the Asherah, and he burned them outside Jerusalem, in the limekilns at Kidron. He also did away with those idolatrous priests whom the kings of Judah had ordained to offer sacrifices to the Baal, to the sun, to the moon, and to all the host of heaven. He destroyed the Topheth which was in the valley of Ben-Hinnom, so that no man might make his son or daughter pass through the fire to Molech.

THE DEATH OF KING JOSIAH

AFTER JOSIAH restored the Temple, Neco, the king of Egypt, went up against the king of Assyria to the river Euphrates. King Josiah went up against him. Pharaoh-neco sent messengers to him saying: "What have I to do with you, Judah? I come not against you this day, but I come to fight another house; and God has commanded me to make haste. Cease to provoke God, who is with me, so that we do not destroy

---

◆§ [8] WITH ALL HIS HEART: After Josiah had destroyed the last vestige of paganism and celebrated the Passover properly, he actually made good with his deeds the wrongs which had been committed in his youth. Josiah had come to the throne when he was only eight years old. Now that he was of age, he reexamined all the decisions that had been rendered. "When I judged the people before, did I judge them justly?" He then had a proclamation issued to all the people requesting those who were dissatisfied with his judgments to return

וַיִּקְרָא בְאָזְנֵיהֶם אֵת כָּל דִּבְרֵי סֵפֶר הַבְּרִית הַנִּמְצָא בְּבֵית יְיָ׃

you." But Josiah refused to turn his face away from him. He disguised himself and came to fight in the valley of Megiddo. The archers shot at King Josiah, and the king said to his servants: "Take me away for I am badly wounded." His servants took him out of his chariot and made him ride in the second chariot that he had. They brought him to Jerusalem where he died, and he was buried in the sepulcher of his fathers. All Judah and Jerusalem mourned for Josiah. And Jeremiah lamented after him. And all singing men and women mentioned Josiah in their lamentations. And they made an ordinance in Israel to recite the elegy at a stated time of the year.

Then the people took Jehoahaz, the son of Josiah, and made him king in his father's place. Joahaz was twenty-three years old when he began to rule; and he reigned three months in Jerusalem. Then [Neco], the king of Egypt, deposed him and fined the land a hundred talents of silver and a talent of gold. The king of Egypt made his brother Eliakim king over Judah and Jerusalem, and changed his name to Jehoiakim. And Neco took Joahaz, his brother, and carried him away to Egypt.

THE REIGN OF JEHOIAKIM

JEHOIAKIM WAS twenty-five years old when he began to reign. He reigned eleven years in Jerusalem, and he did evil in the sight of the Lord. In his days Nebuchadnezzar, king of Babylon, came up, and Jehoiakim became subject to him for three years. Then he rebelled against him. The Lord sent against him bands of Chaldeans, and bands of Moabites, and bands of Ammonites. He sent them against Judah to destroy it. Then came up Nebuchadnezzar, king of Babylon, and shackled him in chains to carry him off to Babylon. But Jehoiakim died [9] and his son Jehoiachin became king in his stead.

---

before him. Many did, Josiah heard their cases a second time and it turned out that many were justified in their complaints. To each of those Josiah gave a sum of money as recompense so that they might forgive him.

[9] BUT JEHOIAKIM DIED: Jehoiakim was a vassal of Egypt for seven years. When Nebuchadnezzar defeated the army of Egypt, Jehoiakim became a vassal of Babylon. After three years he rebelled and Nebuchadnezzar came and besieged Jerusalem. The Great Sanhedrin then

וַיְקוֹנֵן יִרְמְיָהוּ עַל יֹאשִׁיָּהוּ. וַיֹּאמְרוּ כָל הַשָּׁרִים וְהַשָּׁרוֹת בְּקִינוֹתֵיהֶם עַל יֹאשִׁיָּהוּ עַד הַיּוֹם. וַיִּתְּנוּם לְחֹק עַל יִשְׂרָאֵל.

THE EXILE OF JEHOIACHIN

JEHOIACHIN [10] WAS eighteen years old when he began to reign, and he reigned three months in Jerusalem. He did evil in the sight of the Lord, as his father had done. At that time Nebuchadnezzar, king of Babylon, came up against the city while his army was besieging it. Jehoiachin went out to the king of Babylon, he and his mother and his servants, his princes and his officers. The king of Babylon took him captive. He carried out all the treasures of the House

---

went to Nebuchadnezzar and asked: "Have you come to destroy Jerusalem?" Nebuchadnezzar answered: "No. Jehoiakim rebelled against me. Deliver him and I will return to Babylon."

The Sanhedrin came to Jehoiakim and said: "Nebuchadnezzar demands that we deliver you."

Jehoiakim answered: "Is it right to buy your own life with someone else's life? with mine? Is it not written: 'You shall not deliver an escaped slave to his master?' (Deuteronomy 23:16)."

The Sanhedrin replied that since the time of his ancestor, David, when Sheba, son of Bichri, rebelled against the king, the law was established that any individual who shall transgress the laws of the king and who is specified by name, may be turned over to the enemy in order for the individuals involved to save themselves.

But Jehoiakim refused to submit to the decision of the Sanhedrin and the court then put him in irons and delivered him up to Nebuchadnezzar. But Jehoiakim was a very delicate man and he died immediately. Then Nebuchadnezzar took his corpse and put it into a hollow wooden donkey and paraded the donkey through the cities of Judah, thus fulfilling Jeremiah's prophecy (22:19): "He shall be buried with the burial of an ass."

&ed; [10] JEHOIACHIN: Nebuchadnezzar made Jehoiachin, Jehoiakim's son, king over Judah, and then returned to Babylon. There his counselors advised him against having done so. Nebuchadnezzar then returned to Jerusalem and demanded that the Sanhedrin surrender the young king to him or he would destroy the city. The

וַיֵּצֵא יְהוֹיָכִין מֶלֶךְ יְהוּדָה עַל מֶלֶךְ בָּבֶל, הוּא וְאִמּוֹ וַעֲבָדָיו וְשָׂרָיו וְסָרִיסָיו וַיִּקַּח אֹתוֹ מֶלֶךְ בָּבֶל.

of the Lord, and all the treasures of the king's house. He also cut to pieces all the vessels of gold, which Solomon, king of Israel, had made in the Temple of the Lord. He also carried into exile the nobles and <u>all the mighty warriors, [11] all the craftsmen and smiths. None was left except the poorest of the people of the land.</u> He exiled to Babylon Jehoiachin, his mother, his wives, his princes and his chief men of the land.

The king of Babylon made Mattaniah, Jehoiachin's uncle, king in his stead; and changed his name to Zedekiah.

THE DOWNFALL OF JUDAH

ZEDEKIAH WAS twenty-one years old when he began to reign, and he reigned eleven years in Jerusalem. He did evil in the eyes of the Lord, just as Jehoiakim had done. The anger of the Lord continued against Jerusalem and Judah, until He had cast them out of His presence.

Zedekiah also did not listen to Jeremiah, the prophet, who spoke in the name of the Lord. He also rebelled against King Nebuchadnezzar, who had made him swear by God. Zedekiah became obstinate and stubbornly refused to turn to the Lord, the God of Israel. All the chiefs of the priests and the people sinned mightily. They polluted the House of the Lord which He had hallowed in Jerusalem. The Lord sent messengers to them early and late, because He had compassion on His people and

---

young king agreed to surrender and all the great scholars and skilled craftsmen were to go into exile with him. Before they surrendered they collected all the keys to the Temple, went to the roof of the Sanctuary and threw the keys up toward heaven, saying, "Lord of the universe, because You have deemed us unworthy to be trustees of Your Sanctuary, here are the keys. Now You keep them." The shape of a fiery hand descended from the heavens and caught the keys, a sign that contact between heaven and earth had been severed.

&ᔆ [11] ALL THE MIGHTY WARRIORS: It is written that Nebuchadnezzar deported all the men of might, the craftsmen, smiths and heroes who make war. What kinds of heroes were they? Can men in chains make war? Our Sages explained that they were great scholars, leaders and artisans, in truth the real warriors and heroes of the people.

וְהִגְלָה אֶת ... כָּל הַשָּׂרִים וְאֵת כָּל גִּבּוֹרֵי הַחַיִל... וְכָל הֶחָרָשׁ וְהַמַּסְגֵּר, לֹא נִשְׁאַר זוּלַת דַּלַּת עַם הָאָרֶץ.

on His dwelling place. But they mocked the messengers of God, and despised His words, and scoffed at His prophets. The wrath of God arose against His people till there was no remedy.

It was in the ninth year of Zedekiah's reign, on the tenth day of the tenth month, Nebuchadnezzar, king of Babylon, came, he and all his army, against Jerusalem and besieged it. The city remained under siege until the eleventh year of King Zedekiah. On the ninth day of the [fourth] month, when the famine was very severe in the city so that there was no bread for the people, the wall of the city was breached. The king and all the men of war [fled] by night, by the way of the gate, which was by the king's garden, while the Chaldeans beleaguered the city. The king went in the direction of the Arabah. But the army of the Chaldeans pursued the king, and overtook him [12] in the plains of Jericho, all his army having scattered from him. They took the king and brought him before the king of Babylon at Riblah. They killed the sons of Zedekiah before his eyes, and then put his eyes out. They bound him in fetters, and carried him to Babylon.

THE DESTRUCTION OF THE TEMPLE

IN THE FIFTH month, on the seventh day of the month, which was the nineteenth year of King Nebuchadnezzar, king of Babylon, came Nebuzaradan, the captain of the guards, a servant of the king of Babylon, to Jerusalem. He burned the House of the Lord, and the king's house and all the houses of Jerusalem. The army of the Chaldeans that were with the captain of the guards, broke down the walls of Jerusalem. The people who were left in the city and the deserters who had deserted to the king of Babylon, and the rest of the people, Nebuzaradan exiled. He also took away all the vessels of the Temple, and carried them away to Babylon. But

---

[12] OVERTOOK HIM: According to legend a secret tunnel ran underground from Jerusalem to the vicinity of Jericho. Through it Zedekiah escaped the besieged city but the Lord was wroth with him for the evil he had done (24:19) and for deserting His people, so He sent a stag to run above the tunnel. The Chaldeans saw the stag with its fine antlers and gave chase. The stag reached the tunnel's opening just as Zedekiah emerged from it and so the Chaldeans leaped upon an even greater prize, the king.

וַיִּשְׂרֹף אֶת בֵּית יְיָ וְאֶת בֵּית הַמֶּלֶךְ וְאֵת כָּל בָּתֵּי יְרוּשָׁלָיִם.

he left the poorest of the land as vine-dressers and plowmen.

So Judah was carried away captive and exiled out of the land. [13]

THE DEATH OF GEDALIAH

OVER THE people who were left Nebu-chadnezzar appointed Gedaliah, the son of Ahikam, the son of Shaphan, gov-ernor. Now when the captains of the forces together with their men heard that the king of Babylon had appointed Gedaliah governor, they came to Geda-liah in Mizpah. Thereupon Gedaliah swore to them and their men, and said: "Fear not the Chaldean warriors. Dwell in the land, and serve the king of Baby-lon, and it will be well with you."

But it was in the seventh month that Ishmael, the son of Nethaniah of the royal house, came with ten men and killed Gedaliah, the Jews and the Chal-deans that were with him in Mizpah.

---

[13] SO JUDAH WAS EXILED OUT OF THE LAND: When the victorious Nebuchadnezzar led his captives from Judah to Babylon, the de-portees of Jeconiah went out to meet the king. They wore white garments, joyful attire, but beneath they wore sackcloth as a sign of mourning for the destruction of the Temple. They met the newly arrived prisoners and asked after their friends and families and were told: "Some died by pestilence, some died by the sword, some died by famine, some you will find among the captives" (Jeremiah 15:2). Then the deportees of Jeconiah raised one hand in salute to Nebu-chadnezzar and with the other smote their thighs as a sign of mourning.

[13] SO JUDAH WAS EXILED OUT OF THE LAND: Rabbi Judah said: "See how beloved are little children before God! When the San-hedrin went into captivity, the Shechinah, God's presence, did not accompany them. When the priests went into captivity, God's pres-ence did not accompany them either. But when the children were taken into captivity, the Presence of God went with them, for it says in Lamentations (1:5): 'Her children are gone into captivity,' and immediately thereafter (1:6): 'From Zion her splendor [that is, the Presence of God] is departed.'"

וַיִּגֶל יְהוּדָה מֵעַל אַדְמָתוֹ.

Then all the people, both small and great, and the captains of the forces arose and went to Egypt, for they were afraid of the Chaldeans.

THE RETURN TO ZION

THOSE WHO escaped from the sword were carried away to Babylon. They were servants to the king of Babylon and his sons until the reign of the kingdom of Persia. In the first year of Cyrus, king of Persia, that the word of the Lord by the mouth of Jeremiah might be accomplished, the Lord stirred up the spirit of Cyrus, king of Persia, who issued a proclamation throughout all his kingdom and put it also in writing, as follows:

"Thus says Cyrus, king of Persia: The Lord, the God of heavens, has given me all the kingdoms of the earth, and He has charged me to build Him a house in Jerusalem, which· is in Judah. Whosoever is among you of all His people, the Lord his God be with him, let him go up."

Then rose up the heads of the families of Judah and Benjamin and the priests and the Levites, and all those the spirit of God had roused, to go to build the House of the Lord which is in Jerusalem; they returned to Jerusalem and Judah, every one to his city.

ḤAZAK, ḤAZAK, V'NIT-ḤAZEK

מִי בָכֶם מִכָּל עַמּוֹ, יְיָ אֱלֹהָיו עִמּוֹ, וְיָעַל.

SOURCES

All references to the tractates of the Talmud are from the Babylonian Talmud unless otherwise indicated.

Sources referred to are in the following editions:

M'chilta d'Rabbi Ishmael, Meir Ish Shalom, editor, Vina, 5630 (1870)

Midrash Rabbah, Epstein edition, Warsaw

Midrash Shohar Tov (Psalms, Samuel & Proverbs), Jerusalem, 5720 (1960). Generally this work is thought to refer only to Psalms. Midrash Sh'muel and Midrash Mishle are sometimes used in referring to the sections dealing with Samuel and Proverbs, but all three works are properly subsumed under the general heading.

Midrash Tanhuma, Rosen edition, Warsaw

Pirké d'Rabbi Eliezer ha-Gadol, Bamberg edition, Warsaw, 5612 (1852)

P'sikta Rabbati, Meir Ish Shalom, editor, Tel Aviv (reprint edition), 5723 (1963)

Sifra, Schlosberg edition, Vienna, 5622 (1862)

Sifri, Meir Ish Shalom, editor, Vina, 5624 (1864)

Tana D'vé Eliyahu Rabbah and Zuta, Tzinkes edition, Warsaw 1883

Zohar, Rom edition (3 vol.), Vilna, 5642 (1882)

CHAPTER ONE

1. T'murah 16a; Yalkut Shim'oni (Yalkut) II §4
2. Homat Anach, Joshua 1, p. 22
3. Deuteronomy Rabbah (Deut. R.) 5:13; Leviticus Rabbah (Lev. R.) 17:6
4. B'rachot 32b
5. Shabbat 33b
6. Yalkut II §7; Tanhuma (Tan.) Sh'lach 1; Ruth R. 2:1
7. M'gillah 14b; Yalkut II §9–11
8. Yalkut II §9; Rashi, Z'vahim 116b
9. Yalkut II §15; Ralbag & Radak, Joshua 3:3

CHAPTER TWO

1. Radak, Joshua 6:23; Josephus, Antiquities of the Jews (Antiquities), Book 5, Chap. 1, §7
2. Tan. Yitro 17; Sifté Hachamim on Rashi, Exodus 20:22
3. Gittin 46a; Numbers (Num.) R. 8:4; 17:5; Deut. R. 5:13; Lev. R. 17:6
4. Yalkut II §22

CHAPTER THREE

1. Z'vahim 101b (see Rashi)
2. Homiletics
3. N'darim 22b
4. Shabbat 105b; Yalkut II §35

CHAPTER FOUR

1. Rashi, Radak & M'tzudat David, Judges 3:2
2. Tana D'vé Eliyahu Rabbah (Eliyahu R.), Chap. 11
3. Eliyahu R., Chap. 11
4. Tan. Va'yhi 14
5. S. Berenfeld, Mavo l'Kitvé ha-Kodesh II, p. 32; M'tzudat David & Ralbag, Judges 3:31
6. Yalkut II §43
7. Eliyahu R., Chap. 9
8. M'gillah 14a; Targum, Judges 4:5; Eliyahu R., Chap. 9
9. Tan. Shofetim 17; Antiquities, Book 5, Chap. 5, §3
10. Targum & Rashi, Judges 5:25

11. Albo, Sefer ha-Ikkarim IV, p. 435, Husik edition

CHAPTER FIVE
1. Yalkut II §60
2. Ralbag, Judges 6:11, 10:4
3. Homiletics
4. Rashi & Radak, Judges 6:11
5. Midrash T'hillim (Buber) Psalms 27:6; Yalkut II §62
6. M'tzudat David, Judges 7:3
7. Yalkut II §62; Ralbag, Judges 6:36; Radak, Judges 7:4
8. Ralbag, Judges 6:36
9. Radak, Judges 7:13; Rashi, Sotah 9a
10. Rashi & Radak, Judges 8:2

CHAPTER SIX
1. Yalkut II §64
2. Yalkut II §63; Radak, Judges 10:1
3. Yalkut II §65

CHAPTER SEVEN
1. Ralbag & Radak, Judges 11:1; Antiquities, Book 5, Chap. 1, §8
2. Gates of Repentance, Second Gate, pp. 31–32
3. Taanit 4a (see Rashi)
4. Yalkut II §67
5. Yalkut II §67–68 (see Zayit Raanan)
6. Yalkut II §68; Eliyahu R., Chap. 11; Targum, Judges 11:39
7. Radak, Judges 11:39; Ralbag, Judges 11:31; Targum, Judges 11:39
8. Eliyahu R., Chap. 11; Yalkut II §68

CHAPTER EIGHT
1. Yalkut II §68; Lev. R. 9:9
2. Num. R. 10:18
3. Yalkut II §69
4. Sotah 9b–10a; Yerushalmi, Sotah, I:8
5. Sotah 10a; Ralbag, Judges 14:2 & 15:20; Malbim, Judges 14:4
6. Shabbat 13a; Malbim, Judges 14:5

CHAPTER NINE
1. Sotah 9b; Num. R. 9:25; Ralbag & M'tzudat David, Judges 14:2
2. Sotah 9b; Malbim, Judges 16:17–18
3. Yalkut II §71; Yerushalmi, Sotah, I:8; Tosefot, Shabbat 55b

CHAPTER TEN
1. Yalkut II §77; Midrash Sh'muel, Chap. 1; Eliyahu R., Chap. 8
2. M'gillah 14a; P'sikta Rabbati 43; Midrash Sh'muel, Chap. 1; B'rachot 31b
3. Yalkut II §97; Gen. R. 58:2; Shabbat 113b (see Rashi); Maimonides' Guide for the Perplexed, II, pp. 204–205
4. Exodus (Ex.) R. 16:4
5. Midrash Sh'muel, Chap. 10; Sifri, Numbers §88
6. Eliyahu R., Chap. 11

CHAPTER ELEVEN
1. Yerushalmi, Taanit, II:7; Yalkut II §103; Midrash Shoḥar Tov 119; Targum & Rashi, I Samuel 7:6
2. Shabbat 56a; Z'vahim 118b–119a (see Rashi); Num. R. 3:7; Rashi & Ralbag, I Samuel 7:2
3. B'rachot 10b
4. Shabbat 56a; Yerushalmi, Sotah, I:4; Yalkut II §105; Midrash Sh'muel, Chap. 7
5. Sanhedrin 20b; Yalkut I §912; Malbim, I Samuel 8:6
6. Ralbag, I Samuel 8:18
7. Midrash Sh'muel, Chap. 11; Lev. R. 9:2; Tan. T'zaveh 8; Yalkut II §108, 110
8. B'rachot 48b; Yalkut II §108
9. M'naḥot 109b; Avot d'Rabbi Natan, 10:3
10. Yoma 22b; Yalkut II §117; K'tubot 17a

CHAPTER TWELVE
1. Num. R. 19:13; Tan. (Buber) Numbers 63b

2. Albo, Sefer ha-Ikkarim IV, p. 242
3. Radak, I Samuel 14:45
4. Yoma 22b; Ecclesiastes R. 7:33
5. Ralbag, I Samuel 15:3
6. Yoma 22b; Num. R. 2:10
7. Taanit 5b; Radak, I Samuel 25:1
8. P'sikta Rabbati 44; Malbim, I Samuel 15:22–23; Eliyahu R., Chap. 31; Maimonides' Guide, III, p. 152; (see Teacher's Resource Book, vol. I, pp. 103–104)
9. Albo, Sefer ha-Ikkarim IV, pp. 240–241
10. Midrash Shoḥar Tov 100; Yoma 22b (see Rashi); Eliyahu R., Chap. 31; Radak & Malbim, I Samuel 15:15

CHAPTER THIRTEEN
1. Moed Katan 27b
2. Radak, I Samuel 16:1
3. P'saḥim 8b; Kiddushin 39b
4. P'saḥim 66b; Tan. (Buber) Genesis 97a
5. Targum, Rashi & Radak, I Samuel 17:8
6. Midrash Shoḥar Tov 36; Yalkut II §725
7. Yalkut II §127; M'chilta d'Rabbi Ishmael B'shalaḥ, Amalek, Chap. 2; Lev. R. 26:8; Tan. Emor 43
8. Radak, I Samuel 17:42, 44, 48
9. Midrash Shoḥar Tov 18; Yalkut II §127
10. A. Hyman, Sefer ha-Torah v'ha-M'sorah, the Prophets, on I Samuel 18:7
11. Sotah 44b; Yalkut II §129; Midrash Sh'muel, Chap. 22
12. Ḥomat Anach, I Samuel 19, p. 27a
13. Yalkut I §168; Yalkut II §432

CHAPTER FOURTEEN
1. M'naḥot 29a; Ḥagigah 26b
2. Midrash Shoḥar Tov 4; Yalkut II §131

3. Num. R. 14:17; Sanhedrin 49a (see Rashi); Yerushalmi, Sanhedrin, X:2; Maimonides' Mishneh Torah, Book 14, Hilchot M'lachim, III:8–9
4. Ralbag, I Samuel 25:3
5. Yalkut II §134; Midrash T'hillim (Buber) Psalm 53

CHAPTER FIFTEEN
1. Midrash Shoḥar Tov 18; Yalkut II §133
2. Lev. R. 23:11; Yalkut I §586
3. Avot d'Rabbi Natan 26:2
4. Lev. R. 26:2; Num. R. 19:2; Midrash Shoḥar Tov 7; Yalkut II §136
5. Yalkut II §139
6. Lev. R. 26:7; Midrash Sh'muel, Chap. 24; Tan. (Buber) Leviticus 41b–42a
7. B'rachot 12b; Yalkut II §139
8. Lev. R. 26:7; Midrash Sh'muel, Chap. 24; Tan. (Buber) Leviticus 41b; Tan. Emor 2 (all with slight variation)
9. Yalkut II §139

CHAPTER SIXTEEN
1. Baba Kamma 92a; Kiddushin 42b; Y'vamot 25b; K'tubot 27b (Rashi); Ralbag, II Samuel 1:14
2. Zohar I, 79b; ha-Mikra v'ha-Aretz II, p. 209
3. Sanhedrin 19b–20a
4. Sanhedrin 20a
5. Pirké d'Rabbi Eliezer, Chap. 36; Yalkut II §28
6. Pirké d'Rabbi Eliezer, Chap. 36
7. Y'vamot 96b; B'chorot 31b; Yalkut II §145
8. M'gillah 15a; Z'vaḥim 116b

CHAPTER SEVENTEEN
1. Sanhedrin 6b
2. Num. R. 4:20
3. Malbim, II Samuel 9:1
4. B'rachot 3b
5. Shabbat 56a
6. Shabbat 56a
7. Sukkah 52b
8. Avodah Zarah 4b–5a

CHAPTER EIGHTEEN
1. Ralbag, II Samuel 1:14; Malbim, II Samuel 15:1–5; Yerushalmi, Sotah, I:8 (see commentary "Korban Edah")
2. Sotah 34b; Num. R. 9:29
3. Yalkut II §151, 142
4. Midrash Shoḥar Tov 3; Yalkut II §151
5. Radak, II Samuel 16:10; Midrash T'hillim (Buber) Psalm 3; Zohar II, 17a & 107b
6. Avodah Zarah 4b–5a (see Rashi)

CHAPTER NINETEEN
1. Sotah 10b
2. M'gillah 13b–14a; Yalkut II §151
3. Shabbat 56b
4. I. B. Levner, Kol Aggadot Yisrael I, pp. 292–293
5. Yalkut II §143 & §145; Midrash Shoḥar Tov 62
6. P'saḥim 117a; Zohar II, 232b (by implication); Yalkut II §165
7. Moed Katan 16b

CHAPTER TWENTY
1. Shabbat 30a–b; (see Ruth R. 3:2)
2. Yalkut II §522; Avot d'Rabbi Natan 4:5; Ruth R. 3:2
3. Sanhedrin 7a; Sifri, Deuteronomy 9; Rashi, Deut. 1:9
4. Midrash Shoḥar Tov 72
5. Ḥomat Anach, I Kings 4, p. 43b; Yalkut II §176
6. P'sikta Rabbati 14

CHAPTER TWENTY-ONE
1. Ḥomat Anach, I Kings 5, p. 44a
2. M'naḥot 86b (see Rashi); Lev. R. 31:16; Num. R. 15:1; Pirké Avot (end of each chapter); see also Teacher's Resource Book, vol. I, pp. 95–96, 98–99
3. Gittin 68b; Yalkut II §182
4. Ralbag, I Kings 6:23
5. Zohar II, 198a

6. Ex. R. 34:1; Num. R. 12:3; Albo, Sefer ha-Ikkarim II, p. 102; Passover Haggadah
7. Tan. T'rumah 9; Tan. (Buber) Genesis 67b; (see Rashi and Radak, I Kings 8:43)
8. B'rachot 30a

CHAPTER TWENTY-TWO
1. Song of Songs R. 1:5; Sanhedrin 104b; Yalkut II §144
2. B'rachot 8a
3. Ḥomat Anach, I Kings 10, p. 46b
4. Shabbat 56b & 54b; Yalkut II §196
5. Sanhedrin 101b
6. Maimonides' Mishneh Torah, Book 4, Hilchot Biah, XIII:16
7. Sanhedrin 102a; Pirké Avot 5:21

CHAPTER TWENTY-THREE
1. Radak, I Kings 17:6; Ḥullin 5a
2. Zohar II, 199a; Genesis (Gen.) R, 5:4; Pirké Avot 5:9
3. P'sikta Rabbati 3; Sanhedrin 113a–b; Pirké d'Rabbi Eliezer, Chap. 33; Yalkut II §207; Sanhedrin 113a; Ex. R. 4:2
4. Midrash Shoḥar Tov 117; (see Isaac Cohen, Perush m'Ari ha-Kohen)
5. Sanhedrin 89b; Num. R. 14:5
6. Yalkut II §214
7. Radak, I Kings 18:30
8. Song of Songs R. 1:39; M'chilta Bo P'siḥta; Yalkut II §15; Zohar I, 209a–b; Eliyahu Zuta, Chap. 8; Antiquities, Book 8, Chap. 13 §7

CHAPTER TWENTY-FOUR
1. Ralbag & Radak, I Kings 19:20 (by implication)
2. Moed Katan 28b

CHAPTER TWENTY-FIVE
1. Sifri, Deuteronomy 34
2. Sanhedrin 105b
3. Zohar I, 191b

4. Eliyahu R., Chap. 5
5. Tosephta Sotah, Chap. 12; Radak, II Kings 2:16
6. Ex. R. 31:3; Tan. Mishpatim 9
7. Zohar 87b; Radak, II Kings 4:4
8. Gen. R. 35:4 (by implication); Rashi, II Kings 4:7
9. Hovat ha-L'vavot, Shaar Heshbon ha-Nefesh, Chap. 3
10. Pirké d'Rabbi Eliezer, Chap. 33; Ralbag, II Kings 4:29; Zohar II, 44b
11. Ex. R. 4:2; Taanit 24a
12. Midrash Shohar Tov 78
13. Sifri, Deuteronomy 52; Yalkut I §875

CHAPTER TWENTY-SIX

1. Sotah 47a; Radak, II Kings 8:7
2. Soncino, II Kings 8:13; Simon, *In Die Teg Fun Die Ershte N'viim*, pp. 215-216

3. Rashi & Radak, II Kings 9:1
4. Sanhedrin 48b; Yalkut II §171
5. Pirké d'Rabbi Eliezer, Chap. 17
6. Midrash Shohar Tov 18
7. Ex. R. 8:3
8. Yerushalmi, Horayot, III:2 (see commentary "Korban Edah")

CHAPTER TWENTY-SEVEN

1. Gittin 88a; Eliyahu Zuta, Chap. 9
2. Homat Anach, II Kings 18, p. 58a–b
3. Pirké d'Rabbi Eliezer, Chap. 38; Tan. Va'yeshev 2
4. Sanhedrin 94b
5. Sanhedrin 95a
6. Yalkut II §241
7. Sanhedrin 95b; Ex. R. 18:5
8. B'rachot 10a (see Rashi & Hagaat ha-Bah)

CHAPTER TWENTY-EIGHT

1. Baba Kamma 17a; Echah Rabbati 25; I. B. Levner, Kol Aggadot Yisrael II, pp. 444–446
2. Deut. R. 2:13; Sanhedrin 103b
3. Yerushalmi, Sanhedrin, X:2
4. Deut. R. 2:13; Sanhedrin 103a; Yerushalmi, Sanhedrin, X:2
5. Sanhedrin 102a–b
6. Rashi & Malbim, II Kings 22:8
7. M'gillah 14b
8. Shabbat 56b
9. Lev. R. 19:6; Yalkut II §249
10. Lev. R. 19:6; Yerushalmi, Sh'kalim, VI:2 (see commentary "Korban Edah")
11. Sanhedrin 38a; Gittin 88a
12. Rashi, II Kings 25:4; P'sikta Rabbati 26
13. Ecclesiastes R. 12:8
13. Lamentations R. 1:33